MEDIA CAPTURE

Media Capture

HOW MONEY, DIGITAL PLATFORMS, AND
GOVERNMENTS CONTROL THE NEWS

Edited by
Anya Schiffrin

Columbia University Press
New York

Columbia University Press
Publishers Since 1893
New York   Chichester, West Sussex
cup.columbia.edu
Copyright © 2021 Columbia University Press
All rights reserved

Library of Congress Cataloging-in-Publication Data
Names: Schiffrin, Anya, 1962– author.
Title: Media capture : how money, digital platforms, and governments
control the news / edited by Anya Schiffrin.
Description: New York : Columbia University Press, [2021] | Includes
bibliographical references and index.
Identifiers: LCCN 2020048105 (print) | LCCN 2020048106 (ebook) | ISBN 9780231188821
(hardback) | ISBN 9780231188838 (trade paperback) | ISBN 9780231548021 (ebook)
Subjects: LCSH: Freedom of the press. | Mass media and business. |
Government and the press. | Press and politics. | Social media—Influence. |
Internet industry—Influence. | Journalism—Objectivity.
Classification: LCC PN4735 .M435 2021 (print) | LCC PN4735 (ebook) | DDC 323.44/5—dc23
LC record available at https://lccn.loc.gov/2020048105
LC ebook record available at https://lccn.loc.gov/2020048106

Columbia University Press books are printed on permanent and durable acid-free paper.
Printed in the United States of America

Cover design: Julia Kushnirsky
Cover image: © istockphoto

CONTENTS

CONTENTS

CONTENTS

MEDIA CAPTURE

PART I
Overview

INTRODUCTION

ANYA SCHIFFRIN

When we think of a press baron, the old-style cigar-chomping, top-hatted William Randolph Hearst–type mogul in his dinner jacket shouting orders at a hapless editor may come to mind. Today, that image takes more varied forms: perhaps a sleazy oligarch in cahoots with an aspiring dictator buying up outlets in central Europe or a fumbling and pale Mark Zuckerberg impatiently answering questions at congressional hearings. Many felt uncomfortable with casino owner Sheldon Adelson's buying up small midwestern newspapers and with Sinclair Broadcasting taking over radio stations. We worry about Jeff Bezos owning the *Washington Post* as well as his behemoth Amazon—it may give him an outsize voice when Congress discusses internet taxation. When we think about what could go wrong, we remember Rupert Murdoch having the *Sun* back the Falklands War as well as the Iraq War and using Fox News to get Donald Trump elected. More recently, the role played by tabloids in the United Kingdom in stirring up fears of immigrants and hatred and mistrust of the European Union's "Brussels bureaucrats" points to the influential role that the media can play in the service of power.

As we think about Bezos and Murdoch, we hope domestic media outlets will not go down the path taken in many parts of Latin America as well as in Turkey, Hungary, the Balkans, and India, where big business controls much of the media and uses them as a mouthpiece for its own interests and those of its buddies in government. We instinctively understand that this kind of media ownership leads at best to soft censorship and a narrowing of the public sphere. Although soft censorship, on its own, may be less physically violent than the hard censorship seen in undemocratic societies, it can nonetheless undermine the role of the media. When journalists come under the control of business and government, they can no longer perform the multiple critical roles the Fourth Estate plays in a democratic society. Journalists and political scientists have elaborated on the essential role that the media play as part of a system of checks and balances, referring, for instance, to the "scarecrow," "watchdog," and "agenda-setting" functions that society needs.[1] But capture is a threat to these roles. Less examined than violence against journalists, capture can lead to soft censorship and a narrowing of freedom of expression.

Soft control can come in many ways, and over the years these have been examined by both media critics and scholars, among others. Because state ownership can give government control over the media, well-functioning democracies have created successful institutional arrangements to make sure that state support does not erode media independence. One example concerns the rules about the placement of government advertising. However, private ownership is no bulwark against state capture; government cronies can buy media outlets and then serve the interests of the state, as the current situation in Turkey and Hungary illustrate. Even philanthropists can control media outlets simply by funding them and requiring certain kinds of coverage.

In *Media Capture*, contributors from journalism and the academy examine the myriad ways in which "media capture" is affecting political and media landscapes around the world. Contributors provide firsthand accounts and analysis of how media capture happens in the digital age and what can be done about it. The voices of the journalists who speak in this book are a valuable counterpoint to research and theory of the academics. The experiences of journalists who have lived through capture and soft control as well as their reporting provide valuable insights into the manifestations of capture in the digital age.

MEDIA CAPTURE: HISTORY OF AN IDEA

Although the idea of soft control of the media is old, the actual term *media capture* was first defined by a small group of economists at the beginning of the twenty-first century. These economists built on previous theories of regulatory capture often associated with George Stigler.[2] Stigler used the term to explain why regulators, instead of doing their jobs, become allied with the entities they are meant to be regulating. For example, it explains why the Federal Communications Commission has such an intimate relationship with media companies.[3]

Defining Capture: Vested Interests Networked with Governments

In the case of the media, the notion of "capture" helps explain how soft censorship takes hold. In 2006, the economists Tim Besley and Andrea Prat used the notion to explain how the media in nominally democratic countries were still not at liberty to do proper investigative and accountability reporting and to function as a fully free and independent entity. Although the old-fashioned censor marking up newspapers with red ink no longer existed (at least in the societies they studied), it had been replaced by softer forms of pressure on journalists. Besley and Prat noted a "combination of formal press freedom and substantial political influence" in a number of democracies, including Thailand, Italy, India, and Mexico.[4] They referred to the phenomenon as "non-coercive media capture." They sought to understand why this had happened and the consequences. Published in the prestigious *American Economic Review*, their seminal paper gave rise to a new school of thought in economics about the media and influenced work being done by scholars in other fields. Indeed, it was the political scientist Alina Mungiu-Pippidi who came up with the best working definition of *media capture*, describing it as a situation in which news media are controlled "either directly by governments or by vested interests networked with politics."[5] But in this definition it is important to focus not just on "government" but on "vested interests." When the media are captured by vested interests, these interests use their influence *to change the politics*, like Murdoch using Fox News to get more voters for the Republican Party. The link with politics is a *result* of the capture—and one of its primary objectives.

Thinking about how the state of media capture has evolved, Mungiu-Pippidi has refined her definition to distinguish between outcomes and mechanisms: "A captive media system occurs whenever the goal of *most media* (regardless if traditional or new, if content producing or advertising, etc.) is in promoting particular vested interests to the detriment of classic media objectives, such as objective information or honest debate. Media capture is a macro concept indicating AN OUTCOME, while soft pressure, self-censorship, etc. are mechanisms operating at a micro level."[6]

Journalists had long been familiar with the consequences of corporate and government control, but the new research coming from economists and political scientists delineates how the consequences of media capture may be felt throughout society. Indeed, because the media are how most citizens come to understand the problems of a society and what can be done about them, incomplete or distorted reporting will have economic, political, and social consequences. Recent research makes bolder claims about the effects of capture. Two studies have argued that media capture can increase wealth concentration and economic inequality. Giacomo Corneo maintains that there may be a vicious circle: media capture may lead to policies—such as greater toleration of market power—that in turn facilitate further media capture. Increased economic concentration in societies makes the occurrence of media bias more likely, and this concentration generally leads to a worsening in the quality of public welfare.[7] Maria Petrova of the Institute for Political Economy and Governance in Barcelona also suggests that media capture can lead to worsening inequality, particularly in a situation in which the media are captured by rich owners. Politicians will likely be voted out of office at some point; the wealthy, in contrast, can retain control for far longer and cause more damage.[8] This new scholarship suggests that the effects of capture are more dire than previously understood.

Media Capture: An Idea Born Before the Internet

Early work done on media capture in 2002 and 2006, of course, did not and could not fully take into account the dramatic effects the internet would have on information. Because the impact of the internet has become impossible to ignore, we argue that it's time to revise theories of media capture, broadening the definition to include how capture works in the digital age. The traditional business model for media has fallen apart, and citizens now rely on largely unregulated internet and social media companies for news and information. The United States offers a powerful and illuminating case study of what happens when monopolists control and profit off the digital sphere with scant regulation, such as laissez-faire policies defended by extreme libertarians. The testimonies of the journalists in this book, who have worked in media for decades, reflect on the consequences for the public sphere of the kind of system that prevails in the United States. We've seen how the election of Donald Trump in 2016 affected the media throughout the world, in part by making global attacks on journalism acceptable. So, too, the growth of unfettered U.S. platforms has had global consequences.

It's remarkable to look back just fifteen years and see that most economists—although not all—assumed that the internet would lower barriers to entry, lead to more competitive media markets, and thus make it more difficult to capture media.[9] Uncaptured media would, of course, provide higher-quality and more diverse journalism and better inform citizens.[10] In hindsight, we can see that some of these predictions turned out to be wrong. Clearly, the internet allowed more information to travel, and this was particularly beneficial in places that had been isolated. But more competition did not lead to better quality. For many outlets, more competition was a disaster. Lower barriers to entry meant the number of online media outlets skyrocketed and caused advertising prices to fall. It turned out that space for advertising on the internet is infinite, and so prices are extremely low. Media outlets became desperate for revenue and rushed to compete for mass audiences; quality declined.[11] Just as in the offline world, if not more so, online media can draw huge audiences despite lower standards of reporting. The financial pressures affected everyone, and many legacy outlets, known for their rigorous editorial standards, welcomed financial arrangements such as sponsored content or native advertising that they might not have accepted twenty years earlier. These kinds of arrangements previously existed mainly in low- and middle-income countries or in the bad old days of the nineteenth century, when newspapers were captured by their owners or advertisers.[12] Two well-known examples from the past exemplify how capture could manifest itself: the influence of advertising by patent-medicine companies affected how quack medicines were covered by newspapers in the late nineteenth century,[13] and *The Brass Check* (1919) by the muckraking author Upton Sinclair describes the capture of newspapers in the United States around the early twentieth century by a variety of industries that supported and subsidized the press through advertising. After writing his famous book *The Jungle* (1906), about labor conditions in Chicago's meatpacking plants, Sinclair faced tremendous opposition from the companies whose business he had exposed.[14]

The Destruction of Traditional Business Models
and the Rise of Capture

Media capture became a greater threat after the collapse of the traditional business model for media. In a climate where the media can make money, media owners have an *economic* reason to own an outlet. But in a climate without these classic economic motives, the incentives for owning media outlets are likely to be more political and ideological.[15] When owning a media outlet is no longer as profitable as it once was, it becomes increasingly likely that rich individuals with a political agenda will seek ownership of media outlets to further their agendas, as billionaire Sheldon Adelson bought Israeli newspapers in order to control public criticism of Prime Minister Benjamin Netanyahu.[16] Even more troubling, rich individuals or corporations seeking legislation that advances their financial (corporate) interests can buy even an unprofitable media outlet with the understanding that using such an outlet to set the agenda and frame the political debate in beneficial ways may be economically advantageous in the long run.[17] Activists working to stop corporate-tax avoidance have long noted that the *Washington Post*—owned by Jeff Bezos, the founder and CEO of tax avoider Amazon—barely covers the topic. Having a major subject ignored by a leading media outlet will make it less likely that government will address the problem.

Thus, instead of providing a new landscape that makes media capture more difficult, digital media may have had the opposite effect: making capture less expensive and more likely and presenting even greater policy challenges for those hoping to prevent it.[18] The extraction of vast wealth by the tech sector and the control exerted by tech platforms over news mean that concentration of media ownership is now far more likely than it formerly was. The lack of regulation in the United States has increased the possibility of political capture and created a climate where media capture may become the norm and not the exception. In this world where a few unregulated tech giants control what people see and watch, anything can happen. The effects of tech wealth were evident in the lawsuit brought by Peter Thiel against Gawker Media.[19] Thiel did not even have to buy Gawker in order to shut it down in 2016. All he had to do was hire lawyers and find a plaintiff. The use of lawsuits to shut down journalism is now common in many parts of the world. It's part of a strategy of intimidating journalists but is also an example of how media capture can be supported by instruments of the state, in Gawker's case the judiciary.

Not only is "direct capture" through ownership easier than it used to be, but so is "indirect capture." In an environment in which the media's financial future is shaky, anyone who helps fund media has influence and power over it. With competition for advertising dollars more intense, the power of the advertiser may be more pronounced. The growth of "native advertising"—that is, advertisements intended to look like legitimate editorial copy—has furthered the erosion of the barriers between editorial and advertising, which began even before Facebook and Google became dominant. However, the use of native advertising has intensified as outlets seek revenue because Google and Facebook have captured an estimated 60–80 percent of advertising dollars. Further, when journalists find themselves in a precarious economic situation, they try to avoid alienating their funders. Sometimes, explicit policies discourage them from doing so. For example, the *Washington Post* prohibited its employees from criticizing on social media the outlet's advertisers.[20]

Moreover, advertisers' dominance has contributed to new forms of media capture, which present novel impediments to the media's ability to perform some of their key societal roles. For instance, platforms such as Google and Facebook act as gatekeepers, making algorithmically based decisions as to which information is made accessible and therefore what news is consumed.[21] As these gatekeepers control or at least greatly affect financial and informational flows and scoop up much of the available advertising revenue, their market power grows. This shift presents a new "capture" problem, which becomes particularly important when issues relevant to these giant platforms' profitability (such as privacy) arise. Privacy is sacrificed when these gatekeepers capitalize on consumer data in order to glean advertising revenues. Ultimately, these large companies exacerbate the capture problem by taking profit for themselves, lessening both the ability and the economic incentives of media owners to perform their traditional roles.[22] These companies also illuminate the capture problem: it may create a scarcity of independent voices willing to criticize their anticompetitive practices, their antiprivacy policies, and their willingness to participate in political manipulation. This is particularly true of the large tech companies that spend millions on lobbying in Washington, DC, and Brussels. It's already clear that their enormous size necessitates new regulations in areas such as antitrust law, competition policy, and privacy.

The fact that it is easier to capture media, that there are more outlets to capture, and that there are a multitude of actors trying—and in many cases succeeding—at capturing either the same or different media might give one comfort. Is it conceivable that a countervailing power (to use John Kenneth Galbraith's phrase) is at play? We may not get the first best nirvana sought by economists, a fully competitive equilibrium, but might we get perhaps a reasonable second best? Unfortunately, the answer is no, especially in a country such as the United States, where money matters so much, especially in politics; where there are so few restraints imposed by laws or norms; and where there is such great inequality. It is clear that in practice some groups of voices are louder than others. Captured media have distorted the flow of information. Whether this is the inevitable outcome does not matter. It is the outcome we have to deal with. Efforts by the Left to produce content discussing economic inequality, such as the Economic Hardship Reporting Project or the investigative reporting by ProPublica on the costs of health care, have had an impact but perhaps not as significant an impact as their stellar reporting deserves.[23]

MULTIPLE PERSPECTIVES ON MEDIA CAPTURE IN THE DIGITAL AGE

The chapters in this book explain how the internet age has created multiple possibilities of capture at multiple levels. Emily Bell (chapter 16), the director of the Tow Center for Digital Journalism at the Columbia Journalism School, studies the impact of digital media, the ways in which we consume news today, and the risks that come with modern platforms. "Our relationship with news is being changed by the convergence of platforms, devices, and content," she observes.

> The mobile social web is revolutionizing production, news gathering and distribution on a global scale, but it is also seeing and causing a consolidation of power in the hands of a few. These distribution platforms now control how people around the world receive information and their access to sources of news. The ease of use and high levels of connectivity are enabling greater

numbers of people to create and consume news media than in the past. However, they are also creating a distribution model for the free press which is potentially embedded within a commercial ecosystem that serves companies and governments alike. What implications do the new mega-gatekeepers have for media independence?[24]

As Josh Marshall notes in chapter 5, in the present situation where the large platforms control much of the revenue stream, media outlets and their audiences are increasingly vulnerable. Not only do the outlets depend on Google and Facebook, but their weakened financial position means they can be more easily captured by a range of funders. Financial desperation means that any two-bit advertiser or small foundation can exert influence over an outlet it helps fund. The result is multiple forms of capture coexisting within outlets as well as a media system that includes different forms of captured outlets. For example, a beleaguered outlet might feel pressure from both advertisers and foundations or from an owner as well as an advertiser. In polarized media climates (such as that of the United States), outlets captured by conservative owners such as Rupert Murdoch exist in a media ecosystem that includes many sites captured by other interests. Other ideological or political motivations might also shape news and media coverage of a particular issue in a way that might be more subtle than Fox's political coverage. Business tycoons have always tried to influence media, and the outlets they control have existed alongside freer titles. What is new in our era is the research showing the effects of such capture. The Republican, now pro-Trump agenda of Fox has real effects. Recent research on Fox News has confirmed what was long suspected: Republicans gain votes in areas where there is strong viewership of Fox, and the network may have been responsible for increasing Republican vote share by six percentage points in the 2008 elections.[25] Its influence may have been even more pronounced in the 2016 elections as Fox moved farther to the right and circulated endless rumors about Hillary Clinton.[26]

Another feature of capture in the age of the internet is the well-documented interplay between extreme outlets on the right and the "established" right-wing press. Entry is easy, so extreme groups can and do create stories that float around the internet; when these stories seem to resonate, they percolate into the mainstream conservative press, eventually forcing the rest of the mainstream press to provide coverage.[27] The deterioration of quality standards referred to earlier feeds into this process. Although at times in the past the "yellow press" had a similar role in "distorting" public debate and sentiment, the internet in a polarized society has resulted in effects likened to "capture on steroids." Captured outlets such as Fox News, which works largely in the service of the right-wing elements of the Republican Party, and—at this writing—of President Donald Trump, become dissemination channels for extreme dis/misinformation found on the outer reaches of the internet. This interplay between capture and mis/disinformation is the next generation of capture that will need to be researched, according to Mungiu-Pippidi.

Yet regulation has been impossible because companies such as Google and Facebook bought themselves a seat at the table through their lobbying and influence peddling precisely to avoid regulation and taxation. In chapter 1, Rana Foroohar describes their influence network and their efforts in Washington, DC, including the vast amount of money they have poured into "partnerships" with journalism organizations and media outlets, thus guaranteeing the tech companies a spot at every journalism conference as well as influence over content and distribution. For example, the tools that Google has designed and pushed at journalism conferences are aimed mostly at exposing government activities, not corporate ones.[28] Facebook Live is another example because although it has helped expose instances of police brutality, it has also undercut the role of the journalist as an ethical gatekeeper of information by streaming to a broad audience regardless of whether the content is authentic or accurate or meets other traditional journalistic norms.[29] Foroohar argues that "Big Tech"—the largest tech companies, Amazon, Apple, Facebook, Google, and Microsoft—has in many respects usurped Wall Street and Big Pharma as a lobbying powerhouse, leading to weakened reporting on the social and economic threats posed by these major corporations. In chapter 4, Noam Cohen argues that in pursuit of scale Facebook, Google, and their ilk distribute journalism edited and organized by algorithm, which removes context and encourages misinformation and political polarization. The result is a news ecosystem ripe for media capture, with clear chokepoints where governments and businesses can apply pressure and without a countervailing belief in truth telling and critical coverage.

Bell (chapter 16) discusses how Google and Facebook have shaped journalism not just through funding research and lobbying but also through the tools and software they have developed, leading to "infrastructure capture"—something that was predicted and has come to pass.[30] "Everyone who has built a successful news product online knows that the technical architecture, tools, software, and analytics applied to journalism inevitably end up shaping aspects of editorial content," she writes in her chapter. As Bell notes, "Facebook, Apple, and Google do things that journalists should be investigating, not profiting from."

More blatantly, the Gates Foundation has funded pop-up outlets on education "reform," a subject that Bill and Melinda Gates feel strongly about. Along with housing and insurance tycoon Eli Broad, they have been funding campaigns against teachers' unions and supporting charter schools for years.[31] Although the issues are complex and controversial, a wealth of serious academic research shows, for instance, that charter schools do not on average perform better than public schools. The worry is that with media capture by biased funders, only one side of the story gets told. This is the subject of chapter 8, by Andrea Gabor, who details the funding of education outlets by moguls.

Felix Salmon (chapter 6) writes on the demise of the "blogosphere," whose early halcyon days of free, open, and networked discourse gave way to increasingly generic and commercialized content as it was captured first by advertisers and then by legacy-media outlets. The hoped-for diversity didn't happen; even when there were more outlets, the blogosphere could hardly be called a robust marketplace of ideas. Further, the commercialized content confused audiences, who were no longer sure what was legitimate news and what had been paid for by advertisers. This uncertainty may have contributed to a decline in media trust.[32]

Relatedly, James Ledbetter (chapter 7) describes how individual journalists are captured through ethically dubious native-advertising schemes, where agencies representing different companies will offer small sums to writers in exchange for a mention in a story. Mary Fitzgerald, James Cusick, and Peter Geoghegan (chapter 11) discuss the political implications of this phenomenon by looking at how formerly storied and respected newspapers in the United Kingdom now take payments in exchange for publishing favorable commentary about Google and Facebook.

Andrew Finkel (chapter 9) and Raju Narisetti (chapter 10) examine capture in two countries, Turkey and India, where media freedom has declined with startling speed. Finkel describes a range of capture tactics used, including hard and soft pressures, and notes that the Turkish government uses both—banning content, imprisoning journalists, and getting government cronies to support government policies. As Finkel explains in his chapter, in Turkey there are still "leakages" in which public opinion cannot be entirely controlled because the relationship between captor and captured is not static.

In India, media capture by cronies of Prime Minister Narendra Modhi has been reinforced by attacks by the ruling party, the Bharatiya Janata Party, on journalism. There have been killings of journalists, massive dissemination of violence and hate speech online, and undermining of the media. The result is a toxic brew that has left journalists afraid to speak out and has created an atmosphere in which the media are not trusted. Across the media landscape in India, there are "growing self-censorship and an unwillingness to pursue and stick with watchdog journalism, unprecedented even for a country with a long history of politicians equating any overtly critical journalism with being negative about India and even unpatriotic." Meanwhile, "trust in India's media has continued to erode as 'play for pay' scandals . . . reinforc[e] . . . what have become enduring, derisive social media hashtags such as '#presstitutes,'" Narisetti writes.

DONORS AND MEDIA CAPTURE: A SOLUTION WITH SOME STRINGS ATTACHED?

Part 3 of this volume deals with solutions, and it's worth noting that foundations and philanthropists have stepped into the breach to fund independent media outlets in many parts of the world in order to alleviate the financial crisis faced by much of journalism and offset the effects of capture. Although the amount being spent annually by foundations and donors goes a long way, it still pales in comparison with the financial weight of the media moguls—spending estimated to be in the hundreds of millions of dollars rather than in the billions. The Open Society Foundation (disclosure: I am on its global board) spends some $25 million a year, as does the Omidyar Network. The Ford Foundation puts about $15 million a year into journalism (rising to some $20 million in 2020 due to the issuance of their "social bonds"), mostly in the United States, and is emphasizing representation and diversity in newsrooms. Much of the funding goes to freedom of expression and business models, but some (particularly from the Gates Foundation, which spends about $25 million a year on journalism) is aimed at strengthening cover-age of particular subject matter, such as corruption, governance, health, and education. Philanthropic funding has supported dozens of websites around the world and many major reporting projects, including the Panama Papers series about tax avoidance published in 2016. But it must be said that an influx of donor funding has the consequence of skewing the editorial decisions of the outlets supported by such funding, leading to fears of donor capture.[33] Even modest amounts of money can have substantial effects.

EFFORTS TO COME UP WITH SOLUTIONS

The practicing journalists in this book offer insights from the field about how media capture plays out in the digital age and how it affects society more broadly. It's clear we don't yet have a solution to fix the problem in an internet age characterized by dominant tech companies and a failing media business model. Some degree of capture may be the inevitable state of the media, and it may not be possible to do away with it completely. However, we conclude the book by describing some of the ways capture can be controlled. The continuing and dramatic difficulties faced by media outlets that try to stay independent as well as the layoffs at "digital-first" outlets such as *Buzzfeed*, *Mic*, and *Vice* in 2019, followed by the decimation of many media outlets in the wake of the COVID-19 pandemic in 2020, make finding financial support for the media urgent. At the same time, the contamination of information ecosystems, the rapid and growing circulation of mis/disinformation and hate speech online, as well as government attacks on journalism standards have contributed to the sense that it is imperative to do something quickly.

The Role of the State in Supporting Free Media

Strengthening free and independent media is a standard solution that is offered by those thinking of how to avoid or at least to counterbalance media capture. The advantage to government interventions is that they can grow and endure. Indeed, some countries have recognized that a strong and independent media are an important public good that have to be publicly supported. Victor Pickard, Robert McChesney, and John Nichols—among others—have repeatedly pointed out that European governments have found many ways to support media pluralism and diversity. To quote a recent report I wrote with Ellen Hume: "Indirect subsidies, which are relatively uncontroversial from a political standpoint and inexpensive, are widespread. Many major Western European countries, including France, Germany, Ireland, Italy, and the UK, among others, have reduced or eliminated VAT (value added tax) rates for newspaper and magazine sales."[34] But indirect subsidies do not ensure long-term sustainability for the media. Instead, several countries have used direct subsidies to preserve their media structure and safeguard media independence.[35]

Public broadcasting is another common form of public support for media. Government funding of quality public-service broadcasting has worked in Sweden and the United Kingdom, among other countries. Public-broadcasting systems enjoy broad popularity among both citizens and governments alike and have been shown to be more resistant to capture by the states responsible for their funding than traditional for-profit media are to capture by advertisers.[36] In some countries, support for public broadcasters is raised from licensing fees (the United Kingdom, Germany, Sweden, Germany, France, Japan, Austria), and a portion of the licensing fees generated by public-broadcasting systems are diverted to private media organizations. Other countries use tax revenue from advertisers on television or radio.[37] Some countries with strong public broadcasters, such as Sweden, tend to have higher levels of trust in media.

New Urgency Breeds Ambitious Solutions

However, in the United States these policies have not been implemented, and in other countries traditional approaches do not seem to have sufficed. As panic about the future of journalism set in, people in media and media development began to plan large-scale solutions. In early 2019, Drew Sullivan, editor and cofounder of the Organized Crime and Corruption Reporting Project, convened a meeting of funders and journalists to think about tapping new revenue sources to create a fund to support investigative journalism. Mark Nelson, senior director of the Center for International Media Assistance (funded by the National Endowment for Democracy), and James Deane, director of policy and learning at BBC Media Action, convened a meeting, also in early 2019, to discuss creating a global fund for media development that would involve earmarking money from Organization for

Economic Cooperation and Development governments that spend money on development assistance. The idea was to persuade governments that part of their development aid money should be directed toward supporting media, including institutions such as public broadcasters and journalism schools. Taxation of Facebook to pay for journalism is another idea that gained traction in 2018 and 2019 thanks to the efforts of Victor Pickard at the Annenberg School for Communication at the University of Pennsylvania.[38] Tim Karr at the Free Press proposed taxing microtargeted advertising and using the money to pay for U.S. investigative reporting.[39] A group of European foundations, Civitates, combined funds to support European journalism and began grant making.[40] A group of economists (I was on the committee) in 2019 proposed giving each U.S. citizen a $50 voucher to donate to news organizations.[41] As an economist might put it, all of these efforts are based on the belief that information provided by a free and effective media sector is a public good from which all benefit. One cannot leave the provision of such public goods to the market; there will be undersupply—and what is provided, as we have seen, may well be distorted.

Building on these initiatives, in chapters 13 and 14 Dean Starkman and Drew Sullivan propose ways of funding voices alternative to those captured or in danger of capture. Starkman suggests that the United States pass a law similar to Hungary's highly successful one percent law, which allows taxpayers to designate one percent of their income tax to a nonprofit of their choice, in order to stimulate a media sector beleaguered by increased productivity strain and widespread financialization of its business model. Drew Sullivan explains why a new fund is necessary and how it can be allocated and administered to support independent journalism. The administration of such a fund would need to be worked out.

Andrea Prat and others have proposed strengthening regulations and updating competition law. The U.K. Competition and Markets Authority, for instance, has "investigated the anticipated acquisition of Sky Plc by 21st Century Fox, Inc on the grounds of media plurality and a genuine commitment to broadcasting standards,"[42] thus taking a step in the direction Prat has called for.

In chapter 12, Mark Nelson argues for going beyond regulation. He writes that though strict enforcement may be difficult in the internet era, formalizing a set of norms and governance principles around the media sector is a vital step to curbing media capture. Such governance of the media sector is needed at the country and global levels and should be worked out through open, democratic processes aimed at preserving freedom of expression and high-quality, independent media institutions. Media governance may include antitrust legislation around media ownership, mandated independence of media regulatory authorities, rules on government advertising, and internet governance at the global level that creates disincentives for dissemination of false information and propaganda. Independent, publicly funded media can also be an effective means of maintaining an uncaptured media presence.

Crucial to the success of these measures, Nelson writes, are civil society groups that help generate public demand for socially responsible, accountable media and raise funds to help pay for alternatives. Active civil society organizations are willing to take on the complicated politics of media freedom and to point out where capture has occurred. The support offered by such organizations is vital to journalists' efforts to stave off capture and concentrated ownership.

At this writing, public opinion has shifted, and regulation of the tech companies seems more likely in both the United States and Europe. In the United States, calls by Republican and Democratic politicians to regulate the platforms have forced the companies to think about how to deal with objectionable right-wing content, political messaging, hate speech, and the tsunami of COVID-19 disinformation seen in 2020. Nikki Usher uses game theory in chapter 2 to argue that even the threat of regulation shapes how the platforms operate. "When these accusations of liberal bias have been applied to mainstream media, the result is an overcorrection as journalists bend over backward to represent conservative viewpoints in order to show that their coverage is impartial. . . . Now Republicans are applying this tactic as a mechanism for platform capture. Platform companies must acquiesce to the demands of partisans, or they will face continued grandstanding by politicians who speak for their partisan supporters, will risk regulation, and will even face withering trust and use of their platforms among the polarized right-wing public."

The United States has been slow to regulate the platforms, and so has the European Union, with the exception of attempts to impose taxes on the platforms. What will become of information in this platform-dominated world? When all else fails and societies are truly closed and captured, brave journalists will continue to do independent journalism. Joel Simon, executive director of the Committee to Protect Journalists, writes in chapter 15 on the lengthy history of media capture by state authorities and criminal networks in Mexico and of the "vanguard journalists" who have an outsize impact by daring to operate outside this framework of capture.

But brave journalism is not likely to be enough. Viable alternatives, funded by nonpartisan public agencies committed to pluralism and diversity and truth telling, are essential. The public good is the most important public good; ensuring that society works for everyone, not just those with the resources to capture the press, should be of vital interest to everyone. And an independent, diverse media *that are not captured* are essential for promoting and protecting the public good.

Much needs to be done, and the time is now. The last few years have seen the problem of media capture spread; it is now regularly discussed at journalism conferences and panels, and there is now a new set of research mostly focused on South Africa and central and eastern Europe. The growth of capture contributes to a feeling of urgency. This book, by documenting the processes by which capture occurs, its consequences, and what can be done about it, will promote public discussion and action. As bad as things are now, it should be clear: we are on a trajectory in which matters could become even worse.

NOTES

1. Christopher William Anderson, Emily Bell, and Clay Shirky, "Post-industrial Journalism: Adapting to the Present," *Geopolitics, History, & International Relations* 7, no. 2 (2015): 1–126; Zhou Yuezhi, "Watchdogs on Party Leashes? Contexts and Implications of Investigative Journalism in Post-Deng China," *Journalism Studies* 1, no. 4 (2000): 577–97; Yunjuan Luo, Hansel Burley, Alexander Moe, and Mingxiao Sui, "A Meta-analysis of News Media's Public Agenda–Setting Effects, 1972–2015," *Journalism and Mass Communication Quarterly* 96, no. 1 (March 2019): 150–72.

2. George Stigler, "The Theory of Economic Regulation," *Bell Journal of Economics and Management Science* 2, no. 1 (1971): 3–21.

3. Emily Badger, "Fixing the FCC, America's Broken Regulator," *Pacific Standard*, May 3, 2017.

4. Timothy Besley and Andrea Prat, "Handcuffs for the Grabbing Hand? Media Capture and Government Accountability," *American Economic Review* 96, no. 3 (June 2006): 720.

5. Alina Mungiu-Pippidi, "How Media and Politics Shape Each Other in the New Europe," *Romanian Journal of Political Science* 8, no. 1 (Spring 2008): 72.

6. Alina Mungiu-Pippidi, correspondence with the author, October 14, 2019, italics and capitalization in the original. For more information, see Alina Mungiu-Pippidi, *The Quest for Good Governance* (Cambridge: Cambridge University Press, 2015), chap. 6.

7. Giacomo Corneo, "Media Capture in a Democracy: The Role of Wealth Concentration," *Journal of Public Economics* 90, nos. 1–2 (2006): 37–58.

8. Maria Petrova, "Inequality and Media Capture," *Journal of Public Economics* 92, nos. 1–2 (February 2008): 183–212.

9. For more hopeful views, see Alexander Dyck, David Moss, and Luigi Zingales, "Media Versus Special Interests," *Journal of Law and Economics* 56, no. 3 (2013): 521–53; and Besley and Prat, "Handcuffs for the Grabbing Hand?" For the other side, see Sendhil Mullainathan and Andrei Schleifer, "The Market for News," *American Economic Review* 95, no. 4 (September 2005): 1031–53; and Julia Cagé, *Saving the Media: Capitalism, Crowdfunding, and Democracy* (Cambridge, MA: Harvard University Press, 2016).

10. Besley and Prat, "Handcuffs for the Grabbing Hand?"

11. Cagé, *Saving the Media.*

12. Marwan M. Kraidy, "State Control of Television News in 1990s Lebanon," *Journalism and Mass Communication Quarterly* 76, no. 3 (September 1999): 485–98; Richard John, "Media Capture: The Long View," keynote address at the conference "Media Capture in an Age of Political Polarization: Preserving Media Independence," Columbia University, New York, April 1, 2016.

13. Marc Law and Gary D. Libecap, "The Determinants of Progressive Era Reform: The Pure Food and Drugs Act of 1906," in *Corruption and Reform: Lessons from America's History*, ed. Edward L. Glaeser and Claudia Goldin (Chicago: University of Chicago Press, 2004), 319–42.

14. Michael Hussey, "Global Muckraking: The International Impact of Upton Sinclair's *The Jungle*," *Teaching History: A Journal of Methods* 34, no. 1 (2009): 29–39.

15. Anya Schiffrin, introduction to *In the Service of Power: Media Capture and the Threat to Democracy*, ed. Anya Schiffrin (Washington, DC: Center for International Media Assistance, 2017), 1–8; and Rasmus Kleis Nielsen, "Media Capture in the Digital Age," in *In the Service of Power*, ed. Schiffrin, 33–42.

16. Ruth Eglash, "How U.S. Billionaire Sheldon Adelson Is Buying Up Israel's Media," *Washington Post*, May 1, 2014.

17. For more information, see Andrew Finkel on Turkey, this volume, chapter 9.

18. Andrea Prat, "Media Power," *Journal of Political Economy* 126, no. 4 (August 2018): 1747–83.

19. Matt Drange, "Peter Thiel's War on Gawker: A Timeline," *Forbes*, June 21, 2016.

20. Josh Delk, "*Washington Post* Prohibits Social Media Criticism of Advertisers," *The Hill*, June 28, 2017.

21. Emily Bell, "Facebook Is Eating the World," *Columbia Journalism Review*, March 7, 2016, https://www.cjr.org/analysis/facebook_and_media.php.

22. April Glaser, "Why Aren't Privacy Groups Fighting to Regulate Facebook?," *Slate*, April 19, 2018, https://slate.com/technology/2018/04/why-arent-privacy-groups-fighting-to-regulate-facebook.html.

23. Connor Sheets, "These Sheriffs Release Sick Inmates to Avoid Paying Their Hospital Bills," ProPublica, September 30, 2019, https://www.propublica.org/article/these

-sheriffs-release-sick-inmates-to-avoid-paying-their-hospital-bills; Akilah Johnson, "Medicare-for-All Is Not Medicare, and Not Really for All. So What Does It Actually Mean?," ProPublica, September 6, 2019, https://www.propublica.org/article /medicare-for-all-is-not-medicare-and-not-really-for-all-so-what-does-it-actually -mean.

24. Emily Bell, "Capture and Convergence," statement for the conference "Media Capture in an Age of Political Polarization," April 1, 2016, https://cgeg.sipa.columbia.edu /events-calendar/media-capture-age-political-polarization-preserving-media -independence.

25. Gregory J. Martin and Ali Yurukoglu, "Bias in Cable News: Persuasion and Polarization," *American Economic Review* 107, no. 9 (September 2017): 2565–99.

26. Yochai Benkler, Robert Faris, and Hal Roberts, *Network Propaganda: Manipulation, Disinformation, and Radicalization in American Politics* (Oxford: Oxford University Press, 2018).

27. Benkler, Faris, and Roberts, *Network Propaganda*.

28. Maha Rafi Atal, "The Cultural and Economic Power of Advertisers in the Business Press," *Journalism* 19, no. 8 (2018): 1078–95.

29. Seth Lewis and Nicole Smith Dahmen, "What Facebook Live Means for Journalism," *The Conversation* (Boston), February 7, 2017.

30. Efrat Nechushtai, "Could Digital Platforms Capture the Media Through Infrastructure?," *Journalism* 19, no. 8 (August 2018): 1043–58.

31. Valerie Strauss, "Why It's a Big Deal That Billionaire Activist Eli Broad Is Opposing Billionaire Activist Betsy DeVos as Education Secretary," *Washington Post*, February 1, 2017.

32. Maha Rafi Atal, "The Cultural and Economic Power of Advertisers in the Business Press," *Journalism* 19, no. 8 (2018): 1078–95; Katherine Grosser, "Trust in Online Journalism," *Digital Journalism* 4, no. 8 (2016): 1036–57.

33. Rodney Benson, "Can Foundations Solve the Journalism Crisis?," *Journalism* 19, no. 8 (2018): 1059–77; Kate Wright, Martin Scott, and Mel Bunce, "Foundation-Funded Journalism, Philanthrocapitalism, and Tainted Donors," *Journalism Studies* 20, no. 5 (2019): 675–95.

34. Ellen Hume and Anya Schiffrin, *Creating a Global Fund for Investigative Journalism*, report, Global Forum for Media Development, April 2019, https://gfmd.info /gfmd-content/uploads/2019/08/Creating-a-Global-Fund-for-Investigative-Jour nalism.pdf.

35. See Francesco Guarascio, "EU Agrees on Lower Sales Tax for E-books, Online Papers," Reuters, October 2, 2018; Corinne Schweizer, Manuel Puppis, Matthias Künzler, and Samuel Studer, "Public Funding of Private Media," London School of Economics Media Policy Project, 2014; Milan Živković, "Who Will Pay for Journalism?," Zagreb: South East European Media Observatory, 2016, goo.gl/ZUrtUQ; Dame Frances Cairncross, *The Cairncross Review: A Sustainable Future for Journalism* (London: Assets, 2019), https://assets.publishing.service.gov.uk/government /uploads/system/uploads/attachment_data/file/779882/021919_DCMS_Cairn cross_Review_.pdf; Mart Ots, "Sweden: State Support to Newspapers in Transition," in *State Aid for Newspapers: Theories Cases, Actions*, ed. Paul C. Murschetz (New York: Springer, 2013), 307–22; Corinne Schweizer, Manuel Puppis, Matthias Künzler, and Samuel Studer, "Public Funding of Private Media," London School of

Economics Media Policy Project, 2014; Karl Erik Gustafsson, Henrik Örne-bring, and David A. L. Levy, "Press Subsidies and Local News: The Swedish Case," working paper, Reuters Institute for the Study of Journalism, September 2009, https://reutersinstitute.politics.ox.ac.uk/our-research/press-subsidies-and-local-news-swedish-case; Rasmus Kleis Nielsen, with Geert Linnebank, *Public Support for the Media: A Six-Country Overview of Direct and Indirect Subsidies*, report, Reuters Institute for the Study of Journalism, August 2011, https://reutersinstitute.politics.ox.ac.uk/our-research/public-support-media.

36. Rodney Benson and Matthew Powers, *A Crisis of Imagination: International Models for Funding and Protecting Independent Journalism and Public Media (a Survey of 14 Leading Democracies)* (Washington, DC: Free Press, 2011), https://sverigesradio.se/diverse/appdata/isidor/files/3938/9445.pdf.

37. Helen Weeds, "Is the Television Licence Fee Fit for Purpose in the Digital Era?," *Economic Affairs* 36, no. 1 (2016): 2–20; Melissa Berger, Gerlinde Fellner-Röhling, Rupert Sausgruber, and Christian Traxler, "Higher Taxes, More Evasion? Evidence from Border Differentials in TV License Fees," *Journal of Public Economics* 135 (2016): 74–86.

38. Victor Pickard, "Break Facebook's Power and Renew Journalism," *Nation*, May 21, 2018.

39. For more information, see "Free Press Calls for Tax on Targeted Ads to Fund Civic-Minded Journalism," Free Press, press release, February 26, 2019, https://www.freepress.net/news/press-releases/free-press-calls-tax-targeted-ads-fund-civic-minded-journalism.

40. For more information, see the Civitates website at https://civitates-eu.org/.

41. For more information on the voucher proposal, see Rick Edmonds, "Academics Craft a Plan to Infuse Billions Into Journalism: Give Every American $50 to Donate to News Orgs," Poynter, September 5, 2019, https://www.poynter.org/business-work/2019/academics-craft-a-plan-to-infuse-billions-into-journalism-give-every-american-50-to-donate-to-news-orgs/.

42. Competition and Markets Authority, "21st Century Fox / Sky Merger Inquiry," March 16, 2017, https://www.gov.uk/cma-cases/twenty-first-century-fox-sky-merger-european-intervention-notice.

Chapter One

HOW SILICON VALLEY COPIED WALL STREET'S MEDIA CAPTURE PLAYBOOK

RANA FOROOHAR

It's fascinating how much the technology industry today mirrors the financial industry in the run-up and aftermath of 2008. Just as Wall Street used corporate mythology, opacity, complexity, and sheer size to distort the marketplace and make us think that what was good for Goldman Sachs was good for America, so Silicon Valley has for many years used its unprecedented economic and political power to convince the world that Facebook's and Google's interests are in alignment with those of individual consumers and citizens. Just as only a handful of journalists saw the financial crisis coming, almost no one predicted the role that the largest technology platforms would play in the election of Donald Trump. And we have only just begun to grapple with the dampening effects of Big Tech on everything from job creation to new business formation, not to mention the way such ubiquitous technology is reshaping our brains.

Since the mid-1990s, when the commercial internet began to come of age, we have been in thrall to the Silicon Valley creation myth, which holds that bright-eyed young innovators working in garages invent wonderful new technologies that make us all richer and happier. Like all myths, there's some truth in it. But it was truer decades ago when firms such as Google, Facebook, Apple, Amazon, and so on were still in garages, literally or metaphorically, rather than on state-of-the-art private campuses that resemble gated communities.

The bigger truth is that Silicon Valley is now the country's power center. It is the single largest global hub for billionaires, a place that regularly spends more on Washington lobbying than the financial industry. In 2018, Google alone spent $21 million on federal lobbying, more than any other company in America.[1] Amazon topped the list for the sheer number of entities lobbied, pushing twenty-one issues areas across forty different federal entities.[2]

The valley is also a hub for the economic bifurcation that plagues the country at large. Bright young millennials fresh from Stanford and Harvard board private buses in San Francisco that whisk them to work, while the city itself struggles to cope with out-of-control housing prices that have left more people homeless than ever before in the region's history.

The valley also reflects the concentration of power that has become a huge headwind to growth. A handful of large companies use the network effect and the power of ring-fenced personal data to winnow out smaller players in ways that many regulators believe is anticompetitive. Silicon Valley is also a place in which, like Wall Street, the largest institutions can pay the massive fines they regularly receive for such behaviors as a cost of doing business. It is a place in which the "greed is good" ethos of the 1980s has combined with liberal entitlement and "disrupt everything" libertarianism to create a toxic environment in which society is all too often viewed as being "in the way."

These trends have been with us since the late 1990s. But the coverage of them has only recently begun in earnest. Why have we missed this shift and all of its profound implications? Because the media themselves—the institution that is supposed to tell us the true narrative—have been both disrupted and captured by Big Tech. First, the disruption: digital advertising overtook print years ago; in 2017, it overtook television advertising, too. Between 2015 and 2016, 90 percent of the growth of digital advertising went to Facebook and Google.[3] These firms are now effectively advertising monopolies. This growth has, of course, decimated the traditional news business. U.S. Labor Department statistics show that in 2005 there were 66,490 newspaper reporters or editors in the United States. In 2015, there were 41,400, a decline of 25,090 journalists, or 38 percent.[4] The number of digital reporting jobs has, of course, risen, but this gain has not offset the larger decline of the industry. Most publications, at least those without robust subscription models, now depend on the platform firms for distribution.

The result is that Big Tech has become the gatekeeper of what content gets the most attention. The disruption has been so extreme that the major platforms themselves have begun funding the beleaguered news business (they have realized, perhaps too late, that they actually need content because that's exactly what their targeted advertising business monetizes). Google and Facebook have given hundreds of millions of dollars to major publications in Europe and the United States to help these media outlets "innovate," but of course those programs come with strings both explicit and implicit. It's hard to imagine such money going to investigative journalism that looks closely into the way Big Tech has lobbied for exceptions from regulations or offshored record amounts of tax or aided autocrats globally.

Companies such as Facebook and Google embed in many top news organizations, just as they do in political campaigns, with programs that "help" major newspapers create content best tailored to the tech companies' own business models (such as Facebook Live). In some cases, they have even directly paid tabloid newspapers in places such as the United Kingdom for favorable coverage on the editorial page, a tactic rarely seen outside of emerging market journalism.

Other types of capture are subtler. There is the problem of "access" journalism, for example. As on Wall Street, it's incredibly difficult to get access to the C-suite of Silicon Valley unless you are viewed as a sympathetic listener. In my own experience in business journalism over the past twenty-five plus years, I have found that Silicon Valley executives are as controlling as they come—even more inclined to try to police the terms of an interview or an article than your typical Fortune 500 executive. For example, a few years back, while working at *Time* magazine, I asked to interview then Yahoo CEO Marissa Mayer for a cover story looking at her efforts to turn around the failing dot-com. I was impressed that she had taken on such an obviously tough assignment and was predisposed to be charitable. But Mayer's public-relations team proceeded to try and control so many details about the piece—where the interview would take place, what questions could be asked, the locations in which we could photograph her, even the language we might use in display type—that we eventually had to cancel the cover. A couple of months later, she gave an interview to *Vogue*, a puff piece accompanied by numerous photographs of Mayer, a couture collector, in her favorite outfits. Not exactly tough journalism. Since I began writing more critical pieces on the power of Big Tech for the *Financial Times*, I have hit similar brick walls elsewhere in the Valley.

These problems are at least transparent. What's more insidious is the way Big Tech, like Big Finance, buys up proxies, including the sources that many journalists turn to when reporting on the Valley, sources including non-profit institutes, technology think tanks, academics, and so on. The fact that these sources are receiving funds from tech titans is very often buried in the fine print. Google alone has thrown money at more than 140 such third-party entities, from the American Library Association (ALA) to the American Association of People with Disabilities, the National Hispanic Media Coalition, and the Center for American Progress, as well as funding several academic institutions and media fellowships.

Such organizations may not seem like natural allies of the tech revolution, but they have also supported some of the regulatory loopholes that Big Tech firms enjoy, such as rules that shield them from liability for what users say and do online. The ALA, for example, unlike many other groups that represent authors or publishers, has supported Google in its fight for the right to scan all the world's books. Although it's true that librarians generally support free speech and want books to be widely accessed, it's also true that Google gives the ALA money. What does the money buy? It's impossible to know.

Big Tech has been known to pull funding from journalists and experts when they don't agree with its positions. Just consider how Eric Schmidt, one of the largest funders of the influential Washington think tank the New America Foundation, squashed the journalist and policy expert Barry Lynn, whose ideas he found threatening. Lynn, who gained his reputation with prescient work on supply-chain economics in which he examined how the United States had lost manufacturing competitiveness to China, was in 2017 running a program at the New America Foundation looking at monopoly power. As part of this project, he had begun looking at the way in which Big Tech firms were dominating the economy and hindering entrepreneurial vibrancy and growth as a result.

Lynn's work went somewhat against the grain of New America, which was the unofficial Clinton think tank and tended to have a fairly hands-off approach to corporate America (undoubtedly due in large part to its donor base). But when Lynn's research group, the Open Markets division, posted an article on the think tank's website in praise of the European Union's antitrust ruling against Google, Schmidt (who was at the time still executive chairman of Alphabet, Google's parent company) called up the head of New America, Anne-Marie Slaughter, a former director of policy at the US State Department under Hillary Clinton, and voiced his disapproval.

That was when Slaughter told Lynn that "the time has come for Open Markets and New America" to part ways—not because of his work, she stressed, but because his lack of collegiality was imperiling the organization as a whole. The episode called to mind an email that Slaughter had sent Lynn a year earlier, in 2016, in the run-up to a well-received conference on the market dominance of companies such as Google, Amazon, and Facebook, which Lynn had organized. Slaughter apparently indicated that Google was concerned that its position wouldn't be represented. "We are in the process of trying to expand our relationship with Google on some absolutely key points," wrote Slaughter in her email to Lynn, urging him to "just THINK about how you are imperiling funding for others."[5]

Lynn was eventually pushed out of the think tank, which he believes was due to Schmidt's pressure (a claim denied by both Google and Slaughter). The resulting press was terrible for New America, Google, and Schmidt, but great for Lynn. He ended up starting what has become an even more influential stand-alone think tank, the Open Market Institute, which works on monopoly issues (full disclosure: I sit on the advisory board of the new entity). And his concerns about Big Tech's monopoly power have come to the forefront of the policy conversation in Washington, influencing liberals and conservatives alike.

Lynn is the rare expert of a journalist who truly understands not only technology but also the political economy in which the Big Tech firms operate. That understanding is crucial to combatting subtle forms of cognitive capture. Technology, like finance, is a complex industry prone to jargon and circular narratives that can repel tough questions. The algorithmic use of data is like the complex securitization of the subprime era. Both are understood largely by industry experts who can use information asymmetry to hide risks and nefarious things that companies profit from—for example, in dubious political ads.

The industry uses this complexity to obfuscate. When journalists try to ask the tough questions—about monopoly, privacy, tech-related job disruption, and so on—reactions can range from defensive to patronizing. Among those I have heard: "Politicians don't understand the Valley," "Universal basic income will make work irrelevant," and, worst of all, the exasperated look that says, "You're not a tech insider, so you just don't get it."

All this is like the financial industry's response to the crisis of 2008. Like the tech industry today, finance did a good job of using its money and political power to hold the debate over reform hostage to its own interests. Policy conversations were made as complicated as possible to keep "insiders" in control, even though the simple questions—Is the financial system helping the real economy and society or not?—were often the best and most important.

Those are the questions we need to be asking. The power of Big Tech—economic, political, and cognitive—isn't going away. Indeed, as we move into what will very likely be a multidecade period of disruption as we transition from a tangible to an intangible economy, they will only grow. Journalists owe it to themselves and to the public at large to look beyond the curtain of complexity and start connecting the dots. We need to think about what exactly people *aren't* talking and writing about when it comes to Big Tech. Privilege and silence are strongly correlated. By looking at the things people don't say and at the connections they don't make, you can usually get to the truth. Here's one of the most important things that hasn't been said enough: we should think of the largest technology platform firms today as we thought of the too-big-to-fail banks. They are the systemically important institutions of our time. They deserve coverage by journalists who aren't captured.

NOTES

1. Nitasha Tiku, "How Google Influences the Conversation in Washington," *Wired*, March 13, 2019, https://www.wired.com/story/how-google-influences-conversation-washington/.
2. David McCabe and Erica Pandey, "Amazon's Vast DC Lobbying Operation Reached Further Than Any Other Public Company," *Axios*, March 13, 2019, https://www.axios.com/amazon-lobbying-washington-wide-reach-0f7253e4-234e-462a-aca1-ca19705b9c39.html.
3. Matthew Ingram, "How Google and Facebook Have Taken Over the Digital Ad Industry," *Fortune*, January 4, 2017, https://fortune.com/2017/01/04/google-facebook-ad-industry/.

4. Alex Williams, "Employment Picture Darkens for Journalists at Digital Outlets," *Columbia Journalism Review,* September 27, 2016, https://www.cjr.org/business_of_ news/journalism_jobs_digital_decline.php.

5. Anne-Marie Slaughter, quoted in Kenneth Vogel, "Google Critic Ousted from Think Tank Funded by the Tech Giant," *New York Times,* August 30, 2017, capitalization in the original, https://www.nytimes.com/2017/08/30/us/politics/eric-schmidt -google-new-america.html.

Chapter Two

FROM MEDIA CAPTURE TO PLATFORM CAPTURE

NIKKI USHER

In the United States, we are moving from media capture to platform capture. This may sound surprising, given that we are seemingly at the apogee of Big Tech's power, with these large, global multinational companies reaching their tentacles into almost all arenas of social life. From how we wake ourselves up in the morning ("Alexa, set our alarm for 7:00 a.m.") to the future of autonomous driving to the ownership of our data to the news and information we see, Big Tech is omnipresent. Big Tech seems to endanger the very fabric of social life, enabling misinformation to spread, fomenting polarization, accelerating the destruction of the news business model in advanced media systems, and beyond. This volume provides ample recognition that media capture is real, it is happening now in the United States and elsewhere, and it is worse than ever before. However, Big Tech is in the early stages of capture; it is vulnerable to being trapped by the same forces that boxed in the news media as well as by new challenges. Welcome, then, to the beginning of platform capture.

Platform capture is defined as the combined influence of bad actors who rig the tech companies for their own gains, the threat of government regulation, partisanship and hyperpartisanship, and Silicon Valley's contradictory ideology that favors libertarian conceptions of privacy, speech, and profit. The word *platform* is used because the five Big Tech companies—Google,

Facebook, Microsoft, Amazon, and Apple—are platform companies that host rather than create the content, products, and services they provide. A platform includes the hard technology of server farms and computer hardware, the software and physical infrastructure that facilitates the sales and distribution of consumer goods, and the underlying code and content-management systems that host the content we create and enables the extraction of our data. Platforms provide the software that hosts our photos, videos, and messages; even the word-processing software used to write this chapter is an example of Microsoft's platform power. When we "save to the cloud," we outsource our computing power and rely on a platform company's hardware.

To be clear: the term *platform capture* does not refer to the way platforms have captured news media. Rather, it refers to how the platforms, now the predominant way through which Americans receive news and information, are themselves subject to "capture." We need to be on high alert to the forces inside and outside these companies that are constraining their ability to adapt in pro-social ways. We might think that curbing the power of Big Tech is desirable, but platform capture stands to do more harm than we might initially anticipate. Media capture is the evolutionary antecedent to platform capture, and although it may seem as if platforms are eating the world (as software is said to), platforms, too, are also being eaten from the inside out.

Platforms are hamstrung by a profit model that values user growth more than any single other indicator of investment value. Political elites threaten platform companies with regulatory action that in turn prompts self-corrections with potentially drastic consequences. Hyperpartisan media producers who distribute their content on these platforms pollute our information environment; bad actors who range from those engaging in state-sponsored propaganda to hate groups use platforms to disrupt our information environment. Big Tech's own ethical foundations also play an almost suicidal role in causing platform capture; Silicon Valley's ideological orientations and blind spots make spotting future problems and correcting existing ones difficult. In this chapter, I explain how platform capture is happening, first by explaining how political communication in a digital era reflects a destabilized information hierarchy and then by elucidating the forces that are contributing to the emergence of platform capture.

ANOTHER THEORY OF MEDIA (AND PLATFORM) CAPTURE

To understand platform capture, it is important to think about how inter-connected platforms are to the flows of information and news. In revising a model of the flows of predigital political communication, my colleague Robert Entman and I attempted to chart the human and nonhuman actors that have inordinate power to direct our information.[1] We argue that platforms, along with strengthened ideological media, digital analyt-ics, algorithms, and rogue actors (hyperpartisans and the do-it-for-the-lulz hackers), might be thought of as "pump valves" that exert pressure on the political communication network in all sorts of up, down, and side-ways directions. Much like a pump valve regulates the flow of liquid through a pump, with the ability to shift pressure in multiple ways depending on the strength and direction of input, our news and informa-tion environment is no longer hierarchical. Instead, producers, consum-ers, and the distribution mechanisms for news and information intersect and influence each other in various directions that both constrain and enable knowledge and action.

Our model argues that political communication flows through a frac-tured media system divided into ideological and mainstream information networks that have reached digital maturity. Platforms play a key role in enabling these divisions through algorithms that may help reinforce echo chambers and information silos. Public communicators, such as partisans and political elites, have varying motivations and abilities to influence the political communication network, much of which depends on bending the affordances of platforms to conform to their will. Similarly, platforms afford these public communicators the chance to selectively target their messages with stunning accuracy. In the case of platform capture, even while plat-forms play a critical role in the distortions we now see, they are also acted upon and influenced by other actors who exert pressure in new directions.

Platforms have designed algorithms to aid in efficiently surfacing infor-mation, goods, and services. These algorithms also introduce considerable vulnerabilities for platforms. As the pump-valve metaphor suggests, dis-tortions and noise can bubble up from all corners, from elite political actors relying on stolen data (e.g., Cambridge Analytica) to the chump at home in his basement using the internet to spread hate to Macedonian teenagers looking to make a buck off digital advertising by creating fake news

33

2FROM MEDIA CAPTURE TO PLATFORM CAPTURE

optimized for maximum virality. It is this opportunity for distortion, when mixed with a toxic partisan environment and an unsustainable profit model, that enables platform capture. Silicon Valley's ideological commitments make it difficult for platforms to evolve, adapt, and strategize against these threats, a form of platform capture that has origins in the tech industry itself, with additional pressure emerging from a business model that demands ever-increasing scale and growth.

PLATFORM CAPTURE . . . BY PLATFORM PROFIT

Platform capture is partially a result of the very business model that drives platform companies' profits. At this point, the major platform companies are no longer startups but publicly traded companies with corporate boards and shareholders who demand profit. The fiduciary duty of these publicly traded companies is to make money for their shareholders; this duty to make a profit does not require ethical decision making, though the failure to conduct ethical business can backfire and create costly messes for companies. Platform companies show investors their value by growing their user base, achieving greater scale. More people mean more user data, which in turn feed the platforms' storehouses of user data, which can be optimized to drive consumer purchases or to sell to third parties.

For example, Facebook and Google's YouTube must show continued user growth and maintain user activity, a corporate motive that favors ignoring much needed audits to spot bad actors, fake accounts, and noise on these platforms. Amazon builds its revenue in part by facilitating the sales of an ever-increasing array of products to people. Alexa, although marketed as a modern convenience for helping with shopping lists or kids' homework, is also listening to us, surveilling our conversations to garner further data about us so Amazon can sell to us more effectively. Microsoft, which makes much of its money from selling server space to provide computing power to other companies, grows by gaining more and more market share. Building these servers requires investments in infrastructure, from buildings to electricity, often resulting in harmful environmental consequences.

In short, pursuing continued user growth at all costs is a market incentive that makes it difficult for platform companies to see beyond the next quarterly earnings report. Consider how the reporting around Apple's profit outlook in the first quarter of 2019 reflects this growth-at-all costs rhetoric.

Apple investors were worried that iPhone sales were slowing, and the rate of uptake of Apple's services such as Apple Pay were insufficient to make up the declining profit from hardware. Analysts have come to expect growth that is not reasonable for Apple's mature market position. As the BBC reporter Natalie Sherman explains, "Analysts will have to adjust to a business driven by smaller, regular payments, instead of [by] big hardware hits."[2] However, user growth, not revenue from apps, has long been the measure of Apple's success. Apple is incentivized to sell hardware and in fact has corporate strategies that favor planned hardware obsolescence. In fact, Apple has had to deal with legal challenges to batteries it deliberately designed to fail so users would be forced to buy more phones.

Platform capture is part and parcel of the very business model designed to keep platform companies profitable. Platforms cannot see beyond the latest quarterly earnings and as a result often make socially irresponsible decisions that harm their companies and the public at large. This observation, that profit models create platform capture, should seem familiar. These same profit demands are also key factors that contribute to media capture. However, the ways in which platform capture proceeds through a disorderly political communication network may be of far greater consequence, especially given the news media's dependency on platforms for distribution.

REGULATIONS AND PLATFORM CAPTURE

We might think that Amazon, Facebook, Apple, Microsoft, Google, and other Big Tech companies don't need to answer to anyone, perhaps other than their investors. After all, they are global in reach and stateless. But avoiding regulation in the United States is a principle way that platforms can continue to do what they get to do, unrestrained. Although platform companies are limited in a few official ways in the United States, regulatory pressure is a component of platform capture. The threat of government regulation acts as a soft and omnipresent threat guiding Big Tech's corporate strategies and tactics. And in seeking to avoid regulations, platform companies actually further damage the public sphere.

Platform companies fear regulation in the United States that they already face in Europe. These regulations include stronger privacy protections and regulations for data transparency, anti-hate-speech laws, stronger regulatory efforts against anticompetitive activities, consumer protection against price discrimination, and even algorithmic transparency. For example, in Germany Facebook has had to subcontract hundreds of employees as content moderators in order to comply with the so-called Facebook law, which aims to delete what Germany defines as criminally relevant content.[3] Protest over campaign interference has led to the creation of a Facebook "war room" to fight misinformation, which includes "engineers, data scientists, threat investigators and other Facebook experts from 20 teams" who work to clamp down on misinformation.[4] In Brazil's presidential election in 2018, one rife with misinformation, a court order mandated Facebook take down thirty-three different fake stories (though the damage was likely already done).[5] The greater evidence that the platform companies' own algorithms and humans aren't catching harmful content increases support for regulatory bodies to enforce new rules.

Platform companies have been able to scale and to grow precisely because their content has been mostly content that they have not had to produce but instead comes from platform users' activities. This is a gigantic labor shortcut that news organizations, for example, cannot take. Filling rooms with human content moderators, staffing up legal teams able to fight court battles across the globe, hiring fact-checkers are the opposite of efficient business for these companies. Giving up their vast collection of personal data would be the death knell to many of these platform companies who make profits from deals with third parties such as brands and politicians who hope personalized targeting will lead to more persuasive messaging. Requiring that platform companies open up their proprietary algorithms to the public might destroy their competitive bottom line.

Evidence of platform capture emerges from these companies' growing need to engage in dark-money political contributions and in lobbying as a way to respond to threats of regulatory pressure. This form of platform capture occurs at the margins of visibility in the U.S. political system and is pernicious in its incentives: money makes politics go 'round, and these companies have more than enough of it to keep regulations at bay. The feds can threaten to exact concessions from platform companies without ever bringing any specific and documented legal regulations into fruition, thus prompting platform companies to dispense cash to keep politicians on their side.

As reporting in the *New York Times* and elsewhere has shown, the more that pressure on Facebook, Google, and other tech companies heats up, the more the dollars start flowing into government offices via lobbying. Following accusations of platform-enabled election interference and the moral panic surrounding fake news, in 2017 Google spent $18 million to lobby Washington—more than any other tech company that year; Facebook, Apple, and Amazon also broke their own spending records on lobbying. After the Left's critique of Facebook heated up, Facebook went so far as to hire the consulting firm Definers Public Affairs, a right-wing firm that applies campaign tactics to corporate public relations.[6] Facebook used Definers to target George Soros, the very same tactic employed by the fake-news creators that Facebook has pledged to fight. The soft charm of Facebook has also been put on full display, with top-level executives such as Sheryl Sandberg visiting the Hill, governors' offices, and the States Attorneys General convention and employing other personal touches designed to smooth over ruffled feathers.

Perhaps even more concerning is the way in which political campaigns and platform companies are working hand-in-hand to advance candidate agendas. Providing helpful campaign services may well be a mechanism these platform companies will use to stay in the good graces of their Republican skeptics.[7] Although the Cambridge Analytica scandal seems to involve a misuse of data beyond what Facebook could have ever predicted, it's possible that platforms will conveniently ignore the misuse of user data so long as it keeps Republicans happy.

Certainly, I realize that arguing that regulatory pressures cause platform capture may seem a bit far-fetched, especially given the lack of formal regulation on these companies. However, this hazy situation where dark-money contributions are offered to politicians as a way to discourage their regulatory actions is deeply concerning. There are both a troubling lack of transparency and a limited opportunity for public debate. Instead, politicians hold platforms captured by the mere threat of action rather than by the reality of any regulatory activities. Platform companies remain in the pockets of government officials, and it is hard to tell what kinds of concessions government officials are able to exact from platforms when there are no open, public conversations about the legal repercussions for tech companies' bad behavior. The threat of regulatory pressure comes from elected political elites, but there are other ways in which partisans, especially those on the right, also are responsible for platform capture.

PARTISANS AND PLATFORM CAPTURE

Of course, partisanship influences the actions of elected officials. But partisan goals are slightly different from platform capture; partisans are motivated by their commitment to spread and to strengthen party messages, positions, and ideological perspectives and, most importantly, to win elections. Partisans, especially right-wing partisans, capture platforms by manipulating platforms to do their partisan bidding, whether through the content that is shared and spread or the ways in which they are able to use platforms to further their political goals.

The right wing is taking a chapter out of its old media-strategy playbook and applying it to the platform era. The way the right wing has put pressure on mainstream media is often referred to as "playing the ref," which as the liberal commentator Eric Alterman explained a few years ago, "Their mau-mauing the other side is just a good way to get their own ideas across—or perhaps prevent the other side from getting a fair hearing for theirs."[8] And as I have explained elsewhere, indeed, as with sports, the more you play the ref, the more hesitant the ref will be to make calls against you— and may even rule in your favor.[9] Now, the right wing is accusing platforms of liberal bias.

When these accusations of liberal bias have been applied to mainstream media, the result is an overcorrection as journalists bend over backward to represent conservative viewpoints in order to show that their coverage is impartial. The *Washington Post* (with "Democracy Dies in Darkness" as its new, often misinterpreted, tagline) has been widely associated with liberal positions. However, the newspaper had far more negative coverage of Hillary Clinton during the 2016 election than any other national outlet than Fox and may well have overcorrected to account for accusations of liberal bias. Consider that 77 percent of its coverage of Clinton was negative compared with 81 percent of Fox's coverage.[10]

Now Republicans are applying this tactic as a mechanism for platform capture. Platform companies must acquiesce to the demands of partisans, or they will face continued grandstanding by politicians who speak for their partisan supporters, will risk regulation, and will even face withering trust and use of their platforms among the polarized right-wing public. Even President Trump has accused Google of being biased against the Right, tweeting, "Google and others are suppressing voices of Conservatives and hiding news and information that is good. They are controlling what we can & cannot see. This is a very serious situation—will be addressed."[11] Trump was echoing a common conservative talking point. Certainly, there is at least a shade of truth to the accusation: when Facebook had human content moderators selecting trending news content, one of them disclosed to the tech publication *Gizmodo* that moderators routinely suppressed conservative content. The story resulted in conservative scrutiny of Facebook, threats of regulation, and apologia from the company. However, the company may have overcorrected in favor of promoting conservative content. Social media data monitored by the *New York Times* journalist Kevin Roose in 2018 showed that the top-ten stories on Facebook regularly skewed conservative.[12]

The largely Republican hyperpartisans of internet conspiracy provide additional heft to partisan goals because of their connections to the right-wing political mainstream. These hyperpartisans are wedged between the category of bad actors and the more predictable partisans and partisan ideologues you might find in the Senate or on Fox. On the edges of what is acceptable, they are well poised to serve as bridges between the bad actors and the partisan elite. The supposedly unfair treatment of them by platforms provides support for political elites to exert further pressure on these platform companies. Their talking points become Fox talking points, which become administration talking points—a well-trodden path that facilitates the insertion of extremism and information disorder into the political information ecosystem. Although hyperpartisans are too smart to show obvious and direct ties to the truly dark corners of the Web, Alex Jones (with InfoWars), the right-wing activist James O'Keefe (with his undercover gotcha journalism), and more established players such as Matt Drudge are important actors within Republican ideological media. Their claims of bias in these platforms enables more established Republicans to threaten action against the platforms.

When platform companies testified on the Hill in 2018, multiple senators brought up the example of right-wing vloggers Diamond and Silk (Lynnette Hardaway and Rochelle Richardson, both black women), who say their content is suppressed on Facebook, YouTube, Twitter, and elsewhere. At one point, Facebook told Diamond and Silk that their commentary was "unsafe,"[13] likely because it was filled with misinformation and conspiracy mongering. However, Diamond and Silk's accusations of content censorship were unfounded, anyway; the duo's reach on Facebook was actually better when they were complaining about censorship.[14] Nonetheless, the accusations led to political backlash, and Facebook retracted its critiques. Other politicians have accused platform companies of "shadow banning" Republican commentators—a term used to describe deliberately making someone's content undiscoverable to everyone except the person who posted it, but unbeknownst to the original poster. Twitter has vociferously denied that it uses this tactic to target Republican hyperpartisans.[15] Any misstep by platform companies that appear to discriminate against these hyperpartisans provides additional fodder for political elites to pressure these companies to do their bidding or else face regulatory scrutiny.

If, indeed, regulation is the only real political threat that stands to curb the power of platforms, then pandering to right-wing partisans is exactly what platform companies will do. What this pandering looks like, however, is much harder to predict. Because the algorithms are proprietary, we won't know if platform companies overamplify conservative messages beyond their actual organic spreading power. We don't know how they will moderate safe and unsafe content—with the application of either algorithms or human intervention—except when journalists are able to dig up evidence of these complicated moderation rules.[16] In short, when it comes to partisan actors, including elites and hyperpartisans, platform capture is indeed in full force, with ideological actors using their political power to bend these massive companies to comply with their political goals. While hyperpartisans are often equated with fake news, another form of platform capture emerges from even more pernicious bad actors whose ill intentions and unpredictability undermine the digital public sphere by seeding mistrust and information disorder.

THE DARK ARTS OF DIGITAL BAD ACTORS

The networked society finds itself in a midlife crisis, the enthusiasm and promise of the early internet marred by the inevitable reality that digital tech will not solve all and the realization that the internet often causes more harm than good.[17] Malevolent citizen actors acting to disrupt the good will of civil conversation—what the scholar Thorsten Quandt has called "dark participation"[18]—is real. The bot creators, the alt-right, the global span of

Gabbers and neo-Nazi subredditors and men's rights incels (involuntary celibates), the 8-channers and 4-channers and Patreon members, and whatever other groups exist or will exist in the future are perhaps the most dangerous of all factors causing platform capture. Add into this mix foreign governments' ability to use cyberwarfare to try to manipulate U.S. audiences, not to mention the opportunists looking to make an easy dime off viral content, all of whom know full well that fake news spreads more quickly than the real stuff, especially content with a right-wing bent. Platform capture is well under way.

Big Tech companies must find ways to clamp down on those who use their technology for evil. Yet with every attempt to stop some new means for manipulation, another effort emerges from the dark arts of digital bad actors. Even with their libertarian ideals, few in Silicon Valley leadership would agree that their platforms should be used for planning mass shootings, manipulating elections, recruiting extremists, doxxing journalists, or intimidating public figures. Mark Zuckerberg at least initially tried to diminish how his platforms enabled the spread of fake news, and Jack Dorsey of Twitter has been accused of underreporting the bot-driven activity on Twitter, but there's little denying that these platforms facilitate the spread of conspiracy and hate. Platforms are now held hostage by bad actors who seek to use their technology to spread disorder—and there is no closing of Pandora's box.

For instance, for every effort Google takes to avoid having Holocaust-denial sites appear at the top of searches for "the Holocaust," bad actors will find another way to game the system. For every Facebook effort to stop the spread of fake news, another fake-news article or fake-news meme will pop up. YouTube's conspiracy rabbit holes may be partially combatted by taking down Alex Jones's website InfoWars, but nine thousand other amateur conspiracy videos remain.[19] For every action intended to stop a bad actor, an unpredictable and unequally strong and opposite reaction results—the fury of the hellish beasts of the internet unleashed. Misinformation spread on platforms becomes a form of political warfare, exemplified by Russian propaganda efforts that aim to create information disorder and seed distrust of democratic institutions and norms. For now, bad actors show that platform capture is happening, but the tech companies' blind spots may limit actions that could serve as correctives.

PLATFORM CAPTURE BY TECH IDEOLOGY

Perhaps the most surprising and confounding aspect of platform capture is the self-capture of platform companies. For all of Silicon Valley's disruptive technology, the ideology around startups and tech innovation has remained remarkably consistent. Richard Barbrook and Andy Cameron's essay from 1996 on the Californian ideology is perhaps the classic articulation of Silicon Valley values as "a mix of cybernetics, free market economics, and counter-culture libertarianism."[20] In the pre-Facebook, pre–Web 2.0 world of tech, this meant a strange fusion of hippies, artists, hackers, and billionaires united by a desire to make and build. A little of this world is still visible at the Burning Man festival, where Mark Zuckerburg shows up in a custom airstream trailer, while other attendees bring school busses remodeled into penises or unicorns. And although this strange fusion can perhaps still exist for five days every year in the desert, it no longer makes much sense for our present reality. Barbrook and Cameron's Californian ideology articulates how these platform companies try to keep two competing premises at the forefront of their company ideologies, "the disciplines of market economics and the freedoms of hippie artisanship"—a "bizarre hybrid only made possible through a nearly universal belief in technological determinism."[21]

The belief that technology can solve all problems, a faith in market self-regulation, and a fervent insistence on freedom of expression no longer go hand-in-hand with creativity and benevolent networked connections. Today, we see the maturation of this ideology as Silicon Valley's own contradictions and blind spots result in platform companies being stuck without any meaningful ability to anticipate harm, much less to self-correct. The disconnect between business values and belief in freedom of expression can get quickly compromised. For example, consider how these companies agree to geoblock content in order to appease authoritarian leaders in efforts to keep highly digitized populations in these repressive regimes part of the platforms' active user base.

These libertarian leaders of Silicon Valley have imagined connecting the world without considering how their own largely white, American, cis-gendered vision of racial, ethnic, national, and global harmony might be unrepresentative. Big Tech's failure to meaningfully include women and people of color, not to mention non-Western perspectives, has limited these companies' ability to anticipate how their strategies might cause more harm than good. For instance, every time a real-name proposal is floated in Silicon Valley as a way to create accountability within platforms (whereby users would be required to use handles that identify them by their legal names), LGBT persons and antiauthoritarian activists bang their heads against the wall. Not everyone has the luxury to be able to use a real name if they wish to use these platforms for meaningful social interactions. Real names can expose people to social sanction—for example, when LGBT individuals are accidentally outed to their intolerant families or employers by their Facebook activities. Real names on profiles would expose activists in authoritarian countries to even more surveillance and possibly endanger their lives.

Simply put, platforms cannot make money, provide maximal opportunities for freedom of expression, and connect the world equally well. With each new innovation driven by trying to achieve these goals all at once, the resulting often foreseeable missteps make these companies vulnerable to platform capture of their own design. The internal contradictions that lead to platform capture set in motion an ever-extending game of whack-a-mole, where flawed "innovations" miss their mark and create new problems. In turn, platform companies respond in panicked ways that create more problems, or in some cases they deal with crisis by means of infuriating nonresponses. If platform companies cannot move away from the Californian ideology, then they will find themselves unable to think seriously about how to change their practices and how to plan for the future. In short, they are captured by their own outdated beliefs and their continued failures to address their own blind spots.

PLATFORM CAPTURE'S MANY CONTRADICTIONS

A platform company's aspiration to "do no evil," as Google once promised in its code of conduct (but does no longer), is far harder than it seems. This dictum suggests that these companies see themselves as bigger and more powerful than anything else in their path and as a result have a responsibility to the public to avoid harm. But platform companies are vulnerable to platform capture. By introducing the idea of platform capture, I hope I have shown how no one actor, human or nonhuman, is invulnerable to impacts by other social actors around it.

Platform capture results from myriad old and new pressures, including profit models that emphasize growth as the most important indicator of a company's market value. In the quest for growth and in order to appease investors, platform companies make short-sighted decisions that can have drastic consequences. Although regulations have the power to help moderate the influence of these platform companies, it is the threat of regulation that wields considerable power over platforms. Lawmakers threaten regulation, and in response platform companies donate, lobby, plead, beg, and bargain with politicians to keep them on their side. Regulatory power over platforms is closely related to partisans' role in platform capture. Platforms have become talking points for conservatives, who accuse them of liberal bias. Because there is little public accountability for the day-to-day decision making inside these companies, we cannot know the exact extent to which platforms are self-censoring or overamplifying conservative content in order to appease Republican partisans. Moreover, bad actors can manipulate platforms to spread misinformation and fracture civil digital discourse. With every tactic a platform comes up with to fight these bad actors, a new, often unanticipated problem is likely to emerge.

Throughout this essay, I have focused on the power of elite actors and bad actors, stressing the ways in which they exert platform capture. The power of Big Tech needs to be moderated, but platform capture stands to incentivize further perversions of the political system and undermine our information environment. The question emerges whether platform capture can ever be pro-social: Can individuals or citizen groups somehow pressure platform companies in ways that actually improve our experiences on these platforms, protect our data, and perhaps serve as a corrective to incivility and misinformation?

The answer to a more pro-social version of platform capture lies not with government regulation but rather with the choices we make each day about how we use these platforms. Platforms live and die based on whether we use them; without us, they are nothing. Although this proposal may be far-fetched, if every American were to give up Facebook, Instagram, Google, YouTube, WhatsApp, Reddit, and Twitter and put away their iPhones and Apple computers and cease using Amazon, if every company were to establish its own servers or create alternative noncommercial forms of cloud computing, platform companies would have to win us back. The threat of the loss of a user base may be one way to exact concessions from these companies and force them to consider their role in fostering democratic engagement and the public good.

Pro-social platform capture will result in specific changes only if we have a clear understanding of the current factors that put pressure on platform companies—taking the power back from platforms by people-powered resistance. We need to equip ourselves with an understanding of how algorithms work, how Silicon Valley rewards particular corporate strategies, and how political elites use platforms to further their political aims. We need to understand how regulatory frameworks used elsewhere can fit into our American political system. How we use these platforms and what we know about the pressures they face give us the power and the vocabulary to exert pressure on platforms to fulfill their aspirations of high-quality social connections and the exchange of reliable information. This chapter is, I hope, the beginning of this conversation.

NOTES

1. Robert M. Entman and Nikki Usher, "Erratum: Framing in a Fractured Democracy: Impacts of Digital Technology on Ideology, Power, and Cascading Network Activation," *Journal of Communication* 68, no. 3 (2018): 298–308, https://doi.org/10.1093/joc/jqy028.
2. Natalie Sherman, "Four Reasons That Apple Shares Have Been Falling," *BBC News*, November 21, 2018, https://www.bbc.com/news/business-46281768.
3. Daniel Stächelin and Max Hoppenstedt, "A Visit to Facebook's Recently Opened Center for Deleting Content," *Vice*, January 2, 2018, https://motherboard.vice.com/en_us/article/qv37dv/facebook-content-moderation-center.
4. Sam Levin, "Facebook Has a Fake News 'War Room'—but Is It Really Working?," *Guardian*, October 18, 2018, https://www.theguardian.com/technology/2018/oct/18/facebook-war-room-social-media-fake-news-politics.
5. Levin, "Facebook Has a Fake News 'War Room.' "
6. Sheera Frenkel, Nicholas Confessore, Cecilia Kang, Matthew Rosenberg, and Jack Nicas, "Delay, Deny, and Deflect: How Facebook's Leaders Fought Through Crisis," *New York Times*, November 14, 2018, https://www.nytimes.com/2018/11/14/technology/facebook-data-russia-election-racism.html.
7. Daniel Kreiss and Shannon C. McGregor, "Technology Firms Shape Political Communication: The Work of Microsoft, Facebook, Twitter, and Google with Campaigns During the 2016 U.S. Presidential Cycle," *Political Communication* 35, no. 2 (2018): 155, https://doi.org/10.1080/10584609.2017.1364814.
8. Eric Alterman, "What Liberal Media?," *Alternet*, February 13, 2013, https://www.alternet.org/story/15187/what_liberal_media?page=0%2C0.
9. Nikki Usher, "How Republicans Trick Facebook and Twitter with Claims of Bias," *Washington Post*, August 1, 2018, https://www.washingtonpost.com/news

/posteverything/wp/2018/08/01/how-republicans-trick-facebook-and-twitter-with
-claims-of-bias/.

10. Thomas E. Patterson, "News Coverage of the 2016 General Election: How the Press
Failed the Voters," Shorenstein Center, December 12, 2016, https://shorensteincenter
.org/news-coverage-2016-general-election/.

11. Donald Trump, tweet, quoted in Darlene Superville and Barbara Ortutay, "Trump
Accuses Google of Biased Searches, Warns 'Be Careful,' " Associated Press,
August 28, 2018, https://www.apnews.com/303cecf1f4fc43c0a466955622c3ecb0.

12. Kevin Roose, tweet, "Today's top stories on Facebook* are from: 1. Ben Shapiro 2.
Ben Shapiro 3. Daily Caller 4. 9Gag 5. TMZ 6. UNILAD 7. Franklin Graham 8. Fox
News 9. The Other 98% 10. Fox News *link posts only, last 24h, ranked by total interactions, data from @crowdtangle," Twitter, November 19, 2018, https://twitter.com
/kevinroose/status/1064633264416219136.

13. Avi Selk, "Facebook Told Two Women Their Pro-Trump Videos Were 'Unsafe,' "
Washington Post, April 18, 2018, https://www.washingtonpost.com/news/the
-intersect/wp/2018/04/10/facebook-accused-of-deeming-black-pro-trump-sisters
-unsafe/.

14. Judd Legum, "Diamond and Silk's Facebook Censorship Claim Is a Hoax," Think-
Progress, April 12, 2018, https://thinkprogress.org/diamond-and-silks-facebook
-censorship-hoax-a764012eed5b/.

15. Vijaya Gadde and Kayvon Beykpour, "Setting the Record Straight on Shadow Banning," Twitter, company blog, July 26, 2018, https://blog.twitter.com/official/en_us
/topics/company/2018/Setting-the-record-straight-on-shadow-banning.html.

16. Julia Angwin and Hannes Grassegger, "Facebook's Secret Censorship Rules Protect White Men," ProPublica, June 28, 2017, https://www.propublica.org/article
/facebook-hate-speech-censorship-internal-documents-algorithms.

17. Nikki Usher and Matt Carlson, "The Midlife Crisis of the Network Society," *Media
and Communication* 6, no. 4 (2018): 107–10, https://doi.org/10.17645/mac.v6i4.1751.

18. Thorsten Quandt, "Dark Participation," *Media and Communication* 6, no. 4 (2018):
36, https://doi.org/10.17645/mac.v6i4.1519.

19. Charlie Warzel, "A Researcher Just Found a 9,000-Video Network of YouTube
Conspiracy-Related Videos," *BuzzFeed News*, February 25, 2018, https://www
.buzzfeednews.com/article/charliewarzel/a-researcher-just-found-a-9000-video
-network-of-youtube.

20. Richard Barbrook and Andy Cameron, "The California Ideology," *Science as Culture* 6, no. 1 (1996): 44, https://doi.org/10.1080/09505439609526455.

21. Barbrook and Cameron, "The California Ideology," 44–45.

Chapter Three

MEDIA CAPTURE AND THE CRISIS
IN LOCAL JOURNALISM

PHILIP M. NAPOLI

As technological and behavioral changes have undermined the economic base for local news organizations, by many indicators the personnel and organizational infrastructure for producing journalism have been declining. These declines have concrete repercussions for civic engagement and government accountability at the local level. This chapter explores these dynamics through the lens of media capture. The declines in local journalism infrastructure create vulnerabilities that can potentially lead to diminished editorial independence between local media and government as well as between local media and other types of institutions. This chapter builds upon this perspective through an analysis of the local journalism infrastructure of all fifty states in an effort to identify states where the dangers of media capture may be most pronounced.

THE CHALLENGING ECONOMICS OF LOCAL JOURNALISM

The economic challenges confronting local journalism have been well documented.[1] As news distribution and consumption have migrated online, it has been difficult for news organizations to attract the same kind of subscription revenue that they were able to attract for their print product. As news became widely available online, news consumers became increasingly resistant to the idea of paying for news. Although we have begun to see some reversal of this trend, the bottom line remains that generating subscription revenues from digital journalism has proven more challenging than generating subscription revenues from print newspapers.

Attracting advertising revenues in the highly competitive online environment has proven equally difficult. Online platforms have siphoned off traditional forms of local newspaper advertising such as classifieds. Social media platforms and news aggregators such as Facebook and Google News have proven capable of siphoning off not only national advertising dollars but also local advertising dollars as well.[2]

And, of course, local journalism is particularly hampered (relative to national or international journalism) by the lack of economies of scale. Local journalism, by definition, serves small geographic markets with relatively small populations, which limits what can realistically be invested in producing local journalism. In the digital space, local, national, and international journalism all compete head to head (particularly within contexts such as news aggregators or social media news feeds). Given the absence of geographic distribution boundaries, the resource imbalances between national/international and local journalism can lead to further audience losses for local news organizations.

This pattern reflects the fact that economic research has shown that for all forms of media content—including journalism—production budgets are an important factor affecting audiences' consumption decisions, with audiences generally gravitating to higher-budget content over lower-budget content. This is why we have historically seen "one-way flows" in news markets, in which journalistic content flows from large markets to small markets (i.e., from cities to the suburbs), but not vice versa. So the *New York Times* reaches readers across the country (and to some extent the world), but few residents of New York City are consuming news produced by the surrounding suburban papers. Larger markets can support larger production budgets than smaller markets, whether movies, music, or news. To the average consumer, all other things being equal, larger production budgets tend to correlate with more appealing content. Thus, it is not surprising that we are seeing the distribution of journalism jobs in the United States increasingly migrating away from small communities and increasingly clustering within a few large cities.[3] The situation has reached a point that *New York Times* executive editor Dean Baquet recently described local news as "the biggest crisis in American journalism."[4]

The documented consequences of these declines in local journalism are wide ranging. Research has shown, for instance, that the demise of local newspapers leads to increases in government costs because the absence of the governmental watchdog allows local governments to operate under less scrutiny and thus, apparently, less efficiently.[5] Other studies have found that declines in the production and consumption of local journalism are related to declines in citizen knowledge, community engagement, and participation in elections.[6] Purveyors of hyperpartisan news and commentary have begun to treat the decline in local news outlets as an opportunity to create local news sites that have the appearance of traditional, mainstream local news outlets but with the ownership and sponsorship of the sites intentionally left opaque.[7] Thus, the gap left by the demise of legitimate local news outlets is being filled by outlets with less journalistic and more partisan agendas. Perhaps, then, it is not surprising that a recent study found that political polarization (as reflected in the prominence of split-ticket voting behaviors) was higher in communities that had experienced closures of their local newspaper.[8] Reflecting this range of consequences, an editorial in the *Washington Post* in 2018 described the crisis in local journalism as nothing less than "a crisis in democracy."[9]

To the extent that contemporary local news organizations operate with fewer resources, they can become more vulnerable to capture because their ability to resist pressures placed upon them by advertisers diminishes, as does their ability to engage as a governmental watchdog rather than as a passive conveyor of governmental news and information (wherein they essentially become more reliant on what journalism scholars have traditionally referred to as *information subsidies*). Reflecting this perspective, the analysis that follows examines the local journalism resources (as measured by personnel) across all fifty states.

LOCAL JOURNALISM INFRASTRUCTURE AND VULNERABILITY TO MEDIA CAPTURE

In light of these economic challenges confronting local journalism and the broader political implications of these challenges, the News Measures Research Project has been assessing the state of local journalism through a variety of methodological approaches. This project (initiated in 2014) focuses on developing indicators of the health of local journalism. The analyses produced by this research initiative can shed light on the types of communities that are most vulnerable to media capture. This chapter presents the results of an empirical investigation that focuses on the individual state as the unit of analysis and the relative robustness of the local journalism infrastructure within each state.

Local Journalism Infrastructure: A State-Level Analysis

For this analysis, the term *local journalism infrastructure* reflects an effort to extract from the entirety of the media outlets within a state those outlets—and their associated personnel—that are focused, at least to some extent, on providing local news and reporting. Thus, within the context of this analysis we approached the notion of infrastructure in terms of the total number of news/journalism-producing media outlets that could be identified within the state and the total number of individuals employed within those outlets.

This approach drew upon what is widely regarded as the best-available commercial database for identifying media outlets and media workers in the United States: the Cision Media Contacts Database (see http://www .cision.com/us/). Well known under its previous name, Bacon's Media Directories, the Cision Media Contacts Database is updated daily and contains information on more than 1.6 million contacts and outlets across the United States and abroad. The scale and scope of the data contained within Cision far exceed what can generally be gathered by academic researchers, which is why the database has frequently been utilized in academic research.[10] For this analysis, we extracted Cision data from the 2016 edition of the database.

With this database, it is possible to perform state-level searches of media outlets and to filter these searches in ways that isolate those outlets engaged in the production of news (the specific filtering criteria are discussed in more detail later). In addition, because one of the key functions of this database is to provide media contacts for public-relations professionals, each outlet entry contains a list of individual contacts within each outlet, across a wide range of occupational categories. These contact lists do not reflect the totality of individuals employed within each outlet, but they do serve as a useful comparative indicator of the human resources associated with each media outlet.

Identifying Local News Sources

The first step for this project involved effectively isolating local news-producing media outlets from the totality of media outlets located within a state to better isolate those outlets actively participating in each state's news ecosystem from the broader media ecosystem operating in each state. Given the extent to which, at this state-level unit of analysis, it is effectively impossible to analyze a sample of the content for every outlet as a means of distinguishing between outlets that produce news and those that don't, this process of outlet filtering based on outlet characteristics obtained from the Cision database was seen as a way of at least superficially tapping into this dimension of media outlets' performance and better zeroing in on the primary concern here, which is to develop a profile of the robustness of the local news media infrastructure in each state.

The Cision Database is organized according to three primary outlet categories (each with many subcategories): print, broadcast, and online. For print media, the following publication categories were included in the analysis: (1) college newspapers; (2) community newspapers; (3) daily newspapers; and (4) magazines. Other available print-media categories, such as newspaper bureaus and newspaper special sections, were not included in order to maintain a focus on the individual outlet as the unit of analysis (and the substantial personnel overlap likely to occur if data on such news organization components were combined with outlet-level data).

For broadcast media, the following types of outlets were included in the analysis: (1) radio stations; (2) television stations; (3) television networks (to account for regional cable news channels); and (4) radio networks (to account for regional radio news networks). Other available categories, such as individual radio and television programs, were not included, once again in order to maintain the focus on outlets as the unit of analysis and to avoid personnel overlap.

For online media, the following types of outlets were included in the analysis: (1) blogs; (2) news websites; and (3) online versions. The term *online versions* refers to the online presence of any print or broadcast outlets (as described earlier). From this standpoint, Cision essentially treats a local newspaper and its website as two distinct outlets. In computing our outlet counts for each state, we combined online versions with their traditional print/electronic-media counterparts into a single outlet. This approach better reflects the reality of the contemporary news ecosystem, in which legacy-media outlets and their digital components represent a single, integrated news outlet rather than separate and distinct entities. However, we did extract contact information from each component separately (as outlined later) because we discovered that the individuals listed as contacts for the online version often were different (with different job titles focused specifically on digital/online responsibilities) from those listed for the associated print or broadcast outlet. Thus, both the print/broadcast and online version contacts were combined to calculate the number of individuals associated with each organization. Other available online categories, such as Social Networking Sites and Photo/Video-Sharing Sites were not included in order to maintain the journalistic focus here.

This process of outlet selection was accompanied by subject-matter filtering. The Cision Database allows for extensive subject-matter filtering across a wide range of subject categories, including Agriculture and Farming, Building and Construction, Fashion and Beauty, Sports, and so on. Most of these categories also have multiple subcategories. For this analysis, the News and Current Affairs category was employed. This is a very broad subject-matter category, and preliminary analysis showed that its use did not lead to the exclusion of individual college, daily, or community newspapers, nor did it lead to the exclusion of individual television and radio stations. Cision essentially tags all outlets of these types with the News and Current Affairs category regardless of whether they actually engage in the *production* of such content (as discussed later). For the purposes of this analysis, the key value in employing the News and Current Affairs category as a content filter was to better filter out various types of blogs (review sites, parenting/lifestyle blogs, and so on) that are quite prevalent in the Cision Database but are not the types of outlets that are the focus of this analysis— those engaged in the production and dissemination of local journalism.

Further Filtering

In order to better narrow the focus of this analysis on local news-*producing* outlets within each state, the project employed additional layers of filtering within each outlet category. First, for news websites and blogs, the list of outlets of these types produced for each state was manually scanned. Any news websites or blogs that did not include explicit mentions of news or current affairs in their outlet profile (a text paragraph provided by Cision describing each outlet) were excluded, primarily to eliminate the many parenting/lifestyle and product-review sites that were still present even after employing the News and Current Affairs filter mentioned earlier. In addition, outlets with a clear national or international focus—rather than a focus on the state or individual communities within the state—also were excluded to maintain a focus on the presence of outlets directed at serving the news needs of residents of the state.

For television stations, Cision provides data that make it possible to determine if the individual station provides a local newscast. For this analysis, stations that provide no local newscasts were not included in the final analysis to maintain the focus on news production. This was determined by examining each station's outlet profile, in which Cision notes if the station has no news department or news director. In some cases, the outlet profile explicitly states that the station produces no local news. Stations of this type were eliminated from the final data set. Further, to better narrow the focus on *sources* of local news, the analysis excluded as well all stations identified as *tower stations* (i.e., repeaters of the signal of another local station) or as *multicasts* (i.e., the secondary or tertiary feed of a local station). Similarly, when a station was described in its outlet profile as a *sister station* that repeats the news broadcast produced by another station, it was eliminated from the final data set. These filtering decisions reflect the intended focus here on outlets engaged in the *production* of news and thus involve excluding those outlets whose capacities are limited to news *dissemination*.

For radio stations, Cision allows filtering according to format/genre. For this analysis, only those stations that included news and/or talk among their genre classifications were included in the analysis. All other programming formats/genres were excluded. Although this is admittedly an imprecise indicator for zeroing in on radio stations engaged in providing news, it seemed a reasonable reflection of the current state of the radio industry, in which investment in local journalism is increasingly rare.[11] We believe the inclusion of state-wide radio networks (discussed later) is an important factor in effectively capturing a state's news infrastructure as it pertains to radio, given that many states have commercial or noncommercial radio networks that produce and disseminate news to affiliated stations.

For radio and television networks, networks whose profiles explicitly identified a focus other than news and information were excluded. Thus, for instance, regional sports networks operated by many cable providers around the country were excluded, as were religious broadcast networks. Also, to maintain the focus on the individual state's local news and information ecosystems, the analysis excluded national radio/television networks located in individual states. State-wide networks were, however, included. Such distinctions are easily made through the networks' Cision profiles.

Finally, with respect to print, the only outlet category for which manual filtering was employed was magazines. Here, the outlet profile of each magazine based in the state was examined to determine (1) if the magazine's subject matter was focused on the state (as opposed to targeting a national or international audience) and (2) if the magazine's focus was at least to some extent news and information. If the magazine in question failed to meet both of these criteria, it was excluded. Thus, all magazines with subject matter of a national and/or international orientation were excluded. For those magazines that were focused on the individual state or on individual cities or geographic/ethnic communities within the state, this process led to the inclusion of magazines such as community-lifestyle and news publications but the exclusion of magazines such as trade association and alumni publications, visitors' guides, and entertainment/nightlife publications. Here, the presence of the term *news* in the magazine's outlet profile and subject-matter categorizations was a primary determining factor in making filtering decisions.

In general, Cision also provides the URL for every outlet's website, allowing for direct examination to provide further information when making determinations regarding inclusion or exclusion. The filtering process was handled by trained research assistants and the author. Cases of uncertainty were resolved through consultation among the researchers.

Once the list of relevant outlets was determined for each state, the list of contacts within each outlet was generated from the Cision Database. As noted earlier, Cision provides an extensive list of the individuals working within each of the media outlets it includes in order to facilitate outreach from the public-relations and marketing communities. For this project, we used these contact lists as an indicator of the outlet's size and scope. The totals provide a useful comparative indicator of the number of "news workers" operating in each state and thus the basis for a useful companion metric to the outlet counts. Thus, the contacts for every outlet in the outlet list generated for each state were extracted, with the total number for all outlets in a state serving as the indicator of the total number of news workers in each state.

For these data, we did not engage in any filtering on the basis of title or occupation because we were interested primarily in developing an indicator of the overall human resources infrastructure associated with the news outlets serving each state. Thus, regardless of job title/responsibilities, individuals listed as contacts for an outlet were counted toward that state's news infrastructure. From this standpoint, the term *news workers* is used throughout the remainder of this chapter somewhat broadly to reflect individuals directly working to produce news as well as individuals working in other supportive capacities for a news-producing media outlet.

These contact lists also were filtered to eliminate multiple counts of single individuals. It was often the case that a single individual served multiple roles within an individual outlet or served in a similar role across multiple outlets in a state. To assess more accurately the human resources infrastructure devoted to local journalism within each state, the analysis counted such individuals only once toward a state's final total. Similarly, all instances in which a contact entry provided no individual name but rather only a department or position (e.g., "Public Affairs Department") were excluded from the final tallies.

This process of data extraction and filtering took place from the spring of 2016 through the fall of 2016 and thus represents Cision's data on the media outlets and workers located in each state at that particular point in time.

RESULTS

State-by-State Comparisons

The data-gathering and filtering protocols described earlier provide a basis from which we can develop metrics for assessing individual states and comparing them in terms of the robustness of their local journalism infrastructure, as defined by the quantity of news outlets and news workers directed at serving states' news and information needs. The basic totals for each state in terms of number of local news outlets and news workers are presented in table 3.1. It is important to emphasize that these totals reflect the database search and filtering protocols described earlier and thus do not represent the full extent of the media infrastructure in each state.

TABLE 3.1
News Outlet and News Worker Totals by State

State	Number of News Outlets	Number of News Workers	State	Number of News Outlets	Number of News Workers
AL	201	1,076	MT	120	504
AK	59	262	NE	198	796
AZ	162	874	NV	78	500
AR	167	766	NH	66	348
CA	946	5,347	NJ	193	1,030
CO	228	1,110	NM	90	427
CT	152	762	NY	658	4,554
DE	30	135	NC	302	1,827
FL	481	3,296	ND	96	389
GA	332	1,668	OH	359	2,497
HI	51	295	OK	243	1,083
ID	77	393	OR	194	1,016
IL	479	2,761	PA	418	3,016
IN	268	1,464	RI	45	287
IA	318	1,260	SC	161	904
KS	125	837	SD	125	432
KY	201	1,054	TN	239	1,395
LA	198	1,080	TX	808	4,423
ME	88	490	UT	74	507
MD	61	413	VT	59	281
MA	273	1,794	VA	260	1,429
MI	337	1,878	WA	262	1,557
MN	350	1,701	WV	107	615
MS	153	661	WI	304	1,525
MO	328	1,703	WY	67	243

The size of a state's news media infrastructure is, of course, a function of the size of the population within that state, which makes direct comparisons across states difficult. Other state characteristics, such as geographic size, population density, number of municipalities, and population demographics, also may have a bearing on the size of a state's local news infrastructure.

In order to develop a clearer sense of how these various state characteristics might be related to news media infrastructure, a multiple-regression analysis was conducted that incorporated the following geographic factors: (1) population; (2) population density (population per square mile); (3) size (square miles); and (4) number of municipalities. In addition, a number of demographic factors were incorporated that could potentially relate to the robustness of a state's news media infrastructure: (1) median household income; (2) African American population percentage; and (3)

Hispanic population percentage. The incorporation of these demographic variables reflected the findings of recent research that suggested that lower-income and more ethnically diverse communities might find themselves comparatively underserved from a local journalism standpoint.[12]

It is important to note that the ratio of independent variables (seven) to cases (fifty) is less than ideal from a statistical power standpoint, though comparable ratios can be found in state-level analyses of other phenomena such as cybercrime victimization and the digital divide.[13] In such situations, the small number of cases can contribute to Type II error (false negative), which would mean that independent variables that did not emerge as significant in the analysis would have done so if the number of cases had been larger. Of course, in this case all fifty states were subjected to analysis; thus, no additional cases could be added to the point in time being analyzed.

The results of these regressions are presented in table 3.2 (news outlets) and table 3.3 (news workers). The results indicate that at the state level the local journalism infrastructure (as reflected in the number of personnel) is overwhelmingly and almost exclusively a function of population size. Analysis of scatterplots of the distribution of cases indicated that this relationship is strongly linear (rather than curvilinear). As can be seen in the tables, the model explains 93 percent of the variance in news outlets by state and 94 percent of the variance in news workers. Almost all of this variance is accounted for by population size; however, the number of municipalities also emerged as a significant explanatory factor (though with far less explanatory power than population size). None of the other state geographic and demographic characteristics incorporated into the analysis emerged as statistically significant.

TABLE 3.2
Regression Analysis of Local News Outlets in a State (N = 50)

	Beta	t
(Constant)		2.29
Population	0.94**	17.08
Municipalities	0.18**	4.05
African American %	−0.05	−0.79
Hispanic %	−0.05	−0.98
Median household income	−0.06	−1.18
Population per square mile	−0.04	−0.67
State size (square miles)	0.02	0.32

** $p < 0.01$. Adjusted $R^2 = 0.93$.

TABLE 3.3
Regression Analysis of Local News Workers in a State (N = 50)

	Beta	t
(Constant)		2.15
Population	0.94**	18.74
Municipalities	0.19**	4.61
African American %	−0.04	−0.89
Hispanic %	−0.06	−1.30
Median household income	−0.07	−1.45
Population per square mile	0.03	0.52
State size (square miles)	0.01	0.12

** $p < 0.01$. Adjusted $R^2 = 0.94$.

In terms of the issue of statistical significance, it is worth noting that despite the fact that this analysis contains data for all fifty states (i.e., the *population* of states), measures of statistical significance are still being employed under the assumption that these data represent a *sample* from one specific point in time (mid-2016, when the data were gathered) and that the models presented here would have predictive value for data gathered at subsequent points in time. We recognize that some might argue that the data presented here represent a population and not a sample and thus that indicators of statistical significance could be considered irrelevant.[14]

Finally, the news outlet and news workers measures proved to be very highly correlated ($r = 0.98$; $p < 0.01$). Given this strong correlation, the resulting similarity in the subsequent analyses, and that the news workers measure better taps into the issue of the vulnerability of existing outlets to media capture (described earlier), the focus from here on is primarily the news workers variable.

The positive relationship between the number of municipalities and news media infrastructure is reflective of what we might expect—that individual municipalities have their own unique information needs associated with their local political processes and civic and cultural institutions. These unique information needs spur and sustain media outlets that serve these needs—though only to an apparently relatively moderate extent. Indeed, despite the statistical significance of this relationship, its modest practical significance is in some ways troubling, particularly given the relatively weak correlation between population size and the number of municipalities ($r = 0.27$; $p > 0.05$), which indicates that these two variables vary independently. From a media and democracy standpoint, it would certainly be preferable to see a state's news media infrastructure be more responsive to variation in the number of municipalities. It would be particularly interesting to explore the nature of this relationship with longitudinal data to see if in the past the number of municipalities had a stronger relationship with the local journalism infrastructure before economic and technological changes undermined the viability of local news outlets.

Based on these findings and the overwhelming significance of population size in explaining variance in the number of news workers and news outlets in a state, controlling for population size would seem to provide a potentially useful way of facilitating more direct comparisons across states, though, of course, relying purely on population neglects various characteristics of the population that might be relevant. Table 3.4 presents the news outlets and news workers per 100,000 residents for each state.

However, even this representation of state news media infrastructure has limitations in terms of allowing us to draw comparisons across states because the number of news outlets/news workers per 100,000 residents also is a function of the size of a state's population. News, like all forms of media content, is what economists call a *public good*.[15] Public goods have very high fixed costs but very low variable costs, which means that there are economies of scale to be realized when the production costs can be spread across a larger audience base. As a consequence, is it reasonable to expect populous states like California and New York to have as many news outlets/news workers per 100,000 residents as less-populous states such as South Dakota and Wyoming? Probably not.

And, indeed, figure 3.1 bears this out. In figure 3.1, we have scatter-plotted each state's news workers per 100,000 residents (the y axis of the graph) according to the state's population (the x axis). As the figure illustrates, the relationship between news workers per 100,000 residents is much more logarithmic (the dotted line) than linear (the solid line). And, as we can also see, less-populous states, such as North Dakota, South Dakota, Wyoming, and Vermont (see the upper-left portion of the graph), have more news workers per 100,000 residents than do very populous states, such as New York, California, Florida, and Texas (see the lower-right portion of the graph).

Figure 3.1 illustrates which states have more—and which states have fewer—news workers per 100,000 residents than their population size

TABLE 3.4
News Outlets and News Workers per 100,000 Residents by State

State	News Outlets per 100,000 Residents	News Workers per 100,000 residents	State	News Outlets per 100,000 Residents	News Workers per 100,000 residents
AL	4.14	22.14	MT	11.62	48.79
AK	7.99	35.48	NE	10.44	41.98
AZ	2.37	12.80	NV	2.70	17.30
AR	5.61	25.72	NH	4.96	26.15
CA	2.42	13.66	NJ	2.15	11.50
CO	4.18	20.34	NM	4.32	20.48
CT	4.23	21.22	NY	3.32	23.00
DE	3.17	14.27	NC	3.01	18.19
FL	2.37	16.26	ND	12.68	51.39
GA	3.25	16.33	OH	3.09	21.50
HI	3.56	20.61	OK	6.21	27.69
ID	4.65	23.75	OR	4.82	25.22
IL	3.72	21.47	PA	3.26	23.56
IN	4.05	22.12	RI	4.26	27.17
IA	10.18	40.33	SC	3.29	18.46
KS	4.29	28.75	SD	14.56	50.32
KY	4.54	23.82	TN	3.62	21.14
LA	4.24	23.12	TX	2.94	16.10
ME	6.62	36.86	UT	2.47	16.92
MD	1.02	6.88	VT	9.42	44.89
MA	4.02	26.40	VA	3.10	17.05
MI	3.40	18.93	WA	3.65	21.71
MN	6.38	30.99	WV	5.80	33.35
MS	5.11	22.09	WI	5.27	26.42
MO	5.39	27.99	WY	11.43	41.46

would lead us to expect. So, for instance, states such as Maryland, New Jersey, and Arizona sit well below the curve, with numbers of news workers per 100,000 residents substantially lower than their population sizes would lead us to expect. We can think of these states as being underserved relative to their population from a local journalism infrastructure standpoint. These states seem less capable of sustaining the expected levels of local journalism infrastructure, and thus communities in those states may be more vulnerable to those forms of media capture that are a function of resource inadequacies.

It should be emphasized that the unit of analysis employed here doesn't tell us anything about the vulnerability of individual media outlets to capture; rather, the point is that it may tell us how vulnerable the local journalism ecosystem in the aggregate may be to capture. States in which the

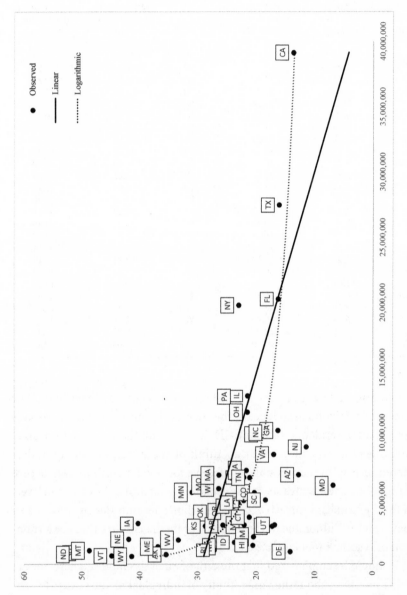

FIGURE 3.1. Scatterplot of news workers per 100,000 residents by population size.

number of journalism professionals fails to reflect the size of the population may be states in which the local journalism ecosystem is less equipped to resist the various forms of media capture.

In contrast, states such as Minnesota, Iowa, and Texas have substantially more local news workers per 100,000 residents than their population sizes would lead us to expect. We can think of these states as being overserved from a journalism infrastructure standpoint relative to what we would expect based on population size. These states thus may have local journalism ecosystems that are better able to resist the various forms of media capture.

In order to provide an additional perspective from which to consider vulnerability to media capture, the size of these deviations from expectations has been plotted in figure 3.2. In this figure, for each state the difference between the actual and the predicted value (i.e., the residual) is divided by the predicted value, which allows us to represent as a percentage the extent to which a state's local journalism infrastructure is larger or smaller than its population size would lead us to expect. We can then compare states in terms of the extent to which their number of news workers per 100,000 exceeds or falls short of expectations based on population size. As figure 3.2 indicates, the states that fare the best in exceeding their population-predicted number of news workers per 100,000 residents include South Dakota, North Dakota, New York, California, and Iowa. At the other end of the continuum are Maryland, Delaware, New Jersey, and Nevada.

We can't confidently say why some states fare better on this measure than others. As our multivariate analyses presented previously illustrated, potential explanatory factors related to a state's geographic and demographic characteristics contributed little to the substantial explanatory power offered by population size. Other factors, perhaps unique to individual states, may be at work here.

To offer another perspective on these data, figure 3.3 presents a map of the United States that is shaded according to the magnitude of a state's deviation from predicted news workers per 100,000 residents. The lightest-shaded states are those with news workers per 100,000 residents that meet or exceed their predicted values. The darker-shaded states are those that underperform on this measure to a magnitude of between −0.1 and −19.99 percent. The darkest-shaded states are those whose deviation from predicted values is −20 percent and lower. These states have local journalism infrastructures

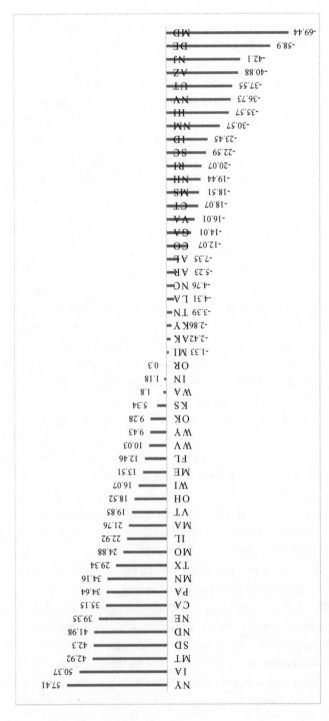

FIGURE 3.2. States ranked by percentage deviation from predicted news workers per 100,000 residents (based on population).

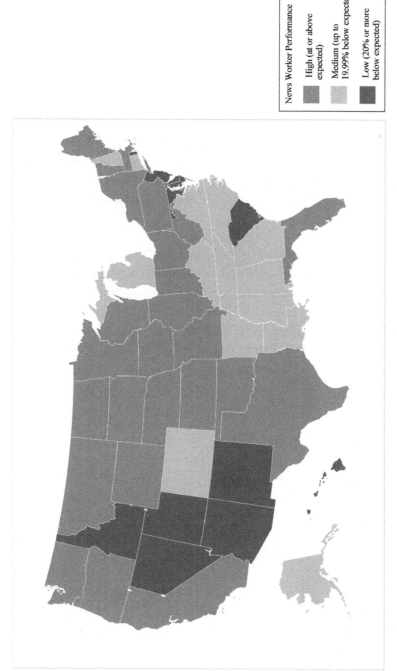

FIGURE 3.3. State map of magnitude of deviation from predicted news workers per 100,000 residents.

News Worker Performance

High (at or above expected)

Medium (up to 19.99% below expected)

Low (20% or more below expected)

that, according to the measure employed here, are in the worst condition and thus potentially the most vulnerable to media capture.

As figure 3.3 indicates, moderately underperforming states are somewhat clustered in the South. The Midwest as a whole performs quite well. There are two primary geographic clusters of very poorly performing states: in the Mountain West region and in the coastal Northeast. Looking at these patterns, one can't help but wonder whether the proximity of geographically small but relatively populous states, such as Maryland, Rhode Island, and New Jersey, to large, out-of-state media markets such as Washington, DC, Boston, New York City, and Philadelphia may explain the significantly lower-than-predicted ratios of news outlets and news workers per 100,000 residents in those states. In such instances, the large media outlets located just over the border may be undermining the robustness of local news outlets in those states. Other unique factors may be at work in relation to other states. The significant underperformance in the Mountain West region is more difficult to explain and merits further research. The primary goal here, however, is to provide comparative indicators that facilitate an assessment of the relative robustness of the local journalism infrastructures across states and thus their relative vulnerability to media capture. According to these data, the two regions of the United States that are most vulnerable are the Mountain West and the coastal Northeast.

This chapter has used an analysis of the robustness of the local journalism infrastructure within each state as a lens through which to consider the vulnerability of states' local media ecosystem to media capture. Future research should take the logical next step and gather state-level indicators of media capture in an effort to determine the extent to which the assumption put forth here, that the robustness of a state's local journalism ecosystem serves as a meaningful indicator of a state's vulnerability to media capture, holds up under empirical testing. As journalism researchers continue to document the range of ramifications associated with the declines in local journalism, such a large-scale exploration into the dynamics of media capture could potentially make a valuable contribution to this growing body of literature.

NOTES

The research presented in this chapter was conducted with the support of a grant from the Democracy Fund's Public Square Program. The opinions contained within this chapter represent those of the author and not the Democracy Fund or its staff.

1. See, for example, Penelope Abernathy, *The Rise of a New Media Baron and the Emerging Threat of News Deserts* (Chapel Hill: University of North Carolina Press, 2016); David W. Chen, "In New Jersey, Only a Few Media Watchdogs Are Left," *New York Times*, January 3, 2017, https://www.nytimes.com/2017/01/03/nyregion/in-new-jersey-only-a-few-media-watchdogs-are-left.html; Rasmus K. Nielsen, *Local Journalism: The Decline of Newspapers and the Rise of Digital Media* (London: I. B. Tauris, 2015).

2. Tom Grubisich, "Why Even Top Local News Sites Can't Compete with Facebook on Ads," *Street Fight*, January 4, 2018, http://streetfightmag.com/2018/01/04/why-even-top-local-news-sites-cant-compete-with-facebook-on-ads/.

3. Jim Tankersley, "Why the PR Industry Is Sucking Up Pulitzer Winners," *Washington Post*, April 23, 2015, https://www.washingtonpost.com/news/wonk/wp/2015/04/23/why-the-pr-industry-is-sucking-up-pulitzer-winners/.

4. Dean Baquet, quoted in James Warren, "*New York Times* Editor: Local News Is the Biggest 'Crisis' in Journalism," Poynter, May 31, 2017, https://www.poynter.org/newsletters/2017/dean-baquet-targets-the-crisis-in-journalism-local-news/.

5. Kriston Capps, "The Hidden Costs of Losing Your City's Newspaper," *CityLab*, May 30, 2018, https://www.citylab.com/equity/2018/05/study-when-local-newspaper-close-city-bond-finances-suffer/561422/.

6. Lisa George and Joel Waldfogel, "Does the *New York Times* Spread Ignorance and Apathy?," unpublished working paper, 2002, http://www.anderson.ucla.edu/faculty_pages/romain.wacziarg/mediapapers/GeorgeWaldfogel.pdf; Danny Hayes and Jennifer L. Lawless, "As Local News Goes, so Goes Citizen Engagement: Media, Knowledge, and Participation in U.S. House Elections," American University School of Public Affairs, Research Paper no. 2014-0004, 2014, https://papers.ssrn.com/sol3/papers.cfm?abstract_id=2452076; Danny Hayes and Jennifer Lawless, "The Decline of Local News and Its Effects: New Evidence from Longitudinal Data," *Journal of Politics* 80, no. 1 (2018): 332–36.

7. Jason Schwartz, "Baby Breitbarts to Pop Up Across the Country?," *Politico*, May 1, 2018, https://www.politico.com/story/2018/04/30/breitbart-tennessee-fake-news-560670.

8. Joshua P. Darr, Matthew P. Hitt, and Johanna L. Dunaway, "Newspaper Closures Polarize Voting Behavior," *Journal of Communication* 68, no. 6 (2018): 1007–28.

9. Steve Waldman and Charles Sennott, "The Crisis in Local Journalism Has Become a Crisis of Democracy," *Washington Post*, April 11, 2018, https://www.washingtonpost.com/opinions/the-crisis-in-journalism-has-become-a-crisis-of-democracy/2018/04/11/a908d5fc-2d64-11e8-8688-e053ba58f1e4_story.html?utm_term=.9867a3ac6bfc. See also Henri Gondreau, "Don't Stop the Presses! When Local News Struggles, Democracy Withers," *Wired*, November 30, 2017, https://www.wired.com/story/dont-stop-the-presses-why-big-tech-should-subsidize-real-journalism/.

10. See George and Waldfogel, "Does the *New York Times* Spread Ignorance and Apathy?"; Michael McCluskey, "Reporter Beat and Content Differences in Environmental Stories," *Journalism & Mass Communication Quarterly* 85, no. 1 (2008): 83–98.

11. See Abernathy, *The Rise of a New Media Baron*; and Tyrone Sanders, "American Local Radio Journalism: A Public Interest Channel in Crisis," PhD diss., University of Oregon, 2008.

12. Philip M. Napoli, Kathleen McCollough, Sarah Stonbely, and Bryce Renninger, "Local Journalism and the Information Needs of Local Communities: Toward a Scalable Assessment Approach," *Journalism Practice* 11, no. 4 (2017): 373–95.

13. Hyojong Song, Michael J. Lynch, and John K. Cochran, "A Macro-social Exploratory Analysis of the Rate of Interstate Cyber-victimization," *American Journal of Criminal Justice* 41 (2016): 583–601; James B. Pick, Avijit Sarkar, and Jeremy Johnson, "United States Digital Divide: State Level Analysis of Spatial Clustering and Multivariate Determinants of ICT Utilization," *Socio-economic Planning Science* 49 (2015): 16–32.

14. Regression diagnostics indicated no problems of multicollinearity of the independent variables (tolerance statistics of between 0.48 and 0.76 for all independent variables) or of autocorrelation of residuals (Durbin-Watson statistics of 2.5 in both cases). However, due to evidence in residual scatterplots of some heteroskedasticity and (as indicated by significant Shapiro-Wilk tests) nonnormality in the distribution of the dependent variables, an alternative specification of these models was run using log-transformed dependent variables. The results were similar, with both population size and the number of municipalities emerging as statistically significant, but with the standardized beta for population slightly reduced and the standardized beta for municipalities slightly increased. The adjusted R-squareds also decreased somewhat to 0.70 for news outlets and 0.75 for news workers. Models employing log-transformed independent variables also were explored but resulted in very high levels of multicollinearity for a number of the independent variables and less overall explanatory power.

15. James Hamilton, *All the News That's Fit to Sell: How the Market Transforms Information Into News* (Princeton, NJ: Princeton University Press, 2004).

Chapter Four

NOBODY HOME

NOAM COHEN

Growth for the sake of growth is the ideology of the cancer cell.

—EDWARD ABBEY, *THE JOURNEY HOME*

One fall afternoon in 1973, three men entered a Seaman's furniture store on Livingston Street in Downtown Brooklyn and demanded that the lone salesman hand over all the cash in the store. The salesman, John J. Hug, came up with $1,200, but the robbers weren't satisfied; two of them pushed Mr. Hug down the freight elevator shaft, and the third sent the elevator car down to smash him. If not for the buffer springs, which gave Mr. Hug twelve inches to spare, he surely would have been crushed. A half-hour later, a porter heard his screams and helped him escape.[1]

On the other side of the country, John McCarthy, the head of the artificial intelligence lab at Stanford University, read in the *New York Times* about Mr. Hug's ordeal and pondered how people make sense of the news: What background knowledge does an ordinary reader have so that the events described on the printed page make sense? And how would you program a computer to have those same capacities? Three years later McCarthy published an extraordinary paper, "An Example for Natural Language Understanding and the AI Problems It Raises," which used the *Times* article as a leaping-off point.[2] In the paper, McCarthy lists no fewer than twenty-two questions that a computer should be able to answer from the five brief paragraphs in the *Times* that he reprinted at the top. Those questions were not only the typical journalistic fare—Who? What? Where? Why?

How?—but also bizarre no-brainers an ordinary reader would never pause to consider, such as "Did Mr. Hug know he was going to be robbed?" "Did he want to be crushed?" "Who had the money at the end, Mr. Hug or the robbers?"

These questions may seem unnecessary to us, but they were vital to McCarthy's purpose. They spelled out in detail many of the facts and insights people carry with themselves unthinkingly. If only computers could be trained to carry these same insights, McCarthy reasoned, they, too, could understand the world the way people do.

Such was McCarthy's take on *artificial intelligence*, a term he coined for a pathbreaking conference in Dartmouth in 1956.[3] His strategy, which made so much sense in the 1950s, was to build an artificially intelligent machine by treating the matter as a reverse-engineering problem. Carefully record, step by tedious step, how a person does a certain task—tying shoelaces, driving a car, reading the newspaper—so you can instruct a machine accordingly. With the right analysis, any human endeavor could be reduced to a straightforward math problem,[4] a hubristic approach to computer science that lives on today in the following Silicon Valley conviction: treat machines as people, treat people as machines.

In this chapter, I trace the recent failures in how news is produced and consumed online—the media capture detailed in the other chapters of this book—to the fundamental category confusion promoted by McCarthy and the other AI pioneers willing to trust algorithms to carry out human tasks. To McCarthy and the others, the benefits from automated news distribution to personal computers were obvious, primarily more knowledge available to more people. With the help of algorithmically empowered computers, indeed, news organizations today deliver oodles of news and information—algorithmically tailored to our interests—to the tiny computers we all carry with us.

What these visionaries hadn't considered was that their faith in algorithms would ultimately change how the news that computers would be "understanding" in the future is produced. Today's news is distributed by a handful of gigantic, journalistically oblivious platforms that rely on algorithms to process and deliver so much information to so many people. Such concentration of power has soaked up the advertising revenue of traditional newspapers, putting under mortal threat the notion of independent journalism. The result is a news media ecosystem that has clear chokepoints where governments and businesses can apply pressure—a key ingredient of media capture—and that has abandoned the project of truth telling and critical coverage.

The brash Silicon Valley titans such as Mark Zuckerberg of Facebook, Jack Dorsey of Twitter, and Sergey Brin and Larry Page of Google didn't necessarily sign up to be modern-day press barons. From the start, they have given themselves a different mission of connecting the people of the world to the world's information. The news, they soon discovered, ties people together and represents much of the information people want to access. Facebook and Google and Twitter inevitably became the world's news services. And, as is their wont, those companies deployed algorithms to analyze the news that passed through their platforms the better to match an article and its potential readers.

Whereas the earlier news barons—loud, larger-than-life characters such as the Murdochs and the Hearsts—reveled in the economic and political power that flows from controlling the news, the Silicon Valley news barons have been introverted and self-effacing, insisting they operate neutral platforms. If they register any thrill from their increasing control over the news, it can be traced to pride that their digital platforms have truly become indispensable. But this shouldn't absolve them of responsibility for the news they spread, as they have hoped. In fact, the quest to be indispensable has made them particularly open to media capture.

Silicon Valley platforms have prospered from the same tactics used by the bombastic, yellow journalists throughout history—inflammatory headlines and stories, anger directed at outsiders, an appeal to tribalism, titillation. In this way, in shunning thoughtful analysis and deep reporting, they have served the powerful. Also, like the press barons of old, they have made deals with politicians and businesses, unburdened by principles about journalism or democracy or anything else that would stand in the way.

In the fall of 2019, Facebook, YouTube, and Twitter with little fanfare agreed to make an exemption to their standards of conduct to allow President Donald Trump, and in some cases his backers, to spread hate and aggression on their platforms that would otherwise be blocked. They all cited the inherent "news value" of those statements, with Facebook going so far as to say that it would allow all manner of lies or hate on any advertisement or page "with the primary purpose of expressing the opinion or agenda of a political figure." (For those looking closely at the role of capture,

Facebook clarified that "only politicians currently in office or running for office, and political parties, are exempt: other political adverts still need to be true." Why cater your rules to those merely seeking power?)[5]

This jury-rigged policy of permitting lies from politicians, but not from others, was defended by Zuckerberg in a speech at Georgetown University a year before Election Day 2020 as standing "for free expression, understanding its messiness, but believing that the long journey towards greater progress requires confronting ideas that challenge us."[6]

The high-mindedness of Zuckerberg's explanation lost much of its potency, however, when word leaked out that only days later he attended a secret dinner with Trump, Trump's son-in-law, Jared Kushner, as well as longtime Facebook board member Peter Thiel, who was a prominent supporter of Trump in 2016. The question, put in a *New York Times* account of these events, was: "Did Mr. Trump and Mr. Zuckerberg reach some kind of accommodation?"[7] As in, Trump gets freedom to spread lies to his supporters, while Mr. Zuckerberg gets the support of a president who has made no secret of using his power to reward friends and punish enemies. (A final reward for Facebook: in the seven months before the 2020 election the Trump campaign spent an estimated $89 million on Facebook ads; the Biden campaign came close, at $85 million in the same period.)[8]

Toward the end of the campaign, Facebook, YouTube, and Twitter issued yet newer rules to block certain campaign "speech" that directly threatened the integrity of the election or encouraged violence.[9] But the application of these rules was haphazard and highlighted how arbitrary these companies' principles, in fact, were: Could it be that the long journey to greater progress didn't necessarily require "confronting ideas that challenge us"?

We learned in 2020 that Big Tech's version of yellow journalism may well represent a greater danger to democracy than yellow journalism of the past. After all, the yellow newspapers, with their political slants and trumped-up causes, were only one part of a journalistic ecosystem that included publications with different values; today, the digital platforms *are* the ecosystem. They succeed not if we believe a certain idea with furious intensity and become transfixed, but if we believe any idea with furious intensity. Conspiracy theories of all stripes and political persuasions are welcome under the big umbrella of a Silicon Valley platform such as Facebook, Twitter, or YouTube.

Sean Parker, the first president of Facebook, recently explained how programmers like himself and Zuckerberg were consciously exploiting "a vulnerability in human psychology" by using the platform "to sort of give you a little dopamine hit every once in a while, because someone liked or commented on a photo or a post or whatever." The goal was clear: "How do we consume as much of your time and conscious attention as possible?"[10]

The current, profit-seeking use of AI—the business model of Facebook, Google, and so many other Silicon Valley companies—is a radical departure from the idealistic ambitions of McCarthy and his young colleague, Marvin Minsky, who together organized the Dartmouth conference. When seeking grants for the conference, the two stated confidently their conjecture "that every aspect of learning or any other feature of intelligence can in principle be so precisely described that a machine can be made to simulate it."[11] Once a machine began to think, the sky was the limit.

This deep faith in science is on the one hand inspiring while on the other fundamentally flawed in its appreciation of human activities, including journalism. McCarthy leaves out so much about being human in his paper from the 1970s as he proposes teaching machines how to read the news. In particular, he ignores the uncomfortable, nonfactual questions we ask ourselves every day to make sense of the world, such as "How does this article make me feel?" "Why do I care?" "What will I do differently after reading it?" To McCarthy, writing a news article is nothing more than gathering facts; reading a news article is the transference of those facts to a brain so it can answer comprehension questions. Notably, McCarthy chose to leave out the final two paragraphs of the *Times* article about the robbery, which do not report the events that occurred but rather the feelings of those involved:

> Mr. Hug said that when he got home he "had several good shots" to calm himself while waiting for his wife, Mary, to return home from her bank job.
> He was alone in the store yesterday was [*sic*] because of the Jewish holidays. He said he was going to request a transfer to another store because he felt he "was afraid he was pressing his luck."

It's not just the idioms and definitions that might challenge a computer: "Excuse me, human friend, how does one *press* one's luck, exactly? Is there a button somewhere? What exactly is *luck*, anyway?" More significant are the complicated and contradictory sentiments. A man has endured a traumatic experience. He's wondering why robberies keep happening to him. Maybe he's even wondering why robberies happen at all. He is considering switching jobs. A reader needs context to understand all of this —not context as in what is the precise meaning of the word *robbery* but context that recognizes that people are often afraid to die, worry they'll miss loved ones, can become angry at the idea that people would hurt them just for money. You know, just the big things.

Yet here we are forty years later with executives from Facebook and YouTube and Google espousing a McCarthy-like belief that artificially intelligent computers can be taught to understand and distribute news and, more importantly, should be *trusted* to understand and distribute news. When Zuckerberg was questioned by members of Congress who criticized Facebook's efforts in policing dangerous posts that appear on its platform—hate speech, false news items presented as if genuine, incendiary arguments—he promised that computer algorithms would come to the rescue. Specifically about hate speech, he told Congress, "I am optimistic that over a five-to-ten-year period we will have AI tools that can get into some of the linguistic nuances of different types of content to be more accurate, to be flagging things to our systems, but today we're just not there on that."[12] This was before Facebook carved out its hate-speech, untruthfulness exemption for politicians and political parties, thus rendering the AI tools irrelevant.

The vice president of Google in charge of news, Richard Gingras, expressed a similar faith in algorithms. He was just being practical. At the size of Google or Facebook, if algorithms can't solve the problem, there really is nowhere else to turn. In an interview with Bloomberg TV in 2018, Gingras said matter-of-factly: "We actually don't make any editorial decisions—this is all done with machines. . . . We look at what all the news organizations are doing, what they are covering, how they are covering it, and algorithmically we make a determination as to what the top stories are."[13]

Google's way from the start has been to use what already exists on the Web to better organize the Web and support an advertising business. The basis of the Google search engine, the PageRank algorithm, which was created by Brin and Page while they were Stanford graduate students, analyzes links by and among web pages to fuel Google's search-result rankings. Today's

Google news algorithm works along the same lines.[14] "You could think of it in a sense as crowd sourcing editors," Gingras says.[15]

The one quality shared by Facebook and Google is that neither wants to take responsibility for what appears on its platform. So just as we can see how these companies are indebted to McCarthy and his fact-based understanding of news, we shouldn't be surprised that they are casual purveyors of false news. He showed the way. When you divorce facts from context— Who wrote this? How do these facts fit into the large narrative of your community, your institutions, your country?—then they become trivial and easily obscured. You say Mr. Hug was robbed at the furniture store, I say it was an inside job. What does a reporter know that I don't?

In practice, algorithms have failed every major test at these large platforms[16]—whether that means banning as pornography images of breast-feeding mothers[17] or the famous photograph of a naked Vietnamese girl frantically running after being set on fire by napalm dropped by the U.S. military[18] or ads placed by and for the Trump campaign to explicitly suppress the African American vote in the 2016 election[19] or allowing fantastic news articles published by fictitious news outlets to reach audiences lacking the news literacy tools to reject them. In terms of profits, however, AI-enabled news distribution has been an unprecedented success.

In the early days of Facebook, when it had barely left the Harvard dorm room where the twenty-year-old Zuckerberg cooked it up, he was given a crucial piece of advice by Thiel, the company's first outside investor. "Here's the one thing that matters," Zuckerberg recalled Thiel saying, "connecting everyone as quickly as possible, because network effects were a massively important part of this."[20] *Network effects* is a term that encapsulates all the benefits from being the biggest platform in town—the efficiencies of operating on a global, billions-of-users scale and the pressure its size puts on the public to join the crowd. Growth is power, Thiel knew, and his advice was quite shrewd, if tautological: to become the biggest in the world, you need to be the biggest in the world. Not the best, the biggest.

Zuckerberg today insists that his motivation in building Facebook isn't greed or power but simply to make the world a better place, specifically to fulfill the company's new motto: "Give people the power to build community and bring the world closer together."[21] Over the decade of Facebook's rise, Zuckerberg has gone back and forth on the issue of how important news should be in an average person's life, which would then be reflected in the news feed Facebook algorithmically produces for each user based on her past likes and dislikes. At times, Facebook has joined with news organizations to promote their work; at other times, it has decided that news is really a source of anger and division and that what people need to see instead is personal updates from family and friends.

At the beginning of 2018, Zuckerberg cited social science to explain Facebook's decision to again retreat from news. According to research, he explained, passively reading articles or watching videos, even informative ones, may not be good for well-being. As a result, Zuckerberg told Facebook users, who now number around two billion, "you'll see less public content like posts from businesses, brands, and media. And the public content you see more will be held to the same standard—it should encourage meaningful interactions between people."[22]

One man's waffling over the importance of news—and entrusting a computer algorithm to carry out an edict that news posts "should encourage meaningful interactions between people"—would be laughable were it not so scary. In a meeting with news executives that was covered by the *Atlantic*, Zuckerberg defended himself by retreating to the convenient position that, "in general, within a news organization, there is an opinion. I do think that a lot of what you all do, is have an opinion and have a view." Facebook, he explained, simply "has more opinions." Joe Kahn, the managing editor of the *New York Times*, called Zuckerberg out: "The institutional values of most really good media companies should transcend any individual opinion." Zuckerberg's denial that there is any such a thing as a professional commitment to informing the public, Kahn said, was "part and parcel of the polarization of society." If there is no authority other than intensity of opinion—a quality that a computer can measure quite accurately—then we are left with two screaming factions. There was a pause after Kahn spoke, Adrienne LaFrance reported in the *Atlantic*, and then Zuckerberg replied, "I think that's fair."[23]

Despite Zuckerberg's concession, Facebook by its actions denies the importance of traditional journalism. Facebook and Google don't go so far as to have an algorithm randomly generate a news article on a certain topic from any of a thousand organizations. No respectable platform would do that, of course—treat a self-published, politically compromised blog the same as a long-standing, long-respected news publication. But the two companies do something similar; they algorithmically send you to sites that have a perspective similar to what you've expressed interest in before. You've read racist conspiracy theories in the past and "liked" them, so, well, that's what you'll get now. Gingras of Google tried to explain: "Some folks say, because of the algorithm at YouTube, if I watch an extremist video, I get another extremist video. And I say, yes that's true." He said that videos that violate YouTube's policies would be removed, but he conceded that plenty of extreme content fits well within the parameters of those policies. He continued: "I have to remind people that that same algorithm that is likely to, in a sense, reinforce your interest in a bad subject is the same one that reinforces my interest as a woodworker in woodworking videos, or someone who is interested in human rights and transgender rights in the same way."[24]

Unlike the random-news generator, sending people material similar to what they have liked before makes business sense. People won't be scared away. Also, this kind of simple analysis is just right for algorithms. There is no insistence that an algorithm understand a new text and assess it for reliability and accuracy in comparison with another text, as McCarthy once imagined. What Google and Facebook ask an algorithm to do is more like matching similar items. A perfect assignment for AI, as it is understood today: that is, not an intelligent machine helping to inform the public but an intelligent machine that keeps the public's attention.

"Let's be honest with ourselves," Gingras said in an interview with the Nieman Journalism Lab, the spread of unreliable, sensationalist news "didn't start with the Internet, right? Frankly, you can go back to tabloid journalism in that regard. I mean, you know, what bleeds leads. Give me a break. These are important issues for society, but when I hear people say 'oh God, Facebook is causing your addiction,' I go wait a second—we've been driving addiction with media since the day we started producing it."[25] Freed from journalistic traditions or codes of conduct, these algorithm-led companies welcome yellow journalism on their platforms and often bend to the special pleadings of right-wing grifters such as Alex Jones of InfoWars, who claims his news reports are unfairly suppressed.[26] If you don't hold the reporting process sacred, rejecting someone's conspiracies can look as if you're picking on that person. After all, lots of people read conspiracy theories.

One writer, Richard Roberts, explored the parallel between the leaders of Silicon Valley and young Rupert Murdoch as depicted in the recent play *Ink* by James Graham. In the early 1960s, Murdoch was less concerned with right-wing politics than with turning his new purchase, the *Sun*, into the most-popular newspaper. "There is no code he lives by, no purpose that motivates him, apart from this single-minded quest to grow *The Sun*'s readership and beat the competition," Roberts writes. The politics came later, and the lesson is that "we didn't get where we are today by design. The undermining of civil society (in both senses) was an unintended side-effect of the pursuit of growth at all costs."[27]

Facebook grows because Facebook must grow to be Facebook, just as Thiel counseled. In an internal memo, one of Zuckerberg's closest confidants, Andrew Bosworth, a senior vice president who also was Zuckerberg's teaching assistant in a computer science class at Harvard, explained the Facebook corporate philosophy:

> The ugly truth is that we believe in connecting people so deeply that anything that allows us to connect more people more often is *de facto* good. It is perhaps the only area where the metrics do tell the true story as far as we are concerned.
>
> That isn't something we are doing for ourselves. Or for our stock price (ha!). It is literally just what we do. We connect people. Period.[28]

Bosworth later denied that he ever believed what he wrote—it was all a thought experiment to encourage impassioned discussion. Upon close examination, however, his apology, which was followed by an apology from Zuckerberg, didn't make any sense. The heart of Bosworth's apology was this line, "I care deeply about how our product affects people and I take very personally the responsibility I have to make that impact positive."[29] Zuckerberg similarly said, "We recognize that connecting people isn't enough by itself. We also need to work to bring people closer together."[30] To disagree with what Bosworth wrote, however, you would have to dispute that growth is something to be pursued no matter what. Yet this is Facebook's belief now and always has been. This is the Silicon Valley ideology distilled: growth is good. You can't connect the world without growth. And connecting the world is good. Journalistic ethics must give way. Media capture is a small price to pay.

Lately there has been some public push back on this question—Could small and local be better? Zuckerberg has a response. "I think that the alternative, frankly, is going to be the Chinese companies," he told an interviewer who proposed breaking up the Big Tech companies. "They do not share the values that we have. I think you can bet that if the government hears word that it's election interference or terrorism, I don't think Chinese companies are going to want to cooperate as much and try to aid the national interest there."[31] In other words, the current algorithm-based capture of the news media cannot be reversed by the people because a worse algorithm-based capture will take its place. Do we want an American-based media capture or—God forbid!—a Chinese-based one?

Of course, Zuckerberg's cynicism is misplaced and self-serving. His is antidemocratic, antiregulatory thinking run amok. No, we can change course. The people can control how the news is created and distributed. Large, automated social networks are not inevitable. Technology is not destiny. That these leaders answer criticism with implicit threats is the best evidence that they—and the algorithms that act in their name—should not be entrusted with delivering the news.

NOTES

1. *New York Times*, "Salesman Robbed and Pushed Down an Elevator Shaft," September 29, 1973.

2. John McCarthy, "An Example for Natural Language Understanding and the AI Problems It Raises," 1976, http://jmc.stanford.edu/articles/mrhug.html.

3. John McCarthy, Marvin L. Minsky, Nathaniel Rochester, and Claude E. Shannon, "A Proposal for the Dartmouth Summer Research Project on Artificial Intelligence," August 31, 1955, reprinted in *AI Magazine* 27, no. 4 (2006): 12–14, https://aaai.org/ojs /index.php/aimagazine/article/view/1904/1802.

4. McCarthy, "An Example for Natural Language Understanding."

5. Facebook, quoted in Alex Hern, "Facebook Exempts Political Ads from Ban on False Claims," *Guardian*, October, 4, 2019, https://www.theguardian.com/technology /2019/oct/04/facebook-exempts-political-ads-ban-making-false-claims.

6. "Mark Zuckerberg Stands for Voice and Free Expression," *Facebook Newsroom*, October 17, 2019, https://about.fb.com/news/2019/10/mark-zuckerberg-stands-for -voice-and-free-expression/.

7. Ben Smith, "What's Facebook's Deal with Donald Trump?," *New York Times*, June 21, 2020, https://www.nytimes.com/2020/06/21/business/media/facebook-donald -trump-mark-zuckerberg.html.

8. Simon Dumenco, "Here's What Trump and Biden Have Spent on Facebook and Google Ads," *AdAge*, October 30, 2020, https://adage.com/article/campaign-trail /heres-what-trump-and-biden-have-spent-facebook-and-google-ads/2291531.

9. Adam Conner and Erin Simpson, "Addressing Social Media's Threat to Democratic Legitimacy and Public Safety After Election Day," Center for American Progress, October 23, 2020.

10. Sean Parker, quoted in Olivia Solon, "Ex-Facebook President Sean Parker: Site Made to Exploit Human 'Vulnerability,'" *Guardian*, November 9, 2017, https://www.theguardian.com/technology/2017/nov/09/facebook-sean-parker-vulnerability-brain-psychology.

11. McCarthy et al., "A Proposal," 12.

12. Mark Zuckerberg, quoted in Dave Gershgorn, "Mark Zuckerberg Just Gave a Timeline for AI to Take Over Detecting Internet Hate Speech," *Quartz*, April 10, 2018, https://qz.com/1249273/facebook-ceo-mark-zuckerberg-says-ai-will-detect-hate-speech-in-5-10-years/.

13. Richard Gingras, *How Alphabet Is Using AI to Combat Fake News*, interview by Emily Chang, Bloomberg TV, video, May 9, 2018, 00:10, https://www.bloomberg.com/news/videos/2018-05-09/how-alphabet-is-using-ai-to-combat-fake-news-video.

14. Noam Cohen, "Conspiracy Videos? Fake News? Enter *Wikipedia*, the 'Good Cop' of the Internet," *Washington Post*, April 6, 2018, https://www.washingtonpost.com/outlook/conspiracy-videos-fake-news-enter-wikipedia-the-good-cop-of-the-internet/2018/04/06/ad1f018a-3835-11e8-8fd2-49fe3c675a89_story.html?utm_term=.e2a15a46ab42. See also Noam Cohen, *The Know-It-Alls* (New York: New Press, 2017), chap. 6.

15. Gingras, *How Alphabet Is Using AI to Combat Fake News*.

16. Noam Cohen, "Facebook Doesn't Like What It Sees When It Looks in the Mirror," *New York Times*, January 16, 2018, https://www.nytimes.com/2018/01/16/opinion/facebook-zuckerberg-public-content.html.

17. Cohen, "Facebook Doesn't Like What It Sees When It Looks in the Mirror"; Mark Sweney, "Mums Furious as Facebook Removes Breastfeeding Photos," *Guardian*, December 30, 2008, https://www.theguardian.com/media/2008/dec/30/facebook-breastfeeding-ban.

18. Mark Scott and Mike Isaac, "Facebook Restores Iconic Vietnam War Photo It Censored for Nudity," *New York Times*, September 9, 2016, https://www.nytimes.com/2016/09/10/technology/facebook-vietnam-war-photo-nudity.html.

19. Noam Cohen, "Facebook Isn't Just Violating Our Privacy," *New York Times*, March 29, 2018, https://www.nytimes.com/2018/03/29/opinion/facebook-privacy-zuckerberg-society.html.

20. "Mark Zuckerberg at Startup School 2013," Zuckerberg Transcripts, paper 160, accessed April 15, 2019, http://dc.uwm.edu/zuckerberg_files_transcripts/160.

21. Mark Zuckerberg, "Bringing the World Closer Together," Facebook, June 22, 2017, https://www.facebook.com/notes/mark-zuckerberg/bringing-the-world-closer-together/10154944663901634/.

22. Mark Zuckerberg, Facebook post, January 11, 2018, https://www.facebook.com/zuck/posts/10104413015393571.

23. Adrienne LaFrance, "Mark Zuckerberg Doesn't Understand Journalism," *Atlantic*, May 1, 2018, https://www.theatlantic.com/technology/archive/2018/05/mark-zuckerberg-doesnt-understand-journalism/559424/.

24. David Skok, "Google's News Chief Richard Gingras: 'We Need to Rethink Journalism at Every Dimension,'" Neiman Journalism Lab, May 10, 2018, https://www.niemanlab.org/2018/05/googles-news-chief-richard-gingras-we-need-to-rethink-journalism-at-every-dimension/.

25. Skok, "Google's News Chief Richard Gingras."

26. Kevin Roose, "Facebook and YouTube Give Alex Jones a Wrist Slap," *New York Times*, July 28, 2018, https://www.nytimes.com/2018/07/27/technology/alex-jones -facebook-youtube.html.

27. Richard Roberts, "The Growth Trap," *Musings of a Young Londoner*, January 13, 2018, https://musingsofayounglondoner.wordpress.com/2018/01/13/the-growth-trap/.

28. Andrew Bosworth, quoted in Ryan Mac, Charlie Warzel, and Alex Kantrowitz, "Growth at Any Cost: Top Facebook Executive Defended Data Collection in 2016 Memo—and Warned That Facebook Could Get People Killed," *Buzzfeed News*, March 29, 2018, https://www.buzzfeed.com/ryanmac/growth-at-any-cost-top -facebook-executive-defended-data?utm_term=.ibxlbG7Ob#.nsOZx3lKx.

29. Bosworth wrote this in a tweet that he has since deleted, but it was covered in Hannah Kuchler, "Facebook Memo Outlines 'Ugly Truth' Behind Its Mission," *Financial Times*, March 29, 2018, https://www.ft.com/content/126b86c8-33ac-11e8-b5bf -23cb17fd1498.

30. Jim Dalrymple II, "Zuckerberg Says He Strongly Disagrees with 'the Ugly' Memo by Top Facebook Exec," *BuzzFeed News*, March 29, 2018, https://www.buzzfeednews .com/article/jimdalrympleii/zuckerberg-says-he-disagrees-growth-memo# .hlo6OGvq5V.

31. Kara Swisher, "Full Transcript: Facebook CEO Mark Zuckerberg on Recode Decode," interview, *Recode*, July 18, 2018, https://www.recode.net/2018/7/18/17575158 /mark-zuckerberg-facebook-interview-full-transcript-kara-swisher.

PART II

Examples of Problems

Chapter Five

A SERF ON GOOGLE'S FARM

JOSH MARSHALL

An unintended effect of Google's heavy-handed attempt to silence Barry Lynn and his Open Markets program at the New America Foundation has been to shine a really bright light both on Google's monopoly power and on the unrestrained and unlovely ways it uses that power. Happily, Lynn's group has landed on its feet, seemingly with plenty of new funding or maybe even with more than it had. I got a press release from them this evening and what seems to be their new site. I've already seen other stories of Google bullying come out of the woodwork. Here's one.

It's great that all this stuff is coming out. But what is more interesting to me than the instances of bullying are the more workaday and seemingly benign mechanisms of Google's power. If you have extreme power, when things get dicey, you will tend to abuse that power. That's not surprising. It's human nature. What's interesting and important is the nature of the power itself and what undergirds it. Don't get me wrong. The abuses are very important. But extreme concentrations of power will almost always be abused. The temptations are too great. But what is the nature of the power itself?

Many people who know more than I do can describe different aspects of this story. But how Google affects and dominates the publishing industry is something I know very, very well because I've lived with it for more than a decade. To say I've "lived with it" makes it sound like a chronic disease or some huge burden. That would be a very incomplete, misleading picture. Google has directly or indirectly driven millions of dollars of revenue to Talking Points Memo (TPM) over more than a decade. Not only that, it's also provided services that are core parts of how we run TPM. So Google isn't some kind of thralldom we've lived under. It's ubiquitous. In many ways, it makes what we do possible.

What I've known for some time—but which became even clearer to me in my talk with Barry Lynn—is that few publishers really want to talk about the depths or mechanics of Google's role in news publishing. Some of this reticence is secrecy about proprietary information; most of it stems from the fact that Google could destroy or profoundly damage most publications if it wanted to. So why rock the boat?

I'm not worried about that for a few reasons: (1) We've refocused TPM toward much greater reliance on subscriptions, so we're less vulnerable. (2) Most people who know these mechanics don't write. I do. (3) We're small, and I don't think Google cares enough to do anything to TPM. (If your subscription to Prime suddenly doubles in cost, you'll know I was wrong about this.) What I hope I can capture is that Google is in many ways a great thing for publishers. At least it's not a purely negative picture. It's a bit like being assimilated by the Borg. You get cool new powers. But having been assimilated, if your implants are ever removed, you'll certainly die. If you're a *Star Trek* fan, you'll understand the analogy. That basically captures our relationship to Google.

Let's discuss the various ways we're in business with Google.

It all starts with DFP, a flavor of Doubleclick called DoubleClick for Publishers (DFP). DoubleClick was one of the early "ad-serving companies" that Google purchased years ago. DFP actually started as GAM—Google Ad Manager. TPM was chosen to be one of its beta users. This was, I think, back in 2006 or 2007. What's DFP? DFP is the application (or software or system—you can define it in different ways) that serves ads on TPM. I don't know the exact market penetration, but it's the hugely dominant player in ad serving across the web. So on TPM, Google software manages the serving of ads. All of our ads drive on Google's roads.

Then there's AdExchange. That's the part of Google that buys ad inventory. A huge amount of our ads come through ad networks. AdExchange is far and away the largest of those for us—often accounting for around 15 percent of total revenues every month—sometimes higher. So our largest single source of ad revenue is usually Google. To be clear, that's not advertising of Google, but advertisers purchasing our ad space *through* Google. But every other ad we ever run also runs over Google's ad-serving system. So Google software/service (DFP) runs the ad ecosystem on TPM. And the main buyer within that ecosystem is another Google service (AdExchange).

Then there's Google Analytics. That's the benchmark audience and traffic-data service. How many unique visitors do we have? How many page views do we serve each month? What's the geographical distribution of our audience? That is all collected through Google Analytics. Now, that's not our only source of audience data. We have several services we use for that in addition to our own internal systems. But we do use it for the big aggregate numbers and long-term record keeping. In many ways, the Analytics data are the canonical data that people on the outside look at to see how big our audience is. Do we have to share those data? No. That is, unless we want potential advertisers to see we have an audience.

Next there's search. Heard of that? There's general search, and then there's Google News, a separate bucket of search. Search tends not to be that important for us in part because we've never prioritized it and in part because as a site focused on iterative news coverage, we produce what tends to be highly ephemeral—at least in search terms. We don't publish a lot of evergreen stories. Still, search is important. For other publishers it's the whole game.

One additional Google implant is Gmail, which we use to provision our corporate email. The backbone of the @talkingpointsmemo.com email addresses is Gmail. Lots of companies now do this.

So let's go down the list: (1) the system for running ads, (2) the top purchaser of ads, (3) the most pervasive audience data service, (4) all search, (5) our email.

But wait, there's more! Google also owns Chrome, the most used browser for visiting TPM. Chrome is responsible for 41 percent of our page views. Safari comes in second at 36 percent. But the Safari number is heavily driven by people using iOS devices. On desktop, Chrome is overwhelmingly dominant.

Google would rightly say now: "Okay, smart aleck, how much do you pay for all of this?" Well, good point. We pay for the email service, but we don't pay for the ad serving or the data. Indeed, using Gmail for our corporate email is the only thing we pay for. (All of these services have paid layers, but in most cases we don't need them. And we're small, so we make do.) This is all true. But as the adage puts it, if you don't pay for the product, *you are the product*. Google isn't doing us any favors. We get these services for free because Google's empire and the vast amounts of money it brings in every year are built on the unimaginable amounts of data that come from, among other places, DoubleClick for Publishers and Analytics. We're just one of a kabillion sites allowing Google to harvest our data.

What all of this comes down to is that we at TPM—and some version of this is the case for the vast majority of publishers—are connected to Google at almost every turn. (I've mentioned only the big points of connection. Some are too minor to mention, and we've chosen not to participate in other very important ones.) Running TPM absent Google's various services is almost unthinkable. I literally would need to give a lot of thought to how we'd do without all of them. Some of them are critical, and I wouldn't know where to start for replacing them. In many cases, alternatives don't exist because no business can get a footing with another version of a product Google lets people use for free.

But here's where the rubber really meets the road. The publishers use DoubleClick. The big advertisers use DoubleClick. The big global advertising holding companies use DoubleClick. Everybody at every point in the industry is wired into DoubleClick. Here's how they all play together. The ad serving (DoubleClick) is like the road. AdExchange is the biggest car on the road. But only AdExchange gets full visibility into what's available. (There's a lot of argument about just what Google does and doesn't know. But trust me on this: it keeps the key information to itself. This isn't a suspicion. It's the model.) So Google owns the road and gets first look at what's on the road. Not only does Google own the road and make the rules for the road, but it also has special privileges on the road. One of the ways it has special privileges is that it has all the data it gets from search, Google Analytics, and Gmail. It also gets to make the first bid on every bit of inventory. Of course, that's critical. First dibs on more information than anyone else has access to. (There are some exceptions, but that's the big picture.) It's good to be the king. It's good to be a Google.

There's more I'll get to in a moment, but the interplay between Double-Click and AdExchange is so vastly important to the entirety of the web, digital publishing, and the entire ad industry that it is almost impossible to overstate. Again: Google owns the road. It makes the rules for the road. It gets special privileges on the road with every new iteration of rules.

In recent years, the big new things are various kinds of private deals and private markets you can set up to do business in different ways with advertisers. They use Google architecture, and it takes a percentage. How much of a percentage does Google take on what I was referring to earlier—the so-called open auction? No one knows.

Now Google can say—and it is absolutely right—that every month it sends checks for thousands and millions of dollars to countless publishers that make their journalism possible. And in general Google tends to be a relatively benign overlord. But as someone who (*a*) knows the industry inside and out—down to the most nuts and bolts mechanics—(*b*) understands at least the rudiments of antitrust law and monopoly economics, and (*c*) can write for a sizable audience, I can tell you this: Google's monopoly control is almost comically great. It's a monopoly at every conceivable turn and consistently uses that market power to deepen its hold and increase its profits. Just the interplay between DoubleClick and AdExchange is textbook anticompetitive practice.

There's one way that Google is better than Facebook. When Facebook is getting a bigger and bigger share of the advertising pie, almost all of that money is going to Facebook. There are some small exceptions, but that's basically the case. When Google is making insane amounts of money on advertising, it's not really the same because a huge amount of that advertising is running on websites that are getting a cut. Still, the big story is that Google and Facebook now have a dominant position in the entirety of the advertising ecosystem and are using their monopoly power to take more and more of the money for themselves.

TPM is basically too small for Google to care about, so I wouldn't say we've had any bad experiences with Google in the sense of Google trying to injure us or use its power against us. What we've experienced is a little different. Google is so big and so powerful that even when it's trying to do something good, it can be dangerous and frightening.

Here's an example.

With the events of recent months and years, Google is apparently now trying to weed out publishers that are using its money streams and architecture to publish hate speech. Certainly you'd probably be unhappy to hear that Stormfront was funded by ads run through Google. I'm not saying that's happening. I'm just giving you a sense of what Google is apparently trying to combat. Over the past several months, we've gotten a few notifications from Google telling us that certain TPM pages were penalized for "violations" of its ban on hate speech. When we looked at the pages referred to, we saw that they were articles *about* white supremacist incidents, most of them tied to Dylann Roof's mass murder in Charleston.

Now in practice all this meant was that two or three old stories about Dylann Roof could no longer run ads purchased through Google. I'd say it's unlikely that the loss to TPM amounted to even a cent a month. Totally meaningless. But here's the catch. The way these warnings work and the way these particular warnings were worded, you get penalized enough times, and then you're blacklisted.

Now, certainly you're figuring we could contact someone at Google and explain that we're not *publishing* hate speech and racist violence. We're *reporting* on it. No, we tried that. We got back a message from our Google rep not really understanding the distinction and cheerily telling us to try to operate within the no-hate-speech rules. And how many warnings until we're blacklisted? Who knows?

If we were cut off, would that be off AdExchange (the ads) or off DoubleClick for Publishers (the road) or both? Who knows?

If the first stopped, we'd lose a big chunk of money that wouldn't put us out of business but would likely force us to retrench. If we were kicked off the road, more than half of our total revenue would disappear instantly and would stay disappeared until we found a new road—i.e., a new ad-serving service or technology. At a minimum, it would be a devastating blow that would require us to find a totally different ad-serving system, make major technical changes to the site to accommodate the new system, and likely not be able to make as much from ads ever again. That's not including some unknown period of time—certainly weeks at least—in which we would go with no ad revenue.

Needless to say, the impact of being kicked off the road would be cataclysmic and could easily drive us out of business.

Now, that's never happened. And this whole scenario stems from what is at least a well-intentioned effort by Google not to subsidize hate speech and racist groups. Again, it hasn't happened. So in some sense the cataclysmic scenario I'm describing is as much a product of my paranoia as something Google could or might do. But when an outside player has that much power, often acts arbitrarily (even when well intentioned), and is almost impossible to communicate with, a significant amount of paranoia is healthy and inevitable.

I give this example only to illustrate the way that Google is so powerful and so all-encompassing that it can actually do great damage unintentionally. As a general matter, I'd say our worst experiences with Google—and to be fair, none has been that bad—have been cases like this one, where Google is so big and its customers and products (people are products) are so distant from its concerns that we've gotten caught up in or whiplashed by rules or systems that simply don't make any sense or are affirmatively absurd in how they affect us. One thing I've observed about Google over the years is that it is institutionally so used to its "customers" actually being its products that when it gets into businesses where it actually has customers, it has little sense of how to deal with them.

Here's another comical example. One day a couple years or so ago, we noticed that we weren't getting any of our TPM emails. This is, needless to say, a pretty big deal. We didn't get the over-the-transom emails from you, the readers, and we weren't getting the individual emails that we all get at our personal TPM email addresses. Reporters have sources. We have business partners who need to contact us. It's really, really bad when we don't get our emails.

This provoked a mad rush to find out what was going on. Remember, we use Gmail for our email service. We're not the product in this case. We pay for it. I'll spare you the ins and outs we had to go through to find out what was happening and just tell you what happened. Many of you know that we have one company email address here at TPM. It's the one linked at the top of the site. It's the lifeblood of the whole operation. Those emails go to everyone on the editorial team. It's a key part of what we do. We want every member of the team to be seeing that mix of comments, tips, criticism, links you're sending into us. It's a key part of our management that we make clear that we want everyone to immerse themselves in those emails, to look at what's coming in. As many current and former TPMers will attest, looking through all that email can be overwhelming, but it's a core part of what we do. Those emails don't sit in an inbox no one reads. We live in them.

Now the mechanics of how that works is that the email is actually a distribution list that forwards the incoming emails from that one address to everyone on staff. And here's the catch. Over the years, a lot of spam has started coming into the address. It's mostly weeded out by filters, so we don't even see it, but some we do. It's sort of a pain, but it is what it is. But according to Google's algorithm, the fact that we took a lot of spam that came to us and forwarded it to our staff meant that TPM was a major spammer. Again, let me repeat that. Because we were *forwarding to ourselves* spam that other people sent to us, Google decided that the owner of the TPM URL was a major spammer, and so it blocked TPM emails from being sent to anyone. When we were notified of this . . . okay, I'm sorry. That was a joke. *We were never notified!* We just disappeared from Gmail. Fun, right?

So let's review. We are paying customers of Google. We were forwarding emails from the site's main address to all staffers. But because we receive a lot of spam, the spam that we were forwarding to ourselves marked us as a major spammer and led to Google banning all our emails with no notice in advance or notification after the fact.

You might imagine that once we got through to someone at Google and explained this ridiculous situation, they'd fix it. Well, no. Once we got through to someone, that person explained what happened and told us a few remedial actions we could take. Once we did that, over time the algorithm would cease to think we were spammers.

Now, in practice I think we were back to normal in a couple days. Obviously we survived. And everyone's life—personal and professional—is filled with various inanities that make life frustrating and yet somehow also entertaining. I share this story in part because it was so surreal and absurd but more because it's an illustration of how Google is so vast and all-pervasive that it can be dangerous even when it's not trying to be.

Of course, the real issue is the monopoly and how it applies to money. Is your favorite website laying off staff or "pivoting to video"? In most cases, the root cause is not entirely but to a significant degree driven by the platform monopolies—in this case, Google and Facebook—taking a bigger and bigger slice of the advertising dollars. It's going to their profits and being taken away from publishers, who of course are also trying to maximize their profits but do it through paying for journalism.

When I discussed a few of these issues on Twitter a couple days ago, some people said: "Well, the publishers brought it on themselves. They went for the cheap clicks or gaming Facebook's or Google's algorithms. So they brought it on themselves."

This is true to an extent, but I think it misses the point. It's not about anyone's individual morality. Not the publishers or the platform monopolies. It's a structural issue. Monopolies are bad for the economy, and they're bad politically. They also have perverse consequences across the board. The money that used to fund your favorite website is now going to Google and Facebook, neither of which produces any news at all.

We could see this coming a few years ago, and we made a decisive and long-term push to restructure our business around subscriptions. So I'm confident we will be fine. But journalism is not fine right now. And journalism is only one industry the platform monopolies affect. Monopolies are bad for all the reasons people used to think they were bad. They raise costs. They stifle innovation. They lower wages. And they have perverse political effects, too. Huge and entrenched concentrations of wealth create entrenched and dangerous locuses of political power.

So we will keep using all of Google's gizmos and services and keep cashing its checks. But we hope they won't see this post and get mad. In the microcosm, it works for us. It's good money. But in the big picture . . . Google is a big, big problem. So is Facebook. So is Amazon. Monopolies are a big, lumbering cause of many of our current afflictions. And we're only now slowly beginning to realize it.

NOTE

A version of this chapter was previously published on *TPM*, September 1, 2017, https://talkingpointsmemo.com/edblog/a-serf-on-googles-farm. The edited version here is published with permission by Josh Marshall.

Chapter Six

THE RISE AND FALL OF BLOGGING IN THE 2000s

FELIX SALMON

I was recently having drinks with the editor in chief of a major website, who was talking about the young journalists he's hiring, many of them straight out of J-school. They're good at straight-down-the-line reporting, he said, but when he encourages them to add a little voice, to be a bit *bloggier*, he generally gets blank stares. Dropping the name "Gawker" doesn't help; although it maybe rings a bell somewhere, none of these young journalists considers it to be a useful touchstone.

The reason is that blogging is dead; indeed, it was dead long before Peter Thiel put the final nail in Gawker's coffin back in 2016. Blogging had a brief and glorious life before it was captured by forces much greater than it could ever muster on its own, most of which represented some kind of larger and more capitalist media ecosystem. Blogging, ultimately, was too pure to survive, and so it didn't.

Who killed blogging? As in *Murder on the Orient Express*, it's hard to keep count of the suspects. Or maybe this story is more akin to *A Case of Exploding Mangoes* (2009), the Mohammed Hanif novel about the attempted assassination of Pakistani general Zia ul-Haq. By the end of the book (spoiler alert!), Zia is dead, but it's hard to say exactly what killed him, given the sheer number of ingenious plots against him, all of which converge at much the same time.

Blogging, as a medium, died because it was captured by forces bigger than itself. Ultimately, it was too small, too fragmented, too recondite to be able to resist the internet's grand transition from an open, distributed network to a place dominated by winner-takes-all economics.

Blogging started in 1994 but didn't really take off until the turn of the century, when freely available software such as Blogger and Movable Type allowed almost anybody with a computer and an internet connection to create her or his own web publication at little or no expense. The attacks of September 11, 2001, especially, precipitated millions of words of commentary and helped to jump-start a vibrant blogosphere, much of which was centered on American politics, both foreign and domestic.

Blogging, as it emerged in the early years of this century, was in many ways unique in the history of media. At its height, the blogosphere was an online ecosystem unrivaled, before or since, in breadth, depth, independence, honesty, and many other characteristics that are generally valued in journalism.

The ecosystem had no hub; there were no gatekeepers. Anybody could start a blog, and millions of people did. Those blogs were published on the open web for free: you didn't need to log in to read them, there were no paywalls, and, indeed, there was precious little advertising. It was Tim Berners-Lee's dream realized: everybody reading, everybody writing (even if only in comments sections), everybody linking to each other and playing a small part in a much grander project.

The blog itself was very simple. At heart it was just a single column on a single page, with posts appearing in strict reverse-chronological order. There were some group blogs, but most were single-author affairs, written by people who made no secret of their opinions and biases. Many blogs had lively comments sections, but the blogosphere itself was the liveliest comments section of all: almost all bloggers would quote and link to many other bloggers, who would do likewise, with conversations evolving at high speed across many different sites. Conventions such as pingbacks and permalinks made it easy for readers to keep track of who was saying what about whom, while the humble bookmark made it easy to check in on your favorite blogs to see what new things were being talked about. For power users, most blogs published something known as an "untruncated RSS (Really Simple Syndication) feed," which allowed people to read (or at least to skim) a huge

number of posts very quickly and which also allowed for incredibly valuable search functionality.

The effect on public discourse was electric and was one of the earliest
examples of the true power of a distributed internet. The gatekeepers of
old didn't go anywhere: their publications remained august and well read
and, indeed, were often linked to by bloggers. But the conversation on and
around the news brought in a slew of new voices, many of whom were
expert practitioners in their field. Rather than scoring an occasional op-
ed once or twice a year, people with deep knowledge started blogging
weekly, daily, or even sometimes more often than that. They could share
their expertise in as much detail as they wanted and receive immediate
feedback while doing so, often at an extremely high level of sophistication.
In areas such as foreign policy, health-care policy, and economics, the
blogosphere often became a real-time public graduate seminar, featuring
many of the foremost academic and real-world practitioners along with
many enthusiastic amateurs. Almost none of them got paid directly for
blogging: in that sense, the "business model" of the blogosphere was just
that there wasn't one.

Indeed, the desire to monetize the blogosphere was one of the early forces
that ultimately led to its capture and then its demise. The rise of the blogosphere caused blog ad networks to be formed, foremost among them John
Battelle's Federated Media, which started placing ad units across hundreds
of blogs. At the time, the arrival of advertising was considered a great idea,
allowing bloggers to be paid for the large amount of time and effort they
put into their blogs. Ideally, it would have paved the way for blogging to
become a viable income source for smart writers around the world, many
of whom had few other opportunities to earn valuable dollars.

The problem, however, was that ads started to corrode the blogosphere.
Blogs, in a sense, started to become captured by the very product they were
looking to as their salvation. Once ads arrived, incentives started being
skewed. Rather than simply trying to contribute as best they could to the
conversation, bloggers now had a clear financial incentive to try to maximize the amount of traffic coming to their own sites. Driving traffic to
someone else paid nothing; engaging in someone else's comments section
likewise paid zero. Serving up ads alongside your own blog posts, however,
made money, and the more posts that people read, the more money you
could make. Bloggers quickly realized that the main way to boost traffic was

simply to write more frequently: more posts meant more income. Posts therefore started becoming shorter and punchier in an attempt to boost pageviews and ad revenue. In general, for any given amount of time spent blogging, the less time you spent *per post*, the more money you would make in total.

More profoundly, the mindset at many blogs rapidly morphed from "I can make money from my blog!" to "I blog in order to make money." Some bloggers, including Heather Armstrong, the mommy blogger known as Dooce, as well as Pete Rojas, who founded both Gizmodo and Engadget, became millionaires just from blogging; many others became professionalized, working either for themselves or for blog publishers. Either way, where previously blogging had been characterized by an excess of linking out generously to other blogs, now bloggers started trying to link wherever possible to their own archives. Internal links were always good (recirculation!), but external links were valued much less highly.

The result was a slow replacement of generosity with selfishness and a growing attitude of "Why should I link to you if you don't link to me?" The "blogroll"—a list of favorite blogs that was often found in the right-hand rail—started to disappear or to be replaced with ad units or, at best, a formalized system whereby sites would "drive traffic" to each other. And although many successful blogs still linked out a lot, especially in the news space, those links were increasingly seen as currency. Only with a steady stream of inbound links could any new blog make a success of itself, and so bloggers started spending much of their time emailing their posts to people with bigger traffic in the hope of receiving one of those precious links in return.

The holy grail was to become part of thousands of readers' muscle memory, to earn a spot in their bookmarks bar, to be that place they would go for a few minutes when bored at work. Ideally, you would become so central to their lives that if you spent too long at lunch, you would come back to multiple emails asking what had happened to you.

But even if you achieved that coveted position, you still had almost no relationship with your advertisers. Battelle says that the technological gulf between editorial and advertising was "the truly original sin of the internet," going back to when he helped introduce the very first banner ad on hotwired.com in 1994 and hosted it on a separate ad server. (Yes, he's blaming himself for creating the very structure that ultimately destroyed the blogosphere.) The result was that even successful bloggers found themselves at the mercy of an incredibly opaque and infernally complex ad-tech system where media buyers had much more interest in clickthrough rates than they did in deep contextual affinity.

After all, the blogs were tiny compared to what legacy publishers produced. Bloggers had almost no negotiating leverage, even if in the barren years following the dot-com bust they were well placed to become the mammals that replaced the portal dinosaurs. They had no aspirations to becoming multi-billion-dollar global corporations centered on a web page that had to be all things to all people; instead, they would create microcommunities held together by social bonds and personal familiarity. Bloggers became familiar to their readers not only through enormous quantities of first-person writing but also because they would invariably reply to smart responses in the comments section or on other blogs. Those ongoing conversations made it easy to find things to write about and helped to cement bonds with readers.

Then, however, the entrepreneurs arrived, seeing gold in all that traffic and hoping to capture it all for themselves. Blogging was never an obvious road to riches—the number of self-employed bloggers making the kind of money they could make as full-time journalists probably never exceeded more than a few dozen at any given time. They often had other gigs and would supplement their day-job income with maybe $3,000 in online ad revenue.

With scale, however, the economics changed. If you got four or five bloggers together on the same blog, they could collectively make $30,000 a month or more, sometimes as much as $100,000 a month. And once revenues hit between $100,000 and $200,000 per month, then the venture capitalists would arrive bearing large checks. Instead of outsourcing ad sales to Federated Media, companies would raise equity capital, hire their own sales staffs, and get onto a growth trajectory that (if all went well) would lead to a multi-million-dollar exit.

The race to scale worked. Backed with relatively modest investments, companies started to take blogging to a commercial level, with frequent posts, paid employees, and often substantial revenues. By 2005, giants such as AOL were paying tens of millions of dollars to acquire blogging start-ups, and the purchase prices went up sharply: $25 million each for Weblogs,

Inc. and Techcrunch, $315 million for the *Huffington Post*, $450 million for *Business Insider*.

Independent blog companies also existed—Gawker Media, Gothamist, Breaking Media, and many others—based on a multisite business model where each site would have an editor and many writers.

The personal relationships that readers had with bloggers morphed slowly into a qualitatively different relationship with sites and brands. Some tenured academics still kept up the spirit of the original blogosphere, but even they became institutionalized, setting up multiblogger sites that would aggregate content and sometimes get licensed out to larger media companies. Again, ambitions changed: instead of trying to make money by monetizing their blogs, writers now wanted to make money by getting full-time jobs, with benefits, in which they would provide grist for someone else's blog. The careerist rule of thumb: the bigger and more successful the blog—that is, the more readers it had—the more attractive it was as a place to work.

Thus did the blogosphere set itself up for capture again, this time by legacy news organizations. If you're going to write for someone else's publication, if you're going to have to adopt someone else's house style, then at that point you might as well do so with the added prestige of, say, the *Wall Street Journal*. That made the next step both inevitable and very easy. Once newspapers and other legacy-media outlets decided they needed blogs and bloggers to complement their core offerings, they found it very easy to hire from the blogosphere: Gawker's founding editor, Elizabeth Spiers, for instance, moved to *New York* magazine to start a blog there as early as 2003.

The problem was that it's almost impossible to maintain the distinctiveness of a blog within the context and bureaucracy of a much larger publication. At big media companies, journalists would find themselves going back and forth from the main newsroom to the blogs section, and it felt increasingly weird for the two to be separate. Why couldn't bloggers do reporting? Why couldn't reporters be a bit more conversational in tone? And the toughest question of all: Why were we linking to our competitors?

Top editors at these publications found it very hard to answer complaints about their blog coverage by trying to say that bloggers were held to a different standard. The result was that standards inevitably started converging—which is to say the blogs became more and more indiscernible from the rest of the reporting, effectively captured by the legacy media they had come to disrupt.

Pretty soon journalists themselves started moving back and forth between big blog-only companies, such as Gawker Media and *Business Insider* and the *Huffington Post*, on the one hand, and legacy print-media organizations, on the other, with the result that norms on both sides started making their way across the divide. One of the main differences between blogging and traditional journalism had historically been that blogging was a real-time effort that would start with a simple post and then iterate through comments and updates and a whole new round of posts; traditional journalists, by contrast, generally thought of published material as the end of the process rather than the beginning. As those traditional journalists increasingly found themselves in positions of authority at blogs and blog companies, they started implementing traditional protocols about, say, editing a post before publishing it (rather than afterward) or calling people for comment before publishing rather than just putting up a post and using that as a means of eliciting a comment. The implementation of such protocols was probably a good idea, given the power that large blogs increasingly wielded, but it did serve to diminish the degree to which having blogs would really diversify a media outlet's offerings.

It didn't take long before the main difference between blogs and other forms of online written journalism was simply technological. Blogs generally ran on a blog content-management system such as Movable Type or WordPress, which would present a blogger's work in reverse-chronological order; more traditional outlets would place stories in more or less prominent positions on the home page and might even have other in-story visual cues that served to convey how seriously the piece should be taken. (One such *New York Times* project about a fatal avalanche, entitled "Snow Fall: The Avalanche at Tunnel Creek," was so successful that it resulted in a brand-new verb, *to snowfall*, meaning to present a longform article with multimedia elements that constitute an integral part of the storytelling.)

The blogs' reverse-chronological approach was not superior to the legacy product. For one thing, it couldn't cope with big scoops, such as when Gizmodo got its hands on an unreleased iPhone 4. That scoop meant that the blog had to stop publishing new stories just so that its iPhone coverage could stay at the top of its home page. Meanwhile, as organizations updated their content-management systems, old-media organizations realized that they didn't need separate blogs at all and that the technological headaches involved in running two parallel content-management systems were almost never worth it. Some bloggy DNA remained sprinkled across the newsroom, but the journalistic media capture story was the same as the technological one. Once blogs and legacy media converged, the final result looked much more like legacy media than it did like blogs, and blogs had largely disappeared.

All of this was happening at the same time as the rise of social media, which alone was more than sufficient to kill off the blogosphere on its own and to capture its conversational vibrancy. At most media companies, social media has been a mixed blessing: an invaluable source of traffic but also a place where advertisers can find a degree of scale and targeting far beyond anything that most media company websites can deliver. The result, for traditional journalism, has been a combination of higher traffic (good), lower per page ad revenues (bad), and the emergence of a seemingly invincible competitor (Facebook) for every ad dollar (terrible).

For blogs, the capture was different. To a certain degree, they too saw an increase in traffic from social media, but even that increase required a certain degree of debloggification. In the early blogosphere, bloggers would link to each other, but they would rarely just copy and paste each other's headlines. "Megan has an interesting argument about skewed incentives in the French antibiotics industry," they might write, linking the word *Megan* or the word *argument* to Megan's blog, where the post might easily include a phrase such as *negative externalities* in its headline. After the rise of social media, however, Megan's actual headline would start showing up on Twitter and Facebook, and she would spend a lot of time trying to work out how to make it clickable. "Cows are killing thousands of French women every year," perhaps. Never mind the accuracy; feel the effects of all that traffic!

The bigger problem with the rise of social media, however, was that Twitter and Facebook captured the heart of the blogosphere, the conversation, for themselves. No longer was it necessary for a blogger to open up her content-management system, write out an argument, put a headline on it, find a photograph to illustrate it, and then hit "publish." She could engender just as much conversation or even more by publishing something much more quickly and much more easily on Twitter or Facebook. And so the fast-and-breezy aspect of the blogosphere—the fact that it enabled a back-and-forth that was not (and is not) possible in traditional media—was effectively disrupted by social media upstarts that were faster and breezier and had vastly greater reach.

Worse, much of that conversation, insofar as it took place on Facebook, would happen entirely out of the public view. If Alan the pharmacist wanted to weigh in on Megan's post, he'd probably do so on Facebook, and his friends and family might well have an interesting and well-informed debate there. But Megan couldn't see it, nor would she ever likely find out that the debate happened. By fracturing the conversation and placing it behind login walls, Facebook did a great job of destroying the public commons around blog posts.

The rise of social media also coincided with the rise of podcasts, which were in most cases *literally* conversational. People who a few years ago would have conversed with their audience by writing a blog moved over to recording podcasts, which feel even more intimate and which aren't prone to hateful comment spam. The connection that listeners feel to podcasters is even more intense than the connection they feel to bloggers, and so blogging naturally paled in comparison.

There was also the unexpected rise of the email newsletter, another personal, intimate means for communication that started to feel fresh and unsullied in comparison to an increasingly messy and ugly Web.

Then there was the death of Google Reader. As social media grew in size and scope, fewer people spent much time using the world's most popular RSS reader. Eventually, in 2013, Google gave up entirely and killed the one web app that was crucial to the continued survival of the blogosphere. Without it, people lost track of the blogs they liked to read, had no easy way of scrolling through them, and certainly couldn't search across them. If any one event can be blamed for killing off blogs entirely, it is surely Google's decision to get rid of Google Reader, much more than it was any jury verdict in Florida.

Still, even the blame for the Google Reader decision can in large part be ascribed to social media. Once Twitter and Facebook took off, people just didn't head to the open web to find news and opinion. Instead, they logged in to their own bespoke social media accounts. The idea of visiting a blog's home page to see if there was anything new there eventually became outdated. If there was something new, you'd trust someone else to find it for you and share it on social media.

That was particularly bad for blogs because the unit of quality for a blog was always the blog as a whole, not any individual post. Ta-Nehisi Coates, for instance, had a great blog for many years; his posts were often just one line long and might say nothing but "Open thread." The point was to create a community, one that was familiar with the blog as a whole, rather than to try to get a large number of anonymous social media users to click on a single post and share it with their friends. No one ever shares blog home pages on social media; at best, they share individual blog posts. Those posts, then, can't really be bloggy—they can't rely on people understanding that they make sense only in the blog's broader context. After all, in the age of social media many of the post's readers might never have previously come across the blog. Even if they love it, they're not going to bookmark it because, well, no one bookmarks anything anymore. And a world without bookmarks or Google Reader is, to a first approximation, a world without blogs. Today, if you want to be part of discussion on a topic, you go to Reddit; you don't start your own blog.

That's probably smart because it's incredibly rare that anybody gets sued for something they say on Reddit, and even if they do get threatened with a lawsuit, they can often make everything go away just by taking down the post in question.

In the blogosphere, by contrast, as Peter Thiel has demonstrated, enmities can fester and grow over time, and a billionaire with a grudge who's willing to play the long game can take down anybody who doesn't have an effectively unlimited legal budget. For all that there were many different forces that killed off blogs, Thiel was the most overt, the most deliberate, the most determined to capture his prey at any cost. Because he had so many broader trends behind him, not to mention a fair amount of luck, he triumphed unambiguously; in doing so, he not only killed Gawker Media but also wrote a playbook that effectively ensured that no one else would dare attempt to re-create anything like Gawker.

Thiel was a frequent target of Gawker Media's *Valleywag* blog, which outed him as gay and then went on to detail the dreadful performance of his hedge fund, Clarium Capital. None of those posts was actionable, but Thiel, burning with righteous indignation, was not willing to let the matter rest. So he took advantage of the main distinguishing feature of the blogosphere, which is that most of its content is put up quickly and sometimes sloppily. With Gawker Media publishing literally millions of posts over its years of existence, he could comb through them all individually to find just one that could act as an Achilles' heel.

The lawsuit *Bollea v. Gawker* was not about a sex tape, was not about invasion of privacy, was not really about Hulk Hogan (Terry Bollea) at all. Hogan was upset at a blog post Gawker published featuring a snippet of his sex tape, but the publication was legal, and there wasn't much Hogan could do about it—until Peter Thiel came along.

Thiel bankrolled Hogan in court after court, appeal after appeal, in return for what would otherwise be utterly incomprehensible and irrational behavior on the part of the former professional wrestler—such as refusing to accept any settlement offers and dropping all the parts of his suit that would cause damages against Gawker to be paid by the blog company's insurers. Hogan's actions made no sense from Hogan's point of view; they made sense only when viewed as part of Thiel's campaign to bankrupt the company out of sheer revenge.

No independent blog could withstand such an onslaught—and Gawker Media, as Thiel intended, ended up filing for bankruptcy, along with its founder and largest shareholder, Nick Denton. Other independent blog companies didn't last much longer: Gothamist got sold to another malign billionaire, Joe Ricketts, who held onto it for a hot second before closing it down; The Awl simply shut its doors one day, unable to make the finances work any longer. (Gothamist would eventually return, without independence, under the aegis of a public radio station.) Today, if you want to start a blog, you try to find a large media company or a deep-pocketed venture capitalist to support you; the go-it-alone route is unthinkable.

True blogs, then, are dead. A few stragglers remain, and while the bloggish voice persists at publications ranging from the *Intercept* to *New York* to *Vox* to the *New York Times*, where Choire Sicha of Gawker and The Awl was appointed editor of the Styles section, it is dying off fast. Glenn Greenwald and Andrew Sullivan and Matthew Yglesias, all bloggers, have left their respective publications, unwilling or unable to work within institutional constraints.

We live in a more cynical world now, filled with sponsored content, a place where no one takes anything at face value any more. It's a world where mistrust in the media has never been higher, a world where red-state juries love to stick it to the coastal elites. The sites that have survived are the sites that have sacrificed the most to the gods of "audience development"; the quirky in-jokes now live much more on obscure YouTube channels than they do in anything text based.

Journalism as a whole lives on, in many ways strengthened by some of the vitality it sucked from the blogosphere, but, then again, blogs were never primarily about the news. They colored the news, annotated it, even occasionally broke it—but they were mostly about conversation and community and the pure love of writing new things on the internet. As Jia Tolentino wrote in "The End of the Awl and the Vanishing of Freedom and Fun from the Internet" in the *New Yorker* in the wake of The Awl's passing in early 2018, "Blogging, that much-maligned pastime, is gradually but surely disappearing from the Internet, and so, consequently, is a lot of online freedom and fun."

To be sure, some things are more important than freedom and fun. But not many. And what's truly depressing is how easy it was to kill off the blogosphere, which was captured by ad dollars, captured by legacy-media organizations, captured by Twitter and Facebook and podcasts and newsletters and a short-sighted Google—and, of course, captured by malign billionaires bearing grudges. With all those forces having been brought to bear, it's hardly any wonder there's nothing left.

Chapter Seven

DIGITAL PAYOLA

Policing the Open Contributor Network

JAMES LEDBETTER

In the spring of 2016, my colleagues at *Inc.* and I began to receive a handful of strange, disturbing messages from our own writers.

These writers forwarded us emails from self-proclaimed professional marketers, although the emails did not look very polished. Their aesthetics were as mercenary as their message: if you agree to mention one of our clients in an Inc.com column, we will pay you money. In some cases, a specific sum was disclosed (typically in the low hundreds of dollars per mention). In other cases, a slightly lower sum was offered to a columnist to go back into a previously published online column and insert a reference and a link for one of the clients. Most troubling were the boasts that these marketers had already successfully placed such mentions on Inc.com, as well as on other prominent websites.

I was flabbergasted. Although I'd been a professional journalist for nearly thirty years, I had never personally encountered an ethical breach this blatant. Moreover, there was no way to know the scope of the problem. Inc.com at the time was publishing approximately seventy articles per weekday, most of which were written by outside contributors who were not on the Inc.com payroll and often not paid for their work. Given this volume, we had published thousands of columns over the past few years that I had never read. Had this pay-for-placement happened once on our site? Twice? Dozens of times?

As we thought about how to respond, I came to understand the problem as a peculiarly twenty-first-century version of a struggle that has been around for much longer than that. Simply put: although this is not always obvious to outsiders, the financial viability of a modern commercial publication relies in no small part on trust. The reader must trust that the publication's content is broadly independent from forces that might seek to control it, be it government or corporations (a reasonable definition of media capture). And on their end, advertisers must trust that the publication will supply content that attracts and engages readers without creating an environment that undermines the advertisers' message.

In this decades-old struggle, there have been infamous examples where trust was strained and even careers ruined. The most direct parallel that occurred to me (and others) was the practice of taking money to play records on the radio, known as "payola." The practice may extend as far back as the 1930s, but it erupted into scandal in the late 1950s and damaged the career of many musicians and disc jockeys, notably Allan Fried, the fierce advocate of rock-and-roll. Congress was moved to change federal communications law to explicitly outlaw the practice (although many have argued that some version of payola has continued in the music industry via subtler means). In more recent instances, established publications have taken a temporary credibility blow by allowing advertisers to have too much sway over what they publish. For example, in 2013 the *Atlantic* was widely criticized for publishing a sponsored webpost from the Church of Scientology and had to issue new guidelines for its "native advertising."[1]

As an ethical challenge, our pay-for-play situation was more insidious because we (and other sites) risked violating reader trust *without knowing where or how we were doing it*. It felt a bit like being hacked—the hackers had found and exploited a vulnerability in the open contributor network we had worked very hard to construct in 2014.

What is an "open contributor network," and why did Inc.com and many other publishing websites decide to create one?

The online contributor network on a mass scale can be traced to the launch of the *Huffington Post* in 2005. Founder Arianna Huffington initially conceived of the site as a group blog for some 250 celebrity figures from literature, media, and Hollywood, including Walter Cronkite, David Mamet,

Nora Ephron, Warren Beatty, Maggie Gyllenhaal, Arthur M. Schlesinger Jr., Diane Keaton, and Norman Mailer.[2] Ten years later, the company had been sold to AOL and claimed to have a network of one hundred thousand contributors—with plans to expand to one million.

Although the *Huffington Post* expanded and evolved in a variety of ways, the massive network of contributors—most of whom were not paid to write—was a significant factor in the company's financial success; at the time of the sale in 2011, AOL estimated the *Huffington Post*'s annual revenues to be at least $60 million. (In 2018, the *Huffington Post* announced that it was moving away from its contributor network; I discuss that announcement in greater depth later.)

The model evolved at Forbes.com in a direction largely attributable to an executive there named Lewis DVorkin. In 2009, DVorkin had launched True/Slant, a general interest website in which contributors were paid not a flat fee per submission but rather based on how much traffic their posts generated. Also crucial to this model was that the contributors, once contracted and trained, published directly to the site, with effectively no editing prior to publication. True/Slant did not stay around for very long, but DVorkin sold the company to Forbes.com (an initial True/Slant investor) and began to remodel Forbes.com along these lines. By the time Inc.com began seriously considering its own network in 2014, Forbes.com had well more than one thousand contributors and had experienced dramatic growth in web traffic (and therefore in digital revenue since the more web pages that are read, the more advertisements are served, meaning more money to the publisher).

We weren't considering this step primarily for editorial reasons. Rather, we recognized in 2014 that while Inc.com traffic was growing, there was a large number of competitors in online business journalism, and our ranking in size—in the middle to lower end of the list—was holding our business back. Moreover, we had a sense that there was ample room to expand not only the volume of what we were publishing but also the range. The publication started in 1979, and in the print magazine, which has a paid circulation of about seven hundred thousand, we keep a fairly tight focus on stories specifically designed to serve people running a business. Online, however, the audience and potential audience were much, much larger, and there was an opportunity to connect our readers to a much broader network of experts than could ever be reached by our reporters. The *Inc.* brand was a credible vehicle for many other types of stories (such as personal finance and product reviews) and formats (such as video) than were feasible in print. Inc.com believed that its readers would benefit by hearing from a much wider group of columnists: company founders, academics, experts in particular business areas (such as law, human resources, and accounting), marketing experts, cutting-edge technology CEOs, and many more.

We began a massive recruitment effort for online contributors, and I was thoroughly impressed with how many we found in a fairly short period of time. Those publishing once a week or less frequently were not paid for their work. To be paid, contributors had to publish a minimum number of posts per month, and, as with Forbes.com, their payment would be tied to traffic—a fixed amount for every thousand page views. Since we were selling ads on those pages for more money than we were paying the contributors, our interests and the contributors' interest were aligned.

It was a dramatic overhaul in *Inc.*'s web strategy, and we spent considerable time thinking about what it meant to open up our system to contributors who were not professional journalists. Vetting the contributors beforehand was crucial to the process. Even in those early days, we definitely anticipated the potential for conflicts of interest; all contributors were required to sign an agreement covering rights, libel, and ethics. Specifically, our original columnist guidelines stated: "Being paid by a third party for writing about them as an Inc. contributor is an absolute no-no, and will result in immediate revocation of your posting privileges."

But, in all honesty, I recall no lengthy conversations about this scenario because I don't think my colleagues and I envisioned that a pay-to-play business would be worth anyone's time or money. (I still think the idea of paying someone hundreds or thousands of dollars for a one- or two-sentence mention in an online column is a waste of money.) Far more frequent were discussions about what topics we wanted to cover; how we would recruit columnists; how we would handle the substantial increase in copy flow; and how to control the quality of contributions, especially from those with little to no experience as professional writers.

For the most part, Inc.com's strategy has been very successful. Over the course of approximately eighteen months, Inc.com doubled the volume of stories it published daily, and in three years it effectively tripled its monthly traffic. This growth was very helpful to the company's bottom line and also meant that a few of our online contributors were making very good incomes. There can be no question that the strategy introduced the *Inc.* brand to consumers who would not obviously have encountered it otherwise. It also gave us lots of insight into what types of stories readers do and don't respond to.

Furthermore, most of the fears we had as journalists about letting outsiders publish on our platform without editing did not come to pass. One virtue of online publishing is that typographical errors and inartful headlines are easily corrected. The vast majority of our contributors took their responsibility very seriously, and we experienced next to no instances of people using their columns for libel or undue criticism of competitors.

Yet, as we learned in 2016, the system was vulnerable to abuse. Our vetting process was clearly not perfect, although no obvious fix suggested itself; no one pitches a column by disclosing that they intend to take money to mention companies.

We didn't exactly have a bulletproof seven-point plan to tackle the problem. Instinctively, however, I felt that some form of disclosure was necessary. We wanted to make it publicly clear to our contributors, our readers, and these underhanded marketers that this behavior was strictly prohibited. We also figured that if we didn't write about it, the chances were good that someone else eventually would, and there would likely be some benefit to getting out ahead of the story. So one of the first things we did was to report and publish a story on the phenomenon. A columnist had forwarded to me one of the pitches she had received, and I asked her if she would follow up with the person who sent it: How much was he offering? Could he provide examples of previous placement on Inc.com? This sting operation yielded a couple of columnist names, and when we looked at their work and the companies they had linked to, we severed our ties with them.

We turned over what we found to Jeff Bercovici, *Inc.*'s San Francisco bureau chief and the perfect writer for the assignment—he had come to us from *Forbes* and also had years of experience writing specifically about the media business. (In 2019, Bercovici left *Inc.* for a job at the *Los Angeles Times*.) The resulting article, published in July 2016, carried a headline that summarized the situation succinctly: "How Shady Marketers Try to Deceive Readers, and What We're Doing About It."[3] Bercovici took a pretty aggressive reporting approach—he reached out to as many of the "shady marketers" as he could find, and, well, they didn't disappoint. In one instance, he found someone advertising online who boasted, "I have guest posting privileges on the Inc.com [*sic*]. I will write and publish a post there with a backlink to your website, using your anchor text," and charge the company $697 per post. When Bercovici reached out to this opportunist, "a helpful person wrote back asking if we wanted the listing removed or if we preferred a cut of the action. We opted for the former."

The article was one of the first ever published on the topic and caught many people off-guard, including a few on the *Inc.* staff. Some columnists wrote to us saying that they, too, had been approached by such marketers and now had something they could send back in response. Others applauded us for policing the site's integrity because their own reputations depended in part on ours. We also made sure to notify the Federal Trade Commission (FTC) of what we had learned (more on that later). In addition, we rewrote our ethics policy to prohibit this activity more explicitly, and we posted it on Inc.com so that readers and marketers could see it.

Dealing with suspect columnists was one of the harder steps. Even if a columnist's work contains numerous questionable links, there are no ways to prove that money was paid. One or two columnists seemingly showed their hands by more or less skipping town once confronted, but more common were columnists who maintained their innocence. It is conceivable that some columnists were deceived without knowing it. One practice to which I wish we had paid closer and earlier attention was "guest posting," in which a contributor—rather like a late-night talk show host—would give over his or her column to a friend or colleague or perhaps someone who had simply requested to write it. These guest posters sometimes turned out to be marketers who had taken money to promote a given company. Indeed, in recent years an entire cottage industry has emerged that sells guest posts, helps people identify sites and bloggers that accept guest posts, instructs them how to pitch to editors and columnists, and so on. In late 2017, we decided to prohibit guest posting altogether.

Just as Inc.com was not alone in creating a broad-based contributor network, we were also not alone in discovering people trying to exploit that openness. In an article in the online publication the *Outline* in late 2017, four unnamed writers apparently admitted to *Outline* writer Jon Christian that they had accepted payments to mention companies.[4]

For those of us enmeshed in the issue, the *Outline* story didn't have much that was new, but it did provide a few illuminating details. One was the remarkable, if frustratingly anonymous, candor of the writers. One

Huffington Post writer, for example, told the *Outline* "that he has included sponsored references to brands in his articles for years, in articles on the *Huffington Post* and other sites, on behalf of six separate agencies. Some agencies pay him directly, he said, in amounts that can be as small as $50 or $175, but others pay him through an employee's personal PayPal account in order to obfuscate the source of the funds." (Just as all the mainstream outlets quoted in the story did, *HuffPost* issued a statement saying that such activity violates the network's terms of use and that anyone discovered engaging in such abuse would have posts removed and be banned from future publication.)

Another revelation was the type of company that was supposedly using such services. According to the *Outline*, "The *Huffington Post* writer also described specific brands he'd written about on behalf of one of the agencies, which ranged from a popular ride-hailing app, to a publicly-traded site for booking flights and hotels, to a large American cell phone service provider." I find this assertion surprising, for at least two reasons. One is that in all the cases at Inc.com in which editors suspected that something improper had occurred, the company that had seemingly benefitted from a link or a mention was far from a household name. Second, big public companies have entire public-relations infrastructures and huge advertising and marketing budgets at their disposal. Why would they put their reputations at risk by spending a hundred dollars here or there for a mention in a *HuffPost* story? A conceivable scenario is that the agencies making such payments are subcontracted by larger agencies in order to provide some degree of deniability to the larger companies; indeed, such activity could possibly occur without the big company knowing about it. If that scenario is true, it suggests a problem broader and more intractable than we at Inc .com conceived it in 2016. Alas, it is difficult to answer these questions without further details.

One of the very few instances in which the name of an offending columnist became public involved Forbes.com. In early 2018, the site severed its ties with Ky Trang Ho, a reporter and marketing consultant who had written for the site since 2015 and who claims to have contributed heavily trafficked articles and slideshows. "All contributors to Forbes.com sign a contract requiring them to disclose any potential conflicts of interest," a Forbes.com spokeswoman told a newspaper columnist. "When it came to our attention that Ms. Trang Ho violated these terms, we ended our relationship with her, and we are currently in the process of removing all of her content from Forbes.com."[5]

Perhaps more troubling was an incident in December 2017 in which an unknown party paid a Pakistani company called Steve SEO Services to publish an article on *HuffPost* about Felix Sater, a Russian-born convicted felon and onetime associate of Donald Trump. The article, headlined "Case Against Felix Sater Dismissed by New York Court," appears to have been part of a coordinated campaign to spread positive messages about Sater (it has since been removed from *HuffPost*).[6] The author of the story was listed as Waqas KH, the owner of Steve SEO Services, who had published at least eight other stories on *HuffPost* and had advertised on the freelance website Fiverr that he could place articles on *HuffPost* for an $80 fee, with an additional $50 fee to write the article. (This solicitation has also been taken down.)

What's especially alarming about such stories is that if the payments are not disclosed to readers (and they never are), this payola appears to be outside the law. In 2009, the FTC issued very detailed guidelines about what kinds of journalists and commentators have to disclose what kind of payments for advertising or endorsements. The letter of the guidelines does not specifically address an online contributor who takes payments to write about a given company, but such activity clearly violates the guidelines' spirit. One of many hypothetical scenarios the FTC imagines is a college student who publishes a review of a video-gaming system on a popular gaming blog and has received the system for free. The guidelines say: "Because his review is disseminated via a form of consumer-generated media in which his relationship to the advertiser is not inherently obvious, readers are unlikely to know that he has received the video game system free of charge in exchange for his review of the product, and given the value of the video game system, this fact likely would materially affect the credibility they attach to his endorsement. Accordingly, the blogger should clearly and conspicuously disclose that he received the gaming system free of charge."[7] It is obvious that if receipt of a free video-game service requires disclosure, then accepting a cash payment to mention a company would as well.

Alas, one symptom of capture in this environment is that the FTC seems unable or unwilling to enforce its own rules. An agency spokesperson was unable to point to a single instance of enforcement in this area.[8] As vexing as the FTC's inaction may be to publishers who would like to subject unscrupulous marketers to legal pressure, it is also predictable. The FTC has a notoriously broad brief and a relatively small budget and staff. It has made some efforts to go after social media "influencers," including in one highly publicized case featuring two men who boasted about winnings on an online gambling site without disclosing that they owned the site. And, of course, the Facebook activity involving "fake news" and the tarred political consultant group Cambridge Analytica falls under the FTC purview as well. Like so many government actors, the FTC has abdicated its oversight role for all but the most egregious instances of fraud, so no one should be surprised if the agency is willing effectively to overlook shady payments to online contributors.

Do the persistence and possible intractability of digital payola mean that the open contributor network is no longer viable for any publisher intent on protecting its integrity? Some in the publishing industry began asking this question in January 2018, when *HuffPost* announced that it was putting an end to its large and long-standing contributor network. In a *New York Times* interview announcing the largely unexpected move, *HuffPost* editor Lydia Polgreen did not cite payola per se as the reason, but she clearly had been thinking about related areas. "The environment where fake news is flourishing is one where it gets harder and harder to support the idea of a 'let a thousand flowers bloom' kind of publishing platform," Ms. Polgreen said.[9]

Given what we currently know about the scope of the payola problem, however, I don't believe that it necessarily represents a fatal threat to the integrity of contributor networks. One reason is that manipulation through covert pay-to-play strategies is not unique to open contributor networks. Paying high-priced lobbying firms or well-known public figures to write and place op-eds in influential publications, for example, is a long-standing tactic used by corporations and foreign governments seeking to burnish their reputations in the United States. In such cases, readers are never told the ultimate source and purpose of the material, and editors, too, are probably often unaware. In one well-publicized incident, Donald Trump's soon-to-be national security adviser Mike Flynn published an op-ed on election day in 2016 in the Washington, DC, publication *The Hill* arguing for the need to treat Turkey as a vital strategic ally of the United States and attacking Fethullah Gülen, the exiled cleric who lives in Pennsylvania and is considered by the Turkish government as an enemy of the state. Months later it was revealed that a Turkish businessman with ties to the Turkish government had paid Flynn's lobbying firm more than half a million dollars and that the businessman's company had reviewed Flynn's op-ed prior to publication. In a subsequent editor's note in March 2017, *The Hill* said: "Neither General Flynn nor his representatives disclosed this information when the essay was submitted."[10] At a more mundane level, a veteran of New York City's tabloid newspapers told me that junior associates at a well-known New York City public-relations firm would sometimes show up at press conferences in the 1970s and 1980s and hand out $20 bills to reporters in exchange for a promise to mention a client.

Moreover, although the reputational risk that payola represents to any given publisher is certainly real, it's important to put it in perspective. Digital publishing is rife with other forms of fraud that are both more widespread and more clearly illegal. For example, "click fraud"—using automated bots to drive fake traffic to web pages—is an alarmingly common form of online theft. One industry study estimated that of the roughly $80 billion spent on online advertising in 2017, some $16.4 billion could be attributable to fraud.[11] Put another way, one out of every five digital advertising dollars is effectively stolen. That theft may not matter much to readers, but the scale of the fraud suggests that it is or should be a higher priority for publishers than eliminating digital payola.

Regardless of medium, no publisher of a certain size is ever going to be able to promise 100 percent compliance with any ban on pay-to-play activity. What is true, though, is that compared to most other forms of publishing, unpoliced open contributor networks make payola strategies easier to implement at a mass scale.

There are remedies that digital publishers can thankfully apply, however, and although each one may have limitations, taken together they seem to provide a reasonable defense. The ones we at Inc.com have identified are:

Self-regulation. Since we first learned of the problem, we required our columnists to re-sign an ethics policy that even more explicitly bans payola.[12] Moreover, we banned guest posting and have all but stopped publishing one-off contributions even from people who seem legitimate. These steps probably involve taking some losses to our overall traffic, but the protection of the system's legitimacy is more important.

Legal action. Inc.com has written cease-and-desist and trademark-infringement letters to some marketing organizations that claim to guarantee mentions on Inc.com for pay. Some of the most flagrant offenders have complied swiftly and thoroughly, which encourages us that we are on the right path. There's no easy way to find all the solicitations, however, and even if the unscrupulous marketers take down an offending promotional offer, it is not possible to track and halt all such activity.

Technological tools. Inc.com's development team has built tools that make it easier to spot wrongdoers (and I am confident that other publications have taken similar measures). One obvious method is to keep track of where contributors link most often. If, say, most of a given contributor's links are to articles in the *Wall Street Journal* and *Harvard Business Review,* that's a positive signal; if by contrast there are numerous links to, say, a company called "Obscure Software Systems," that's a red flag. One of our tools then looks for other columnists who have linked to Obscure Software Systems, both on Inc.com and on other sites, because this type of activity tends to happen in clusters.

In addition, steps can be taken to make these links less desirable in the first place. We use various services to make sure that we give "no follow" links to any pages that aren't already ranked fairly high in search engines. These links don't provide any search-engine benefit to the pages they link to, and so the value of having a link from Inc.com or other established sites is much lower.

Cooperation. In February 2018, some Inc.com staffers organized an informal meeting with editors from other publications with open contributor networks. The goal was not to create a blacklist of contributors—in general we are very aware of the cost of making accusations that can't be irrefutably proven—but rather to discuss and share the various tactics our respective publications had taken and were considering. These meetings are ongoing.

Digital publishing is always a work in progress. A website of a certain size is never more than a few minutes or hours away from publishing another story or video. Design and shifts in the business model are similarly in flux—at least compared to print. Indeed, the evolution of digital publishing and advertising has proceeded at a breakneck pace over the past ten to fifteen years, with each new promising model cascading over the previous one. It is vital in such a dynamic environment to experiment and reinvent where necessary, but it is equally vital to resist the temptation to abandon first principles simply to embrace novelty or revenue opportunities. The open contributor network is, I believe, a viable publishing option for many (though certainly not all) publishers. It is possible to run a network that benefits readers, contributors, and publishers alike. The challenges that many of us who run such networks have faced may be thorny and are certainly different than the ones that we anticipated. But they can be met, particularly if those of us who have been through the digital payola experience are open and prepared—and, of course, ready for whatever form the long-standing struggle to maintain independence and integrity takes.

NOTES

1. Lucia Moses, "After Scientology Debacle, *The Atlantic* Tightens Native Ad Guidelines," *Adweek*, January 20, 2013, http://www.adweek.com/digital/after-scientology-debacle-atlantic-tightens-native-ad-guidelines-146890/.
2. Katharine Q. Seelye, "A Boldface Name Invites Others to Blog with Her," *New York Times*, April 25, 2005, http://www.nytimes.com/2005/04/25/technology/a-boldface-name-invites-others-to-blog-with-her.html. The *Huffington Post* contributor numbers should probably not be taken at face value. Some have speculated, for example, that the 100,000 contributor figure represents not the size of the network at any given moment but rather the cumulative number of people who have ever contributed. In addition, some skeptics have argued that *HuffPost* contributors represent as little as 5 percent of the site's overall traffic. See Mathew Ingram, "Arianna Huffington's New Platform Strategy Has One Big Problem," *Fortune*, June 29, 2015, http://fortune.com/2015/06/29/huffington-platform.
3. See Jeff Bercovici, "How Shady Marketers Try to Deceive Readers, and What We're Doing About It," *Inc.*, July 2016, https://www.inc.com/jeff-bercovici/contributor-marketers-ftc.html. A few months before Bercovici's piece was published, the *Guardian* had published a story reporting that *Forbes* was investigating an incident in which one of its online contributors requested a payment of £300 sterling from a British public-relations company in return for writing a company profile. As eyebrow raising as that was, the *Guardian* story did not imply that there was a whole pay-to-play nexus out there, and thus I never made the connection between that story and our own site until our contributors began forwarding the offers for payment. See John Plunkett, "*Forbes* Investigates After 'Contributor' Asks PR for £300 to Write Online Profile," *Guardian*, March 16, 2016, https://www.theguardian.com/media/2016/mar/16/forbes-contributor-pr-agency-company-profile.
4. Jon Christian, "Bribes for Blogs: How Brands Secretly Buy Their Way Into *Forbes, Fast Company*, and *HuffPost* Stories," *Outline*, December 5, 2017, https://theoutline.com/post/2563/how-brands-secretly-buy-their-way-into-forbes-fast-company-and-huffpost-stories.
5. Forbes.com spokeswoman, quoted in Keith J. Kelly, "*Forbes* Cuts Ties with Contributor," *New York Post*, January 11, 2018, https://nypost.com/2018/01/11/forbes-cuts-ties-with-self-proclaimed-biased-journalist/.

6. See "*HuffPost* Deletes Sponsored Trump–Russia Article," *Shooting the Messenger*, December 13, 2017, https://shootingthemessenger.blog/2017/12/13/huffpost-deletes -sponsored-trump-russia-article/.

7. The FTC guidelines can be found at https://www.ftc.gov/sites/default/files /attachments/press-releases/ftc-publishes-final-guides-governing-endorsements -testimonials/091005revisedendorsementguides.pdf.

8. Mitchell Katz, FTC spokesperson, email exchange with the author, March 7, 2018.

9. Lydia Polgreen, quoted in Sydney Ember, "*HuffPost*, Breaking from Its Roots, Ends Unpaid Contributions," *New York Times*, January 18, 2018, https://www.nytimes .com/2018/01/18/business/media/huffpost-unpaid-contributors.html.

10. *The Hill*, quoted in Erik Wemple, "*The Hill* Publishes Editor's Note on Michael Flynn Op-ed Regarding Turkey," *Washington Post*, March 10, 2017, https://www .washingtonpost.com/blogs/erik-wemple/wp/2017/03/10/the-hill-publishes-editors -note-on-michael-flynn-op-ed-regarding-turkey/.

11. Lara O'Reilly, "The Ad Fraud Issue Could Be More Than Twice as Big as First Thought—Advertisers Stand to Lose $16.4 Billion to It This Year," *Business Insider*, March 15, 2017, http://www.businessinsider.com/thepartnership-msix-and-adloox -ad-fraud-2017-2017-3.

12. Inc.com's most recent ethics policy can be found at https://www.inc.com/inc-staff /inc-columnists-code-of-ethics.html.

Chapter Eight

MEDIA CAPTURE AND THE CORPORATE EDUCATION-REFORM PHILANTHROPIES

ANDREA GABOR

Since the start of the new millennium, business leaders from Wall Street to Silicon Valley have funded and promoted—via their philanthropic organizations—the reengineering of American education based on free-market ideas.

This philanthropic agenda converged with the federal education policies of Presidents George W. Bush and Barack Obama, creating what the political scientist Sarah Reckhow calls a perfect storm.

Three top philanthropies have led this activist movement—the Bill and Melinda Gates Foundation; the Walton Family Foundation, the chief philanthropy of the founders of the Arkansas-based big-box retailer; and the Eli and Edythe Broad Foundation, a California philanthropy built by a local housing and insurance entrepreneur. These foundations quadrupled their spending on K–12 education to $400 million between 2000 and 2005. And they channeled their funding to "districts with political and organizational features" that supported the "likelihood of foundation influence," writes Reckhow in *Follow the Money*.[1]

By 2010, the nation's top-fifteen foundations had contributed $844 million to K–12 education.[2] Moreover, the philanthropies were increasingly pooling their resources around national organizations with a common agenda: to manage schools like stocks in a Wall Street portfolio—high performers, usually as measured by test scores, would win further investment, whereas poor performers would lose funding and be closed.

President Bush's No Child Left Behind policy created a market-based accountability framework by demanding that every child reach proficiency on state tests by 2014; if children failed to reach that goal, schools risked being closed. Although the goal was impossible to reach—and in practice the U.S. Education Department gave states waivers if they didn't meet the 100-percent-proficiency requirement—it created an ideal climate for big philanthropy's agenda of educational disruption.

During the Obama administration, federal government policy and the agenda of key philanthropists effectively fused as education secretary Arne Duncan staffed his department with former Gates Foundation officials. At the same time, the Gates Foundation funded policy initiatives such as the development of the Common Core State Standards and teacher-evaluation systems linked to test scores, which were then adopted by the education department.[3]

The big philanthropies increasingly invested in what Harvard's Jal Mehta and Johns Hopkins's Steven Teles call "jurisdictional challengers," working to "empower a different set of actors" to upend traditional educational institutions, in particular public schools and school boards.[4] The big-three foundations instead funded a range of private and public institutions, including charter-management organizations and alternative teacher-development institutions such as Teach for America, as well as school-board candidates who would back the reform agenda and help break the "monopoly" of public-school districts.

To support their larger policy goals, the big philanthropies also ratcheted up their spending on advocacy and, in particular, their investments in the news media. The philanthropies supported education coverage at mainstream publications—an investment that in some cases helped promote the foundations' education-reform agenda. In addition, they have founded publications dedicated to selling those ideas.

Even as big philanthropy's investments in K–12 organizations climbed, its spending on national advocacy "grew more than 23 percent faster than total giving" in the decade leading up to 2010.[5]

The Gates Foundation especially has been explicit in its intention to influence local and national policy. However, as part of comprehensive policy and advocacy campaigns, all three major foundations have funded education coverage at both general news organization as well as specialized education publications.

The three foundations have radically transformed public education in a range of cities, including Los Angeles and New Orleans. In the process, they have pursued a soup-to-nuts funding strategy designed to maximize the impact of their gifts by simultaneously influencing a broad range of institutions, from local school boards and universities to think tanks and government institutions, all the while targeting the news media as a way to shape public opinion.

On May 15, 2014, the Associated Press ran a story about Gates's $44 million bid to support the rollout of the federal education law called the Every Student Succeeds Act in 2015, which gives states flexibility in defining—and meeting—school quality standards, a departure from Bush- and Obama-era federal oversight. The Associated Press explained how the Gates Foundation operates by

> funding everything from policy work on the ground to broader research and analysis, as well as national advocacy groups, community leaders and media coverage both mainstream and niche.
>
> In Tennessee, a Gates-funded advocacy group had a say in the state's new education plan, with its leader sitting on an important advising committee. A media outlet given money by Gates to cover the new law then published a story about research funded by Gates. And many Gates-funded groups have become the de facto experts who lead the conversation in local communities. Gates also dedicated millions of dollars to protect Common Core as the new law unfolded.[6]

For the news media, battered by internet companies such as Craigslist and Facebook, which have siphoned off advertising revenue, funding from philanthropies comes at an opportune time. Nor can private foundations be faulted for supporting the news media, especially given the recent rise in "alternative facts," demagoguery, propaganda, and kompromat (compromising material). However, large contributions to news organizations—many of them earmarked specifically for education coverage—by foundations that explicitly support market-oriented education reforms raise questions about both the intention of the philanthropists giving the funds and the independence of the news organizations that accept the funds.

In particular, this chapter explores how philanthropic support of news organizations—including new publications founded and run by education-reform advocates—is aimed at creating a receptive audience for the top foundations' market-oriented education reforms. The chapter also demonstrates how the foundations' "carefully curated web of influence" allows them to "drive the conversation"[7]—among researchers, government policy makers, and the news media—in support of their vision of market-based education reform.

THE GATES FOUNDATION'S WIDE REACH

In 2011, the *Seattle Times* published an exhaustive article about its leading hometown philanthropic organization and asked: "Does Gates funding of media taint objectivity?" The article showed how the Gates Foundation funds major media organizations, from ABC to the *Guardian*, noting that its philanthropy does much more than fund media organizations as a way to ensure amplification of its message:

> To garner attention for the issues it cares about, the foundation has invested millions in training programs for journalists. It funds research on the most effective ways to craft media messages. Gates-backed think tanks turn out media fact sheets and newspaper opinion pieces. Magazines and scientific journals get Gates money to publish research and articles. Experts coached in Gates-funded programs write columns that appear in media outlets from *The New York Times* to *The Huffington Post*, while digital portals blur the line between journalism and spin.[8]

Indeed, the news media's coverage of education mirrors in many ways what has happened with charter-school research, which has been "severely tainted by ideology." In his book *Spin Cycle*, Jeffrey Henig, a political scientist at Columbia University, found that "framing charter schools in terms of markets versus government . . . raised the stakes, the visibility, and the prospects that findings would be put to political ends whether with the active cooperation of the researchers, their complicit assent, or to their frustration or dismay."[9]

The Gates Foundation alone devoted $1 billion in the decade from 2000 to 2010 to so-called policy and advocacy, a tenth of the foundation's $3-billion-a-year spending, according to the *Seattle Times* in late 2013. Although much of that money went to analyze policy questions—such as the efficacy of vaccine-funding strategies—"the 'advocacy' side of the equation is essentially public relations: an attempt to influence decision-makers and sway public opinion." "The Gates Foundation spends more on policy and advocacy than most big foundations—including Rockefeller and MacArthur—spend in total," concluded the *Seattle Times*.[10]

Indeed, as this article pointed out, rather than providing general support for individual publications, Gates usually "stipulates" that its funding be used for reporting on issues the philanthropy supports—whether curing diseases such as HIV or improving education in the United States.

Although Gates does not appear to dictate specific stories, the *Seattle Times* noted: "Few of the news organizations that get Gates money have produced any critical coverage of foundation programs. *The Guardian* is an exception, with a recent blog post that blasted the foundation's associations with agricultural giant Monsanto, a leader in genetically modified crops."

The *Seattle Times* story was written before the newspaper accepted a $530,000 grant from the Gates Foundation in 2013 to launch the Education Lab. The paper described the venture as "a partnership between *The Seattle Times* and Solutions Journalism Network" that will explore "promising programs and innovations inside early-education programs, K–12 schools and colleges that are addressing some of the biggest challenges facing public education." The project is funded by grants from the Gates Foundation and the John S. and James L. Knight Foundation, with the Gates Foundation providing the bulk of the funding, $450,000.[11]

In a blog post, the newspaper addressed the potential conflict of interest, posing a series of questions and answers. In answer to the question "Do the foundations have any control over what is reported?," the paper wrote: "*The Seattle Times* would neither seek nor accept a grant that did not give us full editorial control over what is published. Generally, when a grant is made, there is agreement on a specific project or a broad area of reporting it will support." The newspaper earmarked its funding for what it calls "solutions journalism." Although the Gates Foundation insists that "solutions journalism" is not about advocacy, it says the aim is to "critically examine potential solutions that could provide powerful insights that change the way people consider our region's education challenges."[12]

Gates's funding of regional education coverage is not unique. Other foundations support a host of local and national education publications with the explicit purpose of influencing education coverage.

THE BROAD FOUNDATION FLEXES ITS MUSCLE IN LOS ANGELES

In the fall of 2015, Howard Blume, an education reporter for the *Los Angeles Times*, published a scoop—the contents of a forty-four-page memo that outlined an ambitious $490 million Great Public Schools Now initiative spearheaded by the Eli and Edythe Broad Foundation to more than double the number of local charter schools to more than five hundred. Los Angeles already enrolls more kids in charter schools—16 percent of the total number of school-age children—than any other city. What's more, the plan seemed destined to "push the nation's second-largest school system into insolvency, according to an independent panel of experts," reported the *Los Angeles Times*.[13]

The new plan would more than double the $144 million Broad had already spent on local charter schools. The preface to the plan declared, "Thanks to the strength of its charter leaders and teachers, as well as its widespread civic and philanthropic support, Los Angeles is uniquely positioned to create the largest, highest-performing charter sector in the nation. Such an exemplar would serve as a model for all large cities to follow."[14]

The plan also included a helpful list of about two dozen philanthropists who could be relied on to help fund the effort. The list gave not only the net worth of each individual and organization but also the amount each they had already given to charter schools. At the top of the list of charter-giving foundations was Gates with $33 million and Walton with $65 million. It's noteworthy that the Annenberg Foundation, once the largest giver to education, had no money earmarked for charter schools.[15]

Leaving nothing to chance, Broad also appeared poised to ensure the kind of messaging in the news media that would support the new plan, which included a "telling-the-story strategy to support this effort and to explain why this transformation matters in Los Angeles." This effort would include a six-year $21.4 million "investment" in "organizing and advocacy," more than a quarter of which would be devoted to "civic engagement and communications," according to the Great Public Schools Now Initiative, "engaging the media, countering the opposition, and building constructive partnerships using data and strategic messaging."[16]

One month before Blume leaked the plan, one of those "constructive partnerships" with the news media was already in place. The *Los Angeles Times* announced that a group of philanthropists would provide $800,000 to fund a new journalism initiative known as "Education Matters" to expand the paper's coverage of K–12 education. "In other words, the *Times*' new education-reporting project is being funded by some of the very organizations the new education-reporting project is likely to be covering," wrote the *Washington Post*, adding that "three of the *Times*' benefactors—the K&F Baxter Family Foundation, the Wasserman Foundation, and the Eli and Edythe Broad Foundation—have been major supporters of charter and school-privatization efforts that are strongly opposed by teachers' unions."[17]

Journalism experts note that when publications accept philanthropic funding, they must at the very least provide "complete, exhaustive, repetitive transparency," disclosing all of their financial connections in news articles, says Steven A. Smith, a journalism professor at the University of Idaho and a former newspaper editor.[18]

Yet the *Los Angeles Times* has not always been transparent about Broad's "connections to the paper," notes the *Washington Post*: "The *Times*' editorial board recently applauded his foundation's school overhaul proposal, headlining its endorsement, 'A charter school expansion could be great for L.A.'" The editorial made no mention of the Broad Foundation's funding of the *Times*'s education reporting. Indeed, the *Times* has reported on Broad-financed opinion polls showing widespread support for charter schools without disclosing the foundation's support for the newspaper. S. Mitra Kalita, the *Times*' managing editor for editorial strategy, responded to a question about this nondisclosure: "The newspaper discloses such relationships when it reports directly on an organization or individual, but not when an individual has a secondary or indirect involvement in a story."[19]

IN EXCHANGE FOR PHILANTHROPIC INVESTMENTS, BROAD EXPECTS "FEALTY"

In a *New Yorker* article in late 2010, Connie Bruck described Eli Broad's wide reach in Los Angeles as well as his willingness to use his connections to exert influence on the art world: "A map of the city dotted with contributions bearing his name looks almost pointillist: thirty-six million dollars to biological research at the California Institute of Technology, fifty million to the Broad Contemporary Art Museum, a hundred million to charter schools, thirty million to stem-cell research at U.S.C., ten million to the Broad Stage, a new performing-arts center, seven million to the Los Angeles Opera." Bruck pointed to Broad's attempt to take over the major artistic institutions in Los Angeles and the way he seeks to control the entities to which he contributes: "He has given large sums of money to L.A. arts institutions—about a hundred and forty million dollars in the past thirty years—but in return he has expected a degree of fealty that many in the art world find unseemly."[20]

Broad appears to wield the kind of influence on local education that he has exerted on the local arts scene. In 2011, John Deasy, a Broad protégé and former deputy director of the Gates Foundation's education division, became superintendent of the Los Angeles Unified School District. Deasy was brought in with the expectation he would grow the charter-school system and confront the teachers' union. But Deasy's tumultuous tenure ended in 2014, when he was forced to resign following, among other things, a $1.3 billion iPad debacle in which he used money intended for school-construction bonds to buy iPads for students. Deasy also was reviled for testifying against his own district in the *Vergara v. California* trial, which sought (unsuccessfully after multiple appeals) to overturn the state's laws governing teacher tenure, seniority, and dismissal.[21]

In 2015, one month before Blume's *Los Angeles Times* article revealed the details of Broad's ambitious charter-expansion plan, *Inside Philanthropy* speculated that Deasy, who went to work for the Broad Foundation after leaving the district, would be instrumental in the foundation's plans to expand charters in Los Angeles:

> Deasy's forced resignation angered a lot of people—probably nobody more
> than Eli Broad himself. Since leaving LAUSD [Los Angeles Unified School

District], Deasy has doubled down on his relationship with Broad, joining the foundation as Superintendent-In-Residence, and leading many to speculate that Broad and Deasy are gearing up for an aggressive campaign to change the landscape of L.A.'s public school system.

This will be interesting to watch—or damn scary, depending on your viewpoint. Eli Broad is passionate about education reform, and passionate about Los Angeles. But he hasn't yet brought those two interests together at the scale that he might, given his resources.[22]

In 2018, Broad had a hand in appointing another superintendent, Austin Beutner, the former publisher of the *Los Angeles Times*. Beutner was the publisher who had struck a deal for foundation funding for Education Matters three years earlier—though a glowing editorial in the paper at the time of Beutner's appointment failed to mention that fact. The *Times* conceded, however, that

> some people—maybe a lot of people—will see the appointment of Austin Beutner to be superintendent of the L.A. Unified school district [*sic*] as a victory for charter school supporters and a loss for the teachers' union.
>
> They aren't entirely wrong. Beutner certainly has ties to charter schools and a close relationship with billionaire school reformer Eli Broad.[23]

Beutner had ambitious goals for "reimagining" K–12 education in Los Angeles, but his plans ran up against a growing backlash against reform efforts—the backlash itself fueled by resentment against big philanthropy's widespread influence. The education-reform funders had overplayed their hand by, among other things, abandoning coalitions with local organizations, concludes Sara Reckhow.[24]

In January 2019, when an estimated thirty thousand Los Angeles teachers and other school personnel took to the picket lines in the city's first teachers' strike in thirty years, the move was widely supported by parents and local communities. Perhaps most noteworthy, among the union's demands was a call for a moratorium on charter-school expansion; unrestricted charter-school growth, labor leaders argued, was starving public schools because education funds follow each child.[25]

By then, the reformers had suffered setbacks. Gavin Newsom had become governor in 2018, defeating a more charter-friendly Antonio Villaraigosa, the former mayor of Los Angeles, and ending more than twenty-five years of unqualified gubernatorial support for charter schools. (In addition, a union-backed candidate for the state's school superintendency edged out a rival who was backed by the charter industry in a high-stakes $60 million race.) One of Newsom's first actions was to sign a transparency law designed to require charter schools to abide by open-meetings and conflict-of-interest rules—legislation that had been opposed by his predecessor, Jerry Brown. The state also convened a task force to consider the fiscal impact of charter schools on public-school districts. Public schools might get their single greatest boost if a ballot initiative in 2020 aimed at scaling back property-tax protections for commercial properties now covered by Proposition 13 passes.

Beutner was forced to scuttle his plans for remaking the Los Angeles school system, but not before a 342-page report revealed that part of the "reimagining" process had called for "'a drumbeat of positive press' around the initiative."[26] The report itself had been prepared by a consulting firm, Kitamba, which had been hired by Beutner and had helped implement the portfolio system in other cities. Kitamba's work was financed in part by the Broad Foundation and other philanthropies.[27]

THE PHILANTHROPIES EXPAND THEIR NEWS MEDIA REACH

The Broad Foundation was helping to fund a veritable orchestra, not just a drumbeat, of positive press for school reform. Broad helped underwrite the *LA School Report*, a publication covering the Los Angeles Unified School District. The publication was founded by Jamie Alter Lynton, the sister of the journalist Jonathan Alter; both brother and sister are ed-reform advocates and are affiliated with a new education news organization, the 74 Million (discussed later). Lynton also has been a campaign contributor to Los Angeles Unified School Board candidates backed by corporate-style reform advocates but says she directed her editors "to play no favorites." (Jon Alter starred in *Waiting for Superman* [Davis Guggenheim, 2010], a pro-reform documentary, and is a grade-school classmate and friend of the author.)[28]

Although the *LA School Report* is seen as "a legitimate and credible news organization" even by Randi Weingarten, president of the American

Federation of Teachers, the 74, which recently acquired the *LA School Report*, is widely viewed as the house organ of the education reformers.[29]

Indeed, the 74 represents one of the most audacious efforts by the foundations to influence coverage of the education-reform story. Founded by Campbell Brown, a former CNN anchor and controversial advocate of corporate-style education reform—among other things, her nonprofit Partnership for Educational Justice backed the *Vergara* lawsuit to end teacher tenure in California—the 74 is geared explicitly to national coverage of education-reform efforts. Brown also served as the website's editor in chief until taking a job at Facebook in 2017.

The 74 was launched in 2015 with a $4 million annual budget; top funders included Bloomberg Philanthropies, the Walton Family Foundation, Carnegie Foundation, and the Dick and Betsy DeVos Family Foundation. It's worth noting that the 74 is the only news organization that receives funding from the DeVos family. However, following Betsy DeVos's nomination as education secretary in 2016, Romy Drucker, cofounder and CEO of the 74, announced that it would not apply for new funding from the DeVos Foundation after the final disbursement of a two-year "general operating support grant" that had been made in 2014.[30]

In 2016, the Walton Foundation spent $730,000 to underwrite the 74, more than it spent on any other media organization besides National Public Radio (NPR). Meanwhile, the Gates Foundation gave the 74 relatively small change—just $26,000.

Here is how the *Los Angeles Times* describes the controversy over the 74:

> Critics call the Seventy Four an advocacy effort on behalf of a pro-charter school, anti-union agenda. The organization, critics say, uses opinion pieces and reported stories to promote charter schools and to find fault with traditional campuses and teachers unions.
>
> Not so, said co-founder and Chief Executive Romy Drucker.
>
> "We try to highlight what's working," Drucker said. "Part of the mission also is highlighting what's broken and needs to be fixed and highlighting the solutions."[31]

The *Los Angeles Times* also reported local concern over the 74's recent takeover of the *LA School Report* following the unveiling of Broad's Great

Public Schools Now initiative: "Is there a connection between the Seventy Four's takeover of *LA School Report* and the Broad–Walmart plan to privatize LAUSD schools? Of course there is," said Alex Caputo-Pearl, president of the local teachers' union, United Teachers Los Angeles.[32]

Local coverage of *Vergara v. California,* a lawsuit backed by Campbell Brown's nonprofit and a major education story, illustrates the problem with media organizations owned by big philanthropy.

When the California appeals court overruled a lower-court finding against the teachers' union in the case, the 74 chose initially not to cover the story at all.[33] Two days after the news broke, Mercedes Schneider, a Louisiana teacher and education blogger opposed to corporate-style education reforms, noted on her blog that although the *LA School Report,* now owned by the 74, had reported the story, the 74 itself had not reported the news. Schneider also reported that the *Los Angeles Times* had changed its original coverage of the *Vergara* decision, omitting any reference to Campbell Brown:

> When the *Los Angeles Times* wrote an April 14, 2016, about the *Vergara* reversal, an early version of the article included the following reference to Brown and her penchant for backing tenure-busting litigation:
> "*Vergara* has caused small ripple effects across the country. A similar suit supported by the Partnership for Educational Justice, an organization founded by former CNN news anchor Campbell Brown, is ongoing in New York."
> By April 15, 2016, all reference to Brown and her Partnership for Educational Justice as instigating tenure lawsuits had been scrubbed from the *LA Times* piece. Here is what remains:
> "Similar litigation was filed soon after in New York; and on Thursday, just before the release of the appellate decision in California, another lawsuit was filed in Minnesota."
> At the bottom of the piece, one can find the tracking of updates to the article, However, no update mentions removing information from the article, just "updating."[34]

The New York State lawsuit is ongoing.[35]

As for the 74, its first story covering the *Vergara* lawsuit appeared in August 2016, four months after the decision. It is a repost of *one version* of an article that had previously appeared in its now sister publication the *LA*

School Report. For those searching for telltale footprints of journalistic bias, two editorial decisions are of particular note. First, the original *LA School Report* story, pegged to the California Supreme Court's decision to let the appeals court ruling stand, carries a "newsy" headline "JUST IN: *Vergara* Ends—California Supreme Court Refuses to Take up Teacher Tenure Case." However, the entire story is told from the perspective of the *dissenting* judges:

> The court was split four to three, with two of the dissenting judges issuing lengthy and forceful statements that laid out why action is needed on the state's tenure laws.
>
> Ted Boutrous, an attorney for StudentsMatter, the nonprofit that supported the nine California public school student-plaintiffs and asked the state Supreme Court to review the appellate court ruling, said in a call with reporters that he has never seen dissenting statements like the ones given Monday in previous Supreme Court denials, "Until today."
>
> "These are two scholars, legal scholars, brilliant scholars, who have explained why these issues are so important, why the statutes are so bad, why the court should have taken this case," he said.[36]

Second, although the *LA School Report* coverage had included an updated version with comment from Steve Zimmer, then president of the LA Unified School Board, as well as the from teachers' union, the 74 included no response from either. A Google search with the key words *the 74* and *Vergara v. California* shows only one story published in August, and it lacks the updates that its sister publication included.[37]

Indeed, the foundations not only worked to erase Zimmer from the 74's coverage but also funded a slew of organizations designed to defeat Zimmer, a former teacher who was viewed as an "independent" voice on the school board. In what became one of the most expensive and most negative school-board races in the country, the reformers spent $14 million—more than half of it to unseat Zimmer. Education reformers outspent the union two to one to elect Nick Melvoin, a charter-school advocate, who once called for "a hostile takeover" of the Los Angeles Unified School District.[38]

To wage this school-board battle, the foundations backed "the Coalition for School Reform, LA's Promise, Parent Revolution, and the Los Angeles Fund for Public Education—all front groups designed to sell their version of 'school reform,' " according to Peter Dreier, the chair of the Urban and Environmental Policy Department at Occidental College.[39]

The Coalition for School Reform describes itself as "a group of parents, educators and business and non-profit leaders dedicated to reforming and improving public schools in the LA Unified School District" and is explicit about its principle mission: "We support reform candidates," including Kate Anderson, Zimmer's opponent in the 2013 race. As recently as August 2018, the group's website included no mention of the sizeable donations by business funders, led by $1 million contributed by former New York mayor Michael Bloomberg and $250,000 from the Broad Foundation. Jamie Alter Lynton, the founder of the *LA School Report*, also contributed $100,000.[40]

In the school-board election in 2013, Zimmer prevailed over his opponent Kate Anderson, the coalition's candidate. However, four years later the reformers finally won their majority on the school board by defeating Zimmer.

Thanks to the recent backlash against big philanthropy's efforts to reshape education in Los Angeles, the reformers' school-board majority appeared likely to be short-lived. In an early school-board race in 2019, Jackie Goldberg, the teachers' union favorite, won more than 48 percent of the vote in a field of nine candidates, in which her two leading opponents garnered a little more than 13 percent each. Goldberg won a runoff election in May, which ended the school board's brief pro-charter majority.

Most curious was the *Los Angeles Times's* refusal to endorse Goldberg for the school-board seat. The paper acknowledged Goldberg's experience in glowing terms:

> She's brimming with experience, smarts and humor—and connections. She's been a teacher and served as a member of the school board, the City Council and the state Assembly, and she knows everyone involved in the world of education in California. To say that her chances of winning the May 14 runoff are high would be an understatement.
>
> Nor would it be a terrible thing if that happened. Goldberg's institutional memory and her talent for digging to the heart of an issue would be of value to the board.[41]

Yet the paper endorsed Goldberg's opponent, Heather Repenning, deeming Goldberg too sympathetic to the teachers' union. Yet in endorsing

Repenning, whose campaign benefited from funding from Eli Broad, the paper implied that the far less knowledgeable candidate would not be compromised by the billionaire's backing.[42]

Meanwhile, the 74's advocacy efforts continue unabated. In 2016, it published *The Founders*, a hagiography of the reform movement by Richard Whitmire. The book, complete with an introduction by Arne Duncan, purports to profile the top 20 percent of charter schools, which have "about as much to do with low-performing charters as dogs have to do with cats." The book is a model of breathless boosterism:

> [T]op charters had changed public schooling forever; most were producing a year and a half of learning for every year a student spent in their schools.
> Take my word for it: In urban education that just doesn't happen.[43]

No footnote or data or any other supporting evidence is provided.

The 74 has served another vital function for the philanthropists—as a Greek chorus of praise for the New Orleans education reforms. The 74 produced more than half-a-dozen articles in the celebratory series "10 Years After Hurricane Katrina" as well as at least three documentaries.[44]

Although Los Angeles has enrolled more students in charter schools than any other U.S. city, New Orleans is the first all-charter urban district in the nation and an archetype for the controversial "portfolio model" that the philanthropists are working to take nationwide.[45] During the summer of 2018, the Laura and John Arnold Foundation and the Hastings Foundation announced that they had raised $200 million for the City Fund—including $10 million from the Gates Foundation—which is intended to bring the portfolio model to forty cities around the country. The details were published on the blog of Neerav Kingsland, managing partner at the City Fund and the former head of New Schools for New Orleans, the city's principle charter-school gatekeeper, which channels funding from top philanthropies to local schools.[46]

BIG PHILANTHROPY AND OLD-LINE MEDIA

The role of the foundations in projects such as the 74 and *The Founders* casts more conventional gifts to mainstream news organizations in an almost benign light.

For example, in 2016 the Walton Foundation doubled its education-related funding to the *New York Times* to $300,000 from the amount it contributed in 2014. Similarly, Walton gave $1.1 million to NPR explicitly for "education improvement," up from $343,000 in 2014.[47]

Meanwhile, the Gates Foundation gave NPR $3 million in 2017, 50 percent more than in 2016, but less than half the $6.3 million it contributed to NPR in 2013. The Gates grant was targeted to "inform and engage communities."[48]

This is not to say that this funding has unleashed a spate of pro-reform coverage by respected outlets such as the *New York Times* and NPR. Indeed, I have published essays in the *New York Times* that are critical of the education-reform movement. However, logic suggests that publications desirous of repeat tranches of funding will at least moderate their critical coverage.

Indeed, the big philanthropies also provide substantial backing to national publications dedicated to education coverage. For example, *Chalkbeat*, which has become a must-read publication for anyone connected to the education field, has received generous support from leading education-reform organizations. The Walton Foundation contributed $384,000 in 2016 to *Chalkbeat*, which constituted more than 10 percent of the publication's total revenue that year. (Foundation and trust revenue for 2016 were $432,556 [unrestricted] and $2,621,985, respectively.)[49]

Chalkbeat describes itself as a "nonprofit news organization covering educational change efforts in communities where improvement matters most." The publication has bureaus in, among other locations, New York, Colorado, Indiana, and Tennessee. And it describes its mission as follows: "to inform the decisions and actions that lead to better outcomes for children and families by providing deep, local coverage of education policy and practice."[50]

Chalkbeat does some excellent education reporting. It also has won journalism awards, including two Society of Professional Journalists first-place citations for stories critical of the portfolio model in Detroit and Denver.[51] A comprehensive look at *Chalkbeat*'s coverage would be necessary to attempt any assessment of whether its coverage has been skewed, which is beyond the scope of this chapter.

However, Elizabeth Green, *Chalkbeat*'s editor, also has written glowingly of New York City's controversial Success Academy charter school. In an article published in both *Chalkbeat* and the *Atlantic*, Green declared the charter-school charter-management organization—including $10 million from the Gates Foundation—"the most impressive education system I've ever seen."[52] One doesn't have to question Success Academy's test prep or discipline practices to wonder how a school that graduated its first class in 2018 (just sixteen students out of an original cohort of seventy-three) could merit such a superlative designation—or how Green's views affect *Chalkbeat*'s coverage.

Green acknowledges in the *Atlantic* article on Success Academy that John Petry, a Success Academy board member (who attended public school in the same Maryland district as Green), helped throw a book party for her book *How to Build a Better Teacher*. The article was published in the *Atlantic* just six months after Laurene Powell Jobs, the widow of Steve Jobs and an ardent charter-school supporter, acquired a majority stake in the *Atlantic*.

Education Week, another must-read education publication, also receives abundant funding from pro-reform sources. Editorial Projects in Education, the nonprofit publisher of *Education Week*, has received generous donations from the Broad, Gates, and Walton Foundations in recent years.[53]

As a nonprofit publisher, Editorial Projects in Education has always relied on philanthropic funding. The organization launched *Education Week* in 1981 with funding from the Carnegie Corp., among other sources, because it "determined that the precollegiate field likewise needed independent, first-rate journalistic coverage of national scope."[54] The organization started out as the nonprofit publisher of the *Chronicle for Higher Education* but later divested the publication.

Similarly, the Hechinger Institute on Education and the Media, which is housed at Columbia University Teachers College, launched the *Hechinger Report* in 2009 with a $1 million grant from the Lumina and Gates Foundations. The publication also lists the Chan/Zuckerberg Initiative as a major funder.[55]

WHEN FLORIDA'S GOVERNOR REDEFINED PUBLIC EDUCATION

The growing role of big philanthropy in education reform has been enabled by government policy under Presidents Bush, Obama, and, most recently, Trump. Indeed, the role of government and philanthropy is becoming increasingly symbiotic, raising concerns about both oversight and accountability. Note Mehta and Teles,

> The government is picking winners and losers among non-profits, and, in particular, favoring politically controversial non-profits that have substantial backing from private philanthropy. From the point of view of strategic philanthropy, this is precisely how reform is supposed to work: philanthropy backs promising efforts on a small scale, and successful ones then develop more sustainable funding streams from the government. But from the point of view of democratic accountability, the government risks being seen as captured by a particular group of school reformers and the philanthropists who fund them.[56]

That risk of government capture took on new meaning in Florida in early 2019 when Governor Ron DeSantis, standing at a lectern at Calvary Christian Academy in Orlando, announced a new school-voucher program that would use public money for private- and religious-school tuition. "If the taxpayer is paying for education, it's public education," regardless of what school a child attends, said DeSantis, effectively redefining the very meaning of public education.[57]

Education secretary Betsy DeVos immediately responded via tweet: "Completely agree, @GovRonDesantis."[58]

Florida had been whipsawed by education reform long before DeSantis took office, though. The growth of charters and voucher programs, which began under Governor Jeb Bush nearly twenty years ago, has drained funding from public-school districts, with the result that per pupil spending and public-school teacher pay are near the bottom of national rankings—one reason the Sunshine State also has a massive teacher shortage.

Florida was also the test site for one of the Gates Foundation's biggest recent ventures, a costly teacher-effectiveness experiment that the foundation eventually abandoned because it failed to improve student performance. The experiment cost the Hillsborough District in Tampa, one of three participating districts, more than $120 million—its share of the innovation bill. Gates's contribution to Hillsborough's part in the experiment was about $80 million. (Indeed, the teacher-effectiveness gambit was just the latest education experiment abandoned by Gates during the past decade because it didn't work out.)[59]

The *Tampa Bay Times*, a newspaper owned by the Poynter Institute for Media Studies, a nonprofit journalism school based in St. Petersburg, has followed this local education story particularly closely. The paper published several articles on the issue, including an analysis of how the proposed voucher law would affect Florida's public schools. The law would, for example, allocate money directly from the state Education Department to pay for private and religious tuition—a plan that could violate the state constitution. Vouchers programs typically are financed with tax credits given to corporations or individuals.[60]

In an editorial, the *Tampa Bay Times* also called DeSantis's definition of public education "absurd," noting, "It redefines the meaning of public education in Florida and the nation. It also flies in the face of the Florida Constitution."[61]

A few national news organizations picked up the story, including the *Washington Post* in Valerie Strauss's mostly anti-reform-education blog. The Associated Press wrote about the voucher laws journey through the Florida legislature.

Ironically, it was the 74 Million's gleeful coverage that best captured why the stakes in Florida are so high. The 74 noted that there is now "an education reform trifecta in Florida, with reform champions in charge of education policy in both legislative chambers, as well as in the governor's mansion. Observers expect an aggressive push for expanded school choice, both public and private."[62]

Yet the rest of the education press remained virtually silent. Only *Education Week* published an article about Florida's voucher expansion, in April, two months after DeSantis's announcement, but mentioned neither the governor's redefinition of public education nor the proposed changes in how the new vouchers would be funded.[63] There is no shortage of important education stories these days, and some publications may have been focused elsewhere. Indeed, the pace and magnitude of the changes being visited on school districts nationwide are historic, with public education in many parts of the country effectively being handed over to private operators at breakneck speed. The irony is that with local news organizations severely compromised by years of financial drain, education coverage often comes via news organizations that are funded by the very philanthropies that have a stake in the outcome of the reforms. It is hard to see how news organizations beholden to big philanthropy can perform their watchdog function adequately, let alone vigorously. Without it, big philanthropy will continue to have an outsize influence on the future of public education, an institution that the Founding Fathers saw as vital both to the development of a democratic citizenry and to the survival of democracy.

NOTES

1. Sarah Reckhow, *Follow the Money: How Foundation Dollars Change Public School Politics* (Oxford: Oxford University Press, 2013), 37, 41.
2. Sarah Reckhow and Jeffrey W. Snyder, "The Expanding Role of Philanthropy in Education Politics," *Educational Researcher*, May 1, 2014, 186–95, https://journals.sagepub.com/doi/pdf/10.3102/0013189X14536607.
3. Andrea Gabor, *After the Education Wars: How Smart Schools Upend the Business of Reform* (New York: New Press, 2018).
4. Jal Mehta and Steven Teles, "Jurisdictional Politics: A New Federal Role in Education," in *Carrots, Sticks, and the Bully Pulpit: Lessons from a Half-Century of Federal Efforts to Improve America's Schools*, ed. Frederick M. Hess and Andrew P. Kelly (Cambridge, MA: Harvard Education Press, 2012), 214–15.
5. Reckhow and Snyder, "The Expanding Role of Philanthropy in Education Politics," 188.
6. Sally How, "AP Analysis Shows How Bill Gates Influences Education Policy," *Seattle Times*, May 15, 2018, https://www.seattletimes.com/seattle-news/bill-gates-gives-44m-to-influence-states-education-plans/.
7. How, "AP Analysis."
8. Sandi Doughton and Kristi Heim, "Does Gates Funding of Media Taint Objectivity?," *Seattle Times*, February 19, 2011, https://www.seattletimes.com/seattle-news/does-gates-funding-of-media-taint-objectivity/.
9. Jeffrey R. Henig, *Spin Cycle: How Research Gets Used in Policy Debates—the Case of Charter Schools* (New York: Russell Sage Foundation, 2008), 53.
10. Doughton and Heim, "Does Gates Funding of Media Taint Objectivity?"
11. Caitlin Moran, "Education Lab Q&A," *Seattle Times*, October 24, 2013, formerly at http://blogs.seattletimes.com/educationlab/2013/10/24/education-lab-qa/.
12. Moran, "Education Lab Q&A."
13. Howard Blume, "The Seventy Four, Founded by Controversial Advocate, Takes Over LA School Report," *Los Angeles Times*, February 1, 2016, http://www.latimes.com/local/lanow/la-me-ln-seventy-four-takes-over-school-report-20160201-story.html.
14. "The Great Public Schools Now Initiative," confidential draft obtained by the *Los Angeles Times*, September 21, 2015, https://documents.latimes.com/great-public-schools-now-initiative/.
15. "The Great Public Schools Now Initiative."

16. "The Great Public Schools Now Initiative."

17. Paul Farhi, "Foundations Fund *L.A. Times*' Education Reporting: A Conflict?," *Washington Post*, October 29, 2015, https://www.washingtonpost.com/lifestyle/style /2015/10/29/fd03d240-79cc-11e5-b9c1-f03c48c96ac2_story.html.

18. Steve A. Smith, quoted in Farhi, "Foundations Fund *L.A. Times*' Education Reporting."

19. S. Mitra Kalita, quoted in Farhi, "Foundations Fund *L.A. Times*' Education Reporting."

20. Connie Bruck, "The Art of the Billionaire," *New Yorker*, December 6, 2010.

21. Brenda Iasevoli, "Why Did the Los Angeles Superintendent Resign?," *Atlantic*, October 17, 2014, https://www.theatlantic.com/education/archive/2014/10/why-did-the -los-angeles-superintendent-resign/381588/; "John E. Deasy Selected as Deputy Director of Education," press release, Bill and Melinda Gates Foundation, September 2008, https://www.gatesfoundation.org/Media-Center/Press-Releases/2008/09 /John-E-Deasy-Selected-As-Deputy-Director-of-Education; Howard Blume and Kim Christensen, "Bonds Should Not Pay for iPad Curriculum, New L.A. Unified Head Says," *Los Angeles Times*, October 23, 2014, http://www.latimes.com/local /education/la-me-ipad-bonds-20141023-story.html.

22. Stephanie Garden, "A Heavyweight Ed Funder Looks to Expand Charters in His Home City—and Gets a Fight," *Inside Philanthropy*, August 12, 2015, https://www .insidephilanthropy.com/charter-schools/2015/8/12/a-heavyweight-ed-funder -looks-to-expand-charters-in-his-home.html.

23. Howard Blume, "Austin Beutner: A Renewed Emphasis on Education at *The Times*," *Los Angeles Times*, August 17, 2018, http://www.latimes.com/local/education/back -to-school/la-me-education-matters-letter-20150817-story.html.

24. Andrea Gabor, "The Charter-School Movement Is Playing Defense," *Bloomberg Opinion*, March 11, 2019, https://www.bloomberg.com/opinion/articles/2019-03-11 /teacher-strikes-put-charter-schools-on-the-defensive.

25. Andrea Gabor, "Los Angeles Teachers Strike Takes Aim at Wall Street," *Bloomberg Opinion*, January 15, 2019, https://www.bloomberg.com/opinion/articles/2019-01-15 /los-angeles-teachers-strike-takes-aim-at-wall-street.

26. Matt Barnum, "Los Angeles Hired Consultants to 'Re-imagine' Its School System. Read Their Confidential Recommendations," *Chalkbeat*, April 9, 2019, https://www .chalkbeat.org/posts/us/2019/04/09/los-angeles-consultants-recommendations -reimagine-kitamba-consultants/?utm_source=newsletter&utm_medium=email &utm_campaign=edsource.

27. Matt Barnum, "As L.A. Teachers Threaten to Strike, Union Leaders Are Fighting a Controversial School Reform Strategy," *Chalkbeat*, January 8, 2019, https://www .chalkbeat.org/posts/us/2019/01/08/la-teachers-strike-portfolio-model/.

28. Blume, "The Seventy Four"; Howard Blume, "Outside Groups Trying to Influence L.A. School Board Races," *Los Angeles Times*, February 10, 2013, https://www .latimes.com/local/la-xpm-2013-feb-10-la-me-school-board-money-20130211-story .html.

29. Blume, "The Seventy Four."

30. Romy Drucker, "Statement: On Education Secretary Nominee (and 74 Supporter) Betsy DeVos," *74 Million*, November 30, 2016, https://www.the74million.org/article /statement-on-education-secretary-nominee-and-74-supporter-betsy-devos/.

31. Blume, "The Seventy Four."

32. Blume, "The Seventy Four."

33. Brenda Iasevoli, "Lawsuit to Overturn New York's Teacher-Tenure Laws Heads to Trial," *Education Week*, March 29, 2018, http://blogs.edweek.org/edweek/teacherbeat /2018/03/lawsuit_to_overturn_new_yorks_teacher_tenure_laws_to_trial.html.

34. Mercedes Schneider, "Campbell Brown's 74 Noticeably Silent About *Vergara* Reversal," *deutsch29: Mercedes Schneider's Blog*, April 16, 2016, https://deutsch29 .wordpress.com/2016/04/16/campbell-browns-74-8noticeably-silent-about-vergara -reversal/.

35. Patrick Wall, "What Does California's Teacher Tenure Ruling Mean for New York? Depends Whom You Ask," *Chalkbeat*, August 23, 2016, https://www.chalkbeat.org /posts/ny/2016/08/23/what-does-californias-teacher-tenure-ruling-mean-for-new -york-depends-whom-you-ask/.

36. Sarah Favot, "JUST IN: *Vergara* Ends—California Supreme Court Refuses to Take Up Teacher Tenure Case," *LA School Report*, August 22, 2016, http://laschoolreport .com/just-in-vergara-ends-california-supreme-court-refuses-to-take-up-teacher -tenure-case/.

37. "*Vergara v. California*: Inside the State Supreme Court's Refusal to Hear the Teacher Tenure Case," 74 Million, August 22, 2016, https://www.the74million.org/article /vergara-v-california-inside-the-state-supreme-courts-refusal-to-hear-the -teacher-tenure-case/.

38. Nicholas Melvoin, "Opinion: Maybe a 'Hostile Takeover' Is Precisely What the Los Angeles Unified School District Needs," 74 Million, October 1, 2015, https://www .the74million.org/article/opinion-maybe-a-hostile-takeover-is-precisely-what-the -los-angeles-unified-school-district-needs/.

39. Peter Dreier, "Who Are the Out-of-Town Billionaires Wading Into a City School Board Race?," *Huffington Post*, May 12, 2017, https://www.huffingtonpost.com/peter -dreier/los-angeles-public-education_b_2798894.html.

40. Peter Dreier, "Who Are the Billionaires Trying to Defeat Steve Zimmer?," *Huffington Post*, May 3, 2013, https://www.huffpost.com/entry/who-are-the-billionaires -trying-to-defeat-steve-zimmer_b_58b9086fe4b0fa65b844b1c8.

41. "Editorial: Heather Repenning, an Independent Voice, for L.A. Unified School Board," *Los Angeles Times*, April 13, 2019, https://www.latimes.com/opinion /editorials/la-ed-repenning-goldberg-lausd-school-board-election-20190413-story .html.

42. Howard Blume, "Eli Broad Weighs in at Last Minute with $100,000 Donation in L.A. School Board Race," *Los Angeles Times*, March 7, 2019, https://www.latimes .com/local/education/la-me-edu-eli-broad-lausd-school-board-election-20190307 -story.html.

43. Richard Whitmire, *The Founders* (N.p.: 74 Media, 2016),thefounders/the74mi llion.org.

44. See, for example, *New Orleans Schools After Katrina, Part II: The Class of 2015*, video, 74 Million, October 27, 2017, https://www.the74million.org/article/new-orleans -schools-after-katrina-part-ii-the-class-of-2015/.

45. Gabor, *After the Education Wars*, 196–261.

46. Chris Barbic, Gary Borden, Ken Bubp, Beverly Francis-Pryce, Ethan Gray, David Harris, Kevin Huffman, et al., "The City Fund," *Relinquishment: Writing About*

Handing Power Back to Educators and Families – and Other Thoughts, blog, July 31, 2018, https://relinquishment.org/2018/07/31/the-city-fund/.

47. Walton Family Foundation, "990 Tax Filing," 2016, https://990s.foundationcenter .org/990pf_pdf_archive/133/133441466/133441466_201612_990PF.pdf.

48. Bill and Melinda Gates Foundation, "Grantmaking, Awarded Grants," n.d., https:// www.gatesfoundation.org/How-We-Work/Quick-Links/Grants-Database#q /k=National%20Public%20Radio.

49. Walton Family Foundation, "990 Tax Filing, 2016.

50. Chalkbeat, Inc., financial statements, June 30, 2015, and June 30, 2016, https://www .chalkbeat.org/wp-content/uploads/2017/01/2015-and-2016-Financial-Statements -for-Chalkbeat-Inc.pdf.

51. Chalkbeat Awards, https://www.chalkbeat.org/about/awards/.

52. Elizabeth Green, "The Charter-School Crusader," *Atlantic*, January–February 2018, https://www.theatlantic.com/magazine/archive/2018/01/success-academy-charter -schools-eva-moskowitz/546554/; Christina Veiga, "Success Academy Graduates 16 Students at Its Inaugural Commencement," *Chalkbeat*, June 7, 2018, https://www .chalkbeat.org/posts/ny/2018/06/07/success-academy-graduates-16-students-at-its -inaugural-commencement/.

53. Bill and Melinda Gates Foundation, "990 Tax Filing, 2016, https://990s .foundationcenter.org/990pf_pdf_archive/562/562618866/562618866_201612_990PF .pdf; Walton Family Foundation, "990 Tax Filing," 2017, https://990s.foundationcen- ter.org/990pf_pdf_archive/133/133441466/133441466_201712_990PF.pdf; Eli and Edythe Broad Foundation, "990 Tax Filing," 2016, https://990s.foundationcenter.org/990pf _pdf_archive/954/954686318/954686318_201612_990PF.pdf.

54. "About Editorial Projects in Education," *Education Week,* March 3, 2017.

55. Joshua Benton, "Hechinger Announces New Nonprofit to Cover Education," Nie- man Journalism Lab, October 27, 2009, https://www.niemanlab.org/2009/10 /hechinger-announces-new-nonprofit-to-cover-education/.

56. Mehta and Teles, "Jurisdictional Politics."

57. Ron DeSantis, quoted in Jeffrey S. Solochek, "Gov. Ron DeSantis Unveils Plan to Expand State Money for Private School Tuition," *Tampa Bay Times*, February 15, 2019, https://www.tampabay.com/blogs/gradebook/2019/02/15/gov-ron-desantis -reveals-plan-to-eliminate-scholarship-wait-list/.

58. Betsy DeVos, quoted in Valerie Strauss, "Betsy DeVos and Her Allies Are Trying to Redefine 'Public Education.' Critics Call It 'Absurd,' " *Washington Post*, February 28, 2019, https://www.washingtonpost.com/education/2019/02/28/betsy-devos-her-allies -are-trying-redefine-public-education-critics-call-it-absurd/?utm_term=.c0911b1 8f23c.

59. Leslie Postal, "Florida Teacher Shortage: More Than 2,200 Jobs Open Halfway Into School Year, Union Says," *Orlando Sentinel,* January 17, 2019, https://www .orlandosentinel.com/news/education/os-ne-florida-teacher-shortage-midyear -20190116-story.html; Marlene Sokol, "Gates Partnership Leaves Hillsborough Schools Shouldering Millions More Than Expected," *Tampa Bay Times*, Septem- ber 22, 2015, https://www.tampabay.com/news/education/k12/hillsborough-schools -shouldering-millions-more-than-expected-in/2246528/.

60. Emily L. Mahoney and Jeffrey S. Solochek, "DeSantis Aims for Schools Overhaul; Public Education Supporters Fear State Will Divert Millions to Private Schools,"

Tampa Bay Times, March 4, 2019, https://www.pressreader.com/usa/tampa-bay
-times/20190304/281509342487367.

61. *Tampa Bay Times*, "DeSantis Redefines Public Education," editorial, February 18,
2015, https://www.tampabay.com/opinion/editorials/editorial-desantis-redefines
-public-education-20190218/.

62. Bekah McNeel, "With the Governor Issuing Orders and State Lawmakers Filing
Bills, Ed Reform Is Firmly on the Florida Legislature's 2019 Agenda," 74 Million,
March 19, 2019, https://www.the74million.org/article/with-the-governor-issuing
-orders-and-state-lawmakers-filing-bills-ed-reform-is-firmly-on-the-florida
-legislatures-2019-agenda/.

63. Arianna Prothero, "Extending Vouchers Into Middle Class Is Florida's Next Move,"
Education Week, April 16, 2019, https://www.edweek.org/ew/articles/2019/04/17
/extending-vouchers-into-middle-class-is-floridas.html.

Chapter Nine

USING OLD MEDIA TO CAPTURE NEW IN TURKEY

ANDREW FINKEL

In May 2018, Doğan Holding, principal shareholders in what had once been Turkey's largest and arguably most influential media group, sold its remaining newspapers and television stations to a pro-government consortium. Pundit consensus was that the transfer of flagship titles such as *Hürriyet* newspaper and Kanal D television—a little more than a month before joint presidential and parliamentary elections—was politically engineered to ensure blanket support for President Tayyip Erdoğan and his Justice and Development Party (AKP). The sale was reported, certainly in the foreign press, as yet a further erosion of Turkish press freedom, a major trophy in the government's collection of media loyal to its cause.[1] Erdoğan loyalists, the calculation went, were now in complete control of seven of the eight private media conglomerates (in addition to the state broadcasting corporation) and commanded an estimated 90 percent of national newspaper circulation.[2]

As with previous media sales in Turkey, the new owners, Demirören Holding, benefitted from its close ties with the government. The purchase was financed by a state-owned bank, which granted a two-year moratorium on repayment. The Competition Board approved the sale on the nod, and the Turkish Capital Markets Board, in an unusual move, exempted Demirören from the obligation to buy out some U.S.$44 million worth of publicly listed shares of *Hürriyet* newspaper. A leading business columnist on the paper was among a growing list of prominent journalists fired or forced to resign—in his case, after editors refused to publish his account of the injustice being done to minority shareholders.[3]

To hail the demise of the Doğan media group as the "end of an era"[4] is of course to beg the question about the nature of that era and the changes that were to ensue. In practice, the effect of the sale was neither sudden nor immediate. For some years, the Doğan Group's editorial independence had been in retreat, with increasingly bland journalism designed to protect the nonmedia interests of its parent company from political retaliation. Commentators working with *Hürriyet* known to be potentially critical of government policy, for example, were put on special watch (at one stage, notoriously, the paper's arts editor was given the job of wielding the blue pencil), with too many strikes resulting in dismissal. The group's most notorious act of self-censorship had been in 2013 when its CNN Turkish-language franchise broadcast a documentary about penguins even as police were battling demonstrators in the heart of Istanbul during the occupation of Gezi Park.

Those penguins were to become the symbol of a much deeper phenomenon: the nation's media's betrayal of their own integrity and independence. A so-called Gezi generation began to reflect on how their own opinions on major issues—notably the Kurdish situation in the southeastern region of the country—had been filtered for decades by the very newsrooms that were now distorting or simply ignoring events that they themselves were "photographing, tweeting about, and seeing with their own eyes."[5] The Gezi occupation also became shorthand for a phenomenon that went well beyond its stated objective of conserving an inner-city green space, popular parlance for a metric of both the strength and the all too palpable weaknesses of Turkish civil society. "Gezi" was a voice strong enough (as of writing) to save a park but too weak—or perhaps never intended—to present itself as an alternative to machine politics and a hierarchical system of spoils and patronage that the AKP had been able to construct. It was, however, a movement that not just repudiated the credibility of "heritage" media (far from Gezi Park, demonstrators picketed the headquarters of NTV, Turkey's first twenty-four-hour news station, for adhering to government spin that the protests were a well-organized conspiracy; in the park itself, an NTV broadcasting vehicle was attacked and destroyed)[6] but also developed its own alternative channels of communication through Twitter, smartphones, and internet sites.

The government was able to holler its response through the slew of crony-controlled newspapers and televisions stations under its command—what its own supporters referred to as the "pool media," a concept that carries the sense of one "kitchen" serving many outlets. In June 2013, when Prime Minister (later president) Erdoğan, returned from a trip abroad to reestablish control over Gezi, seven national newspapers greeted him with the exact same headline—citing his willingness to sacrifice himself for true democracy.)[7]

At the same time, Gezi alerted the government to a social movement that it was ill equipped to address. It experienced a form of Midas Touch—a debilitating syndrome whereby government could capture the newsstands and the broadcasting environment but at the expense of those media's effectiveness in communicating. It was thus obliged to redraw the rules of engagement in its efforts to control public opinion.

To put events in perspective: A first principle of the analysis here is that the history of Turkish media has been a near perfect ideal-typical account of press capture (which I elaborate on later for the purposes of this particular chapter). At one level, this is a prosaic observation about media that have by and large respected state-drawn red lines—particularly on such sensitive issues as the coverage of Kurdish minority rights—and that (to my certain knowledge, gained from working in the Turkish language press during the 1990s) have even tolerated agents answerable to national intelligence among its editorial cadres. This history is hinted at by the Turkish word *jurnal*, derived from the French, which does not mean "newspaper" but refers to the police intelligence reports assiduously compiled from informants for the nineteenth-century monarch Sultan Abdulhamid II.

The more useful starting point for this essay, however, is the 1990s, which in Turkey was a time of unstable coalition governments and during which increasingly powerful media organizations vied for the role of political kingmaker. Although the onus here is the much later impact of social and digital media on press freedom, it is worth remembering that the 1990s was also a decade of dramatic technological transformation—in web offset printing but also particularly for broadcast news. The introduction of satellite transmissions proved effective in breaking the broadcasting monopoly of state-run TRT. That the first private television station, launched in 1990, was a pirate operation founded by Ahmet Özal, the son of the then president of Turkey, in partnership with the scion of a family whose fraudulent business practices were to land them in the New York courts for racketeering, typifies the trajectory this history was to take.

At the same time, it is impossible to underestimate the eye-opening effect of a new style of news coverage and presentation of current affairs that resulted from the intense competition for ratings among the new private stations.[8] The contrast was with the diet of "protocol" news that the Turkish public continued to be served in the aftermath of the 1981–1983 period of martial rule (usefully summarized as "the same men in different rooms or the same room with different men"). Viewers were now exposed to live transmissions of Kurdish New Year violent protests in the Southeast and open-ended talk shows that lasted from prime evening viewing time all the way until dawn and where a cross-section of commentators could say what they wanted for as long as they wanted. It may seem ironic that this more liberal atmosphere was the work of media organizations whose owners were using their influence over public opinion to extract from government an array of commercial advantages. The simple point is that to secure this advantage they had first to establish that influence through a more credible media.

At a basic level, this is an all too familiar story of media proprietors flexing their muscles to gain public tenders, privatization issues, cheap land, lucrative changes in urban zoning, as well as government-influenced advertising revenues.[9] A less-expected part of the story is that the business empires thus created were to fail in spectacular fashion. If Turkish media were captured, it was in a trap of their own devising.

A central episode of this narrative is the Turkish financial crisis of 2000–2001, which wiped out the financial sector and a third of gross domestic product. A generation of media proprietors who had over the previous decade managed to extract once lucrative bank licenses from government during a heady era of chronic inflation and high interest-rate spreads saw those banks collapse as they scrambled to repay foreign-denominated debt. Some ten of the twenty-five banks that failed had media connections. Media assets were perforce taken into public receivership in an attempt to repay a Treasury that had indirectly encouraged the lack of due diligence by issuing a blanket guarantee on deposits. From there, it was a short step to transfer that media portfolio to government loyalists. Typical were the massive loans from state-owned banks to assist in the purchase in 2008 of a television and newspaper group by a company whose CEO was Erdoğan's son-in-law. Even then, the loss-making Turkuaz Media Group became a drain on its parent company's resources, threatening its credit rating. It was sold five years later to the construction company in the consortium that won the U.S.$29 billion tender to build Istanbul's third airport. In a secretly taped phone conversation leaked on social media, the new owners are heard complaining in graphic terms that they had been frogmarched into the purchase as the price for doing government business.[10]

The 1990s saw the ascendency of media organizations that became involved in banking, a sector whose risks and culture they poorly understood. The 2000s witnessed the converse of this phenomenon: the rise of a new species of press proprietor for whom media were very far from its core concern, let alone expertise, but who came under pressure to take ownership of such media to retain government grace and favor. This shift is more than suggested in yet another illicitly released tape in which the then prime minister Tayyip Erdoğan reduces the elderly head of the Demirören Holding to tears over a story that appeared in *Milliyet* (another paper purchased from the Doğan Group in 2011). "How did I get into this business?" Erdoğan Demirören is heard asking between sobs. Notoriously, that same proprietor had been publicly praised by the prime minister for having asked who would be suitable to his government's liking for the position of editor in chief for *Milliyet*.[11]

The financial crisis at the beginning of this century transformed Turkish media but had a similarly devastating effect on the country's political landscape, virtually eradicating a post–World War II political generation. No political party in Parliament at the time of the crisis was able to return representatives at the parliamentary election of 2002. The AKP was, of course, the chief beneficiary of this wide-scale disillusionment. It emerged victorious from that election without the backing of any mainstream media support, relying instead on grassroots activism and neighborhood organization.[12] A case could be made to depict the earlier election in 1995 as not between the two secular right parties, the True Path and the Motherland, but between the two dominant media groups that supported each party. Public disillusionment with this spectacle meant that in the end a religious-right party, the Welfare Party, snuck through the middle. The Welfare Party, shut down through military pressure on the Constitutional Court, thus broke ground for the rise of the AKP—a successor party. The AKP was in its own mind successful not despite but because of the absence of backing by any well-healed press baron. Resentment toward those proprietors and a disrespect for media in general was thus deeply engrained. To quote Erdoğan, speaking as president in 2018: "I have seen that giant countries are being governed by the media and not by their leaders. . . . What is important for us is how our people judge us. Democracy is empowered by the people. There is democracy if there are people. Democracy is not possible with the media."[13]

The notion of media as a cherished institution, holding government to account and therefore deserving of the privileged status embodied in the concept of press freedom, was thus redefined to mean mere cover for rapacious private interests trying to hold government at their mercy. This redefinition in turn became justification for attempts, covert and overt, to suppress media not entirely under the government's control.

More unusually perhaps—certainly in the international context of the current crop of populist politicians who simultaneously brand critical heritage media as purveyors of false news and revel in Twitter as a direct communication between leader and followers—is that Turkey's leaders extended their suspicion of traditional media to the new digital platforms. In the wake of the Gezi demonstrations, Erdoğan famously described social media as "the worst menace to society." Twitter he labeled "a scourge," and access to that platform was blocked through court rulings in the buildup to the local elections in March 2014.[14] How effective this ban was is open to question. By some reckonings, Twitter usage actually went up after the ban, with users easily able to sidestep it through virtual private networks or by changing domain-name server settings. The government could not risk banning Facebook, a medium popular among its own followers.

In time, the government realized that it could not deny itself use of such a powerful tool as Twitter and that it would have to force an accommodation with social media. And so in February 2015, Erdoğan dispatched his first tweet.[15] Although he now has a formidable Twitter presence (more than thirteen million followers), most of the posts are of official events and pronouncements, and their tone and content suggest they were not composed by Erdoğan personally. A curious exception was a reply to the archtweeter President Donald Trump in October 2018 to defend the independence of the Turkish judiciary.[16]

A quick spin of the globe would indicate that Turkey is far from being the only country where media are a political actor or media owners use their access to political power instrumentally. The very notion of "capture" that lies at the heart of this volume has its etymology in the cynicism of neoliberal economics that institutions designed to hold power accountable are inclined to be co-opted by that power. Thus formulated,[17] "capture" refers less to the faltering integrity of the Fourth Estate than to the failings of regulatory agencies, which are compromised by the industries and public institutions they are meant to monitor and which in the last resort restrict rather than augment competition.

A more radical perspective redefines "capture" or "cognitive capture" as ideologically bound—a transfer of loyalty or a surrender of objectivity, unconscious or otherwise. A salient point is that this use of the term *media capture* implies not just complicity between private and state interests but also a degree of subtlety in their convergence, with media in some cases not even bothering to question the "caged" parameters in which they operate. This applies both to war correspondents on patrol and to business editors embedded at their screens—hence, the criticism of a Western financial press that failed to exercise anything like due diligence ahead of the global financial crisis in 2007–2008. The hegemony described in Antonio Gramsci's *Prison Notebooks* and surfacing in Edward Herman and Noam Chomsky's *Manufacturing Consent* (1988) might be regarded as an extreme version of this by holding press freedom to be if not illusory then at least circumscribed by the structure of media ownership and the market rationale behind the production and sale of news. As in the neoliberal view, this perspective holds what might still be called "capture" as the rule or tendency and not the exception.

However, for most commentators (including the present author), recognizing the ideologically bound nature of media is an unnecessary bridge too far, and that capture is useful to describe a historical process (per the narrative given earlier). First, it occurs by degrees, with, for example, "state capture" being an extreme example whereby media facilitate corruption and even organized crime. Second, capture can be both done and undone. *Media Integrity Matters* is the emphatic title of an edited volume depicting the hijacking of media in Southeast Europe and the failure of the market to restore public-service journalism in the post-Communist era.[18] The obvious point is that without a free press, those nations' post–Cold War embrace of democracy has remained open to compromise. The conundrum of how to set captured media free is at the heart of much discussion on the relation of the press to democratic governance and where the challenge is often redefined as creating alternative ways of accessing credible information.

In Turkey, the argument here goes, commercial media overplayed its hand in its eagerness to barter integrity for state favor and financial advantage. Not only did this strategy in many cases backfire and result in the media companies' own financial ruin, but it also undermined the very possibility of media ever credibly "speaking truth to power." In that sense, the process of press capture after 2002 helped usher in a "post-truth" universe. In the Turkish context, this universe is one in which the verification of truth claims loses its market value—as profitability depends on presenting without question the government's version of events—rather than one in which questioning those events in the presumed interest of news consumers holds the greater value. It would be hard to overstate the degree of sycophancy, complicity, and unashamed bias of pro-government media in Turkey. For news integrity to have scant commercial value is, I would argue, a definition of propaganda. Significantly, the erosion of media integrity in Turkey occurred prior to and independently of the rise of social media. (An example of the opposite would be an institution such as the *Guardian*, whose website operates without a paywall, which solicits voluntary subscriptions and thus presents its own integrity as a commodity.)

In other societies, social media are often depicted as Hydra-headed: on one hand allowing for the rapid and unrestricted dissemination of news and opinion and on the other degrading the quality of the public realm. Social media can inform and challenge stale, conventional wisdom, but they can also become their own message, stifle debate, become an echo chamber that reinforces cognitive dissonance. Manipulative and mendacious tweets, cynical clickbait, prejudice concealed as truth—all fly round the globe before fact-checkers have time to clear their throats.

In such circumstances, to reprise the opening example, the initial survival of the Doğan media titles into both the AKP era and the digital age is in part tribute to the parent company's business expertise. The media groups of the 1990s had developed a sense of impunity—their newly acquired banks making illegal loans to the parent company and in one case selling Treasury bills it had yet to purchase. The Doğan-owned DışBank, by contrast, was properly run, weathered the economic crisis, and was sold in 2005 for what was then a record sum of €985 million.[19] That the sale was to the Benelux-based Fortis Bank, which failed to survive the global financial crisis in 2007–2008, is an unfortunate irony. However, by the end of the 2000s the markets had come to the conclusion that Doğan media's uncomfortable relationship with the Erdoğan government was a political albatross affecting its other businesses. In 2009, the parent company had faced down a U.S.$3.3 billion tax fine on its downstream petroleum operations—a business acquired through a leveraged buyout of a privatization offering. This fine was largely reported as punishment for the media arm's attempts to report news embarrassing to the government. The sale price in 2018 for the media group was already only a quarter of the publicly listed value a decade earlier. In the end, it became a moot point whether this sale had actually been forced or whether a much-beleaguered press baron had simply chosen an opportune moment to cash in his chips.

Doğan-owned media were not the only media to attempt the transition to a new era. The Gülenist movement, a religious-oriented and highly organized business and social community, had a variety of loosely interconnected companies, including an Islamic banking house, schools, private universities, as well as television stations and newspapers. At one stage, it gave close support to the AKP—taking the government side against the Gezi Park occupation. By the end of 2013, however, it withdrew that backing—as far as one can make out, it did so as part of a power struggle within the AKP for control of key institutions.[20] Members of the Gülen movement were well represented in the senior ranks of the judiciary and police, and these high-placed officials mounted a wave of arrests and prosecutions against figures close to the government, including sons of ministers, on what appeared to be well-documented charges of massive corruption. These allegations were supported by Gülen media, although the most incriminating revelations came as anonymous leaks onto social media, including the phone conversations referred to earlier. The government was able, through the media at its disposal, to brand these accusations as the work of "dark forces" and a "parallel state" trying to stage a coup against the elected government.[21] Government wrath appeared to wax even greater at an "apostate" media that had once sided with the AKP but were now trying to tell what the government considered to be unpalatable truths. The Gülen movement was depicted as a terrorist organization, a cryptoagent of "false" allies—notably the United States (Fethullah Gülen, the group's founder, lived in self-exile in rural Pennsylvania)—who wanted to unseat a democratically elected government. This attack on the movement was followed in December 2016 by a police raid on the movement's *Zaman* newspaper group.[22] The justification for this raid was an actual attempted coup in July 2016, responsibility for which was laid firmly at the Gülenist door. The coup led to the twenty-four-month imposition of emergency rule, during which opposition journalists in general, not just those associated with the Gülen movement, became fair game. Many were held for long periods in pretrial detention, some waiting more than a year even for an indictment.

The state of emergency was lifted only after many of the extraordinary powers it bestowed upon the government became statute and after the Constitution was altered to allow for a largely unchecked presidential rule. The judiciary fared little better than the press, with even high-court judges being arrested and with courts under intense pressure to avoid verdicts that might be deemed contrary to the government way of thinking.

Thus, as of 2020 and the foreseeable future, the commercial sustainability of independent media not entirely loyal to the Turkish government is precarious. Typical is the plight of *Karar* newspaper, which represented a dissident wing within AKP that tried to oppose the ascendency of the strongman presidential rule. It issued a front-page public complaint against an unofficial embargo designed to scare off potential advertisers.[23] More remarkable is the fate of the country's oldest surviving newspaper, *Cumhuriyet*. The paper is held in trust through a foundation whose executive board was deposed by court decision in September 2018. The board, which had been elected in 2013, oversaw the paper's transition to a more liberal and antiestablishment focus, reversing a highly nationalist albeit left-wing editorial line. Many of the key journalists and editors of this interregnum paid a price for this shift, with one former editor in chief forced into exile outside Turkey and his successor serving 495 days in pretrial detention. The latter was just one of a dozen key editorial staff to be detained and sentenced—although subsequently released pending final appeal. In all, some thirty journalists resigned or were dismissed when the new board took control. Their situation became untenable because the new board was headed by someone whose testimony for the prosecution had resulted in the imprisonment of his own colleagues.[24]

A second element of this analysis is the observation that Turkish press capture during the 2000s coincided with the rise of digital media and the transformation of the news industry. The details of that transformation, obviously not unique to Turkey, are well rehearsed. The millisecond it takes to flick between Twitter and the online edition of the *New York Times* is emblematic of the perception that business models as well as editorial policies for creating news have been in in a state of upheaval. With virtually no distribution or direct material costs, such digital media allow for easy market entry; at the same time, they decommoditize their own content by habituating consumers to expect it for free. Even more disruptive, digital media rechannel advertising revenues away from those who actually produce the news to the platform providers that make that news accessible. It may be a truism mired in the banal to see digital technology and the media it has inspired as the new Gutenberg, a technological-led metamorphosis in the way citizens access information. Unraveling the civic implications of that transformation is more complex and, as argued here, society specific.

If print journalism helped forge the nation-state, or what Benedict Anderson described as "imagined communities,"[25] social media made a different set of loyalties all too tangible. They not only created ad hoc communities who alerted one another of what to read or watch (and, just as effectively, whom to mock) but also warned of police water canon around the next block. This was a community, moreover, whose numbers could be measured and habits mapped. At the height the Gezi Park demonstrations, there were a reported three thousand tweets per second.[26]

In Turkey, the response of new pro-government media owners to the disruption heralded by social media was blunt and even old-fashioned—to finance their industry through corruption. The recent history of Turkish press capture corresponds in history to the technological transformation of the news industry, but in many way key features of that transformation— the search for new models of profitability and the pop-up of a less commercially fungible social media—remained a less-visible side of the story. The key variable in media viability remained closeness to government and vulnerability to political pressure.

Although difficult to state definitively, given the unreliable nature of circulation figures in Turkey,[27] the assumption must be that the passage of quasi-independent media into pro-government hands negatively affects both sales and influence. At the same time as press capture occurred, there was a modest, countervailing trend of "breakout" in the form of news portals operating on a modest budget. Disillusionment with the "penguin press" encouraged low-cost operations that aggregated (i.e., stole) news from other sources as well as created their own. These operations were run by limited staff out of what were little more than broom cupboards in comparison to the lavish press headquarters—or, as the Turkish would have it, "media plazas"—that sprouted in the 1990s. So although internet news portals had long existed in Turkey—many of the most popular belonged to heritage media such as *Hürriyet*—the new generation of sites provided a home for the household names that were now being excluded from the mainstream press: writers and commentators (in many cases now working for free or at much reduced salaries) whose followers on social media numbered in the hundreds of thousands—easily equivalent to the circulation numbers of a major European newspaper.

The financing of these enterprises remains a challenge, with many advertisers still wary about being seen to associate with anything that might be described as dissident. Thus, one perhaps unexpected difference between these more independent news sites in Turkey and sites elsewhere is the attitude toward Google ads. Whereas elsewhere in the world Google seems to be a leach, syphoning a disproportionate share of revenue through advertising that is far less lucrative than dedicated ads placed by an agency, in Turkey the "individually tailored" nature and anonymity of Google ads (visible to the end user alone) are their particular virtue. Such ads evade government pressure.

A news site such as T24 (according to interviews with its proprietor) saw the number of its hits double during the Gezi Park occupation (to some 70,000 individual hits per day) as it began to publish columnists exiled from the mainstream press. A more recent figure (March 2019) is 460,000—again, what would have been a highly ambitious target for a print newspaper a decade earlier.

For the government, Gezi was a watershed in the creation of a narrative that told of a confrontation with a well-organized conspiracy. At some level, the government felt the need to confront a tangible enemy rather than, as what was almost certainly the case, an amorphous resistance and discontent and thus something it could not eradicate totally. Indeed, the irritating potency of Gezi to the AKP is suggested by the series of prosecutions initiated six years after the event against civil society activist and philanthropist Osman Kavala and fifteen other allegedly "George Soros–backed conspirators" on charges of attempting to overthrow the government through the Gezi Park protests—with the prosecutor demanding sentences of life imprisonment without possibility of parole.[28] This new narrative goes some way toward explaining the paradox of a government so firmly in control of heritage titles, so adept at undermining the economic viability of media outside its direct control, yet still possessed by an animus to oppress expression of discontent.

A further irony is that when faced with an actual conspiracy, the failed military coup of July 15, 2016, the government appeared to adopt the very methods of the Gezi Park demonstrators. The coup plotters' principal communication strategy appeared to be the antediluvian one of seizing the state-owned TRT television stations. The government, however, was able to rally its supporters with Twitter and Periscope as well as with the more time-honored method of summoning people to the streets to defend the regime—a perpetual call from the mosque minarets. President Erdoğan was famously able to assure the nation he was still in control via FaceTime as a news presenter on the Turkish CNN affiliate held his visage on her iPhone up to the camera.

If the government has accepted the challenge of controlling social media, it has done so largely by organizing an army of trolls and embracing the postmodern rhetoric of "perception management."[29] It attributes, for example, dips in the value of the Turkish currency to the work of those manipulating perception rather than to the consequences of its own economic mismanagement.[30] Media under its control churn out the messages it wants to hear. Yet the government's most effective response has arguably been low-tech censorship and oppression. Turkey has become a country where schoolchildren are detained for insulting the president on Twitter, where more than 150 journalists and press workers have been put behind bars, and where access to countless websites is blocked arbitrarily by administrative fiat—a restriction applied even to *Wikipedia*.[31] According to one study, some 408,494 websites were blocked from 2014 to the end of 2019.[32]

A good example not because it is so egregious but because it is so obsessively trivial is the ban in 2020 on access to 273 internet news reports that the head of the presidential communications directorate had built an illegal structure in the garden of the house he rented from the state in an architecturally protected historical neighborhood of Istanbul. The justification given by the court was that the reports served to "disrupt or obscure our country's success in the fight against the global coronavirus pandemic despite many European countries' failure." A criminal investigation was launched against the reporter and photographer for *Cumhuriyet* newspaper, which had reported the building violation.[33]

Such restrictions play havoc with Turkey's efforts to reorient its economy to being information led. But they also muddy the waters in the ruling party's attempts to capture media. The resort to open intimidation is acknowledgment of limitations on an ability to impose through capture a monopoly on information. At the same time, the abuse of judicial process through arbitrary arrest and the manipulation of the courts—in one infamous instance, a lower court refusing to implement the release of an imprisoned journalist ordered by the Constitutional Court—are the product of the sense of impunity that media capture has engendered.

According to official figures announced by Turkey's Interior Ministry, between December 2017 and December 2018 a total of 42,406 social media accounts were investigated for "disseminating propaganda for a terrorist organization, praising terrorist organizations, openly stating their connection with terrorist organizations, inciting the public to hatred and animosity, insulting state officials, attempting to destroy the unity of the state and the security of the public, involving hate speech."[34] Legal action was launched against a total of 18,376 individuals, including 346 persons accused of currency manipulation and "creating the wrong perception" by tweeting alarm in the summer of 2018 when the Turkish lira was plummeting against the dollar.[35]

Attempts by new digital media to bypass the commercial obstacles and regulatory restrictions that block traditional media must now also circumvent Law Number 5651, Regulating Internet Publishing and Combating Crimes Committed via Such Promulgation, first enacted in 2007 but frequently amended since then. According to one internet news publisher, "The core characteristic of the law is its focus on how to control internet publishing, how to limit publication, and how to block access." The same author concludes that although the potentially unbridled nature of online content can raise legitimate concerns, "the special law to regulate the Internet in Turkey, far from being [concerned with] determining ethical principles, is chiefly characterized by being diametrically opposed to rule of law, the principles of freedom of speech and press, and is itself a regulation that is ethically problematic from start to finish."[36]

So although Erdoğan and his party won the elections of June 2018 handsomely, it is perhaps ironic that in a digital age they did so in good measure through an old-fashioned show of authority—physically blocking rivals' access to media, imprisoning opposition candidates, and plastering the streets with apartment-block-size posters of candidate Erdoğan. The object was not to win the argument but to demonstrate there were no others.

In its report for 2014 (i.e., in the wake of Gezi), Freedom House downgraded Turkish media for the first time from being "partly free" to being "not free."[37] However, even before that downgrade, the country was well in the lead of being the worst offender worldwide in terms of the number of journalists and media workers behind bars.[38] A quick flick through more recent cases illustrates their cruel absurdity: the Kurdish reporter Nedim Türfent sentenced to nearly nine years in prison even though twelve of the thirteen prosecution witnesses recanted testimony that they said had been obtained under torture; the best-selling novelist and former editor in chief Ahmet Altan initially sentenced to aggravated life imprisonment for trying to overthrow the constitutional order by using language "evocative" of a coup during a television talk show; the academic Bülent Şık being put on trial for "disclosing restricted information" about carcinogenic pesticides and other toxins found in Turkish food and water in a series of articles for *Cumhuriyet* in April 2018; Pelin Ünker, a member of the International Consortium of Investigative Journalists, sentenced by an Istanbul court for "defamation and insult" for sifting through the voluminous pile of leaked documents known as the Paradise Papers (showing global tax evasion through offshore investment) to discover how senior government figures and their sons maintained companies in Malta as tax havens.[39]

Democracy-promotion agencies identify media capture in order to support strategies to undermine censorship and self-censorship and to bolster editorial integrity. They do so in the accepted belief that the values of independent media—truthfulness, transparency, the questioning of conventional wisdom—are self-evident and enable societies to engage in rational discussion that promote a public good. The rise of populism in Western democracies has, of course, dented confidence in the sustainability of those values and obliged liberal media to look with renewed and fearful respect at the difficulties of getting a citizenry to challenge their own prejudices.

However, if the Turkish example demonstrates anything, it is how quickly the tide can turn. Only the most absolutist would believe that media are so hermetic, cognitive dissonance so absolute, as to admit of no slippage in the way frames of meaning are reproduced. Nor is it obvious that new media can be controlled entirely without the use of fear and legal intimidation. Even then, people's opinions change.

As of 2020, many analysts believe (even if those in Turkey are under pressure to keep such thoughts to themselves) that the Turkish economy is on the brink of a downturn that may in the end prove as debilitating albeit not as dramatic as the banking crisis in 2000–2001 that transformed the media landscape. It is not clear that the construction and other companies that maintain the captured "old" media at a commercial loss will be able to do so in the long run. Indeed, there is evidence that the old media have become less passive and more independent (though not more democratic) as the interests of their parent companies begins to diverge from that of the government. Again, the government ceded control of many of Turkey's metropolitan cities in the nation-wide local elections of March 2019, including the major prize of Istanbul and the capital Ankara. Pro-government media led the howls of protest, demanding recount after recount and then the annulment of the entire Istanbul election. This annulment proved a gross miscalculation when the opposition candidate was subsequently elected with a far greater majority and thus gained far greater legitimacy the second time around. Loss of city government also means the loss of important sources of patronage and will inevitably force a recalculation of the value of the loyalty among the so-called loyalist press.[40]

History is not static, nor is the balance of power between captor and captured. To paraphrase a sentiment attributed—perhaps inaccurately—to an American president who governed more than a century ago, you cannot manipulate all public opinion all of the time.

NOTES

1. See Selin Bucak, "Dogan Media Sale to Erdogan Ally Is Blow to Press Freedom," *Financial Times*, May 30, 2018, https://www.ft.com/content/3273aafc-4317-11e8-97ce -eaoc2bf34a0b.
2. Aykan Erdemir, "Khashoggi Crisis Holds a Mirror to Turkey," *Globalist*, October 12, 2018, https://www.theglobalist.com/jamal-khashoggi-saudi-arabia-turkey-erdogan -press-freedom/.
3. As reported in Murat Sevinç, Azime Acar, Hürrem Sönmez, Nevşin Mengü, and Kemal Göktaş, "Uğur Gürses'i Hürriyet'ten SPK sansürü ayırmış . . . Ve SPK Demirören'e kıyağı yapmış," *Diken*, August 21, 2018, http://www.diken.com.tr/ugur -gursesi-hurriyetten-spk-sansuru-ayirmis-ve-spk-demirorene-kiyagi-yapmis/. In fact, minority shareholders who held onto those shares would have more than recovered short-term losses inasmuch as the market recognized that an unequivocally pro-government *Hürriyet* would be a more profitable investment.
4. As the current author was quoted as saying at the time in the following articles: Orhan Coskun, "Pro-Erdogan Group Agrees to Buy Owner of *Hurriyet* Newspaper, CNN Turk," Reuters, March 21, 2018, https://www.reuters.com/article/us-dogan

-holding-m-a-demiroren/pro-erdogan-group-agrees-to-buy-owner-of-hurriyet
-newspaper-cnn-turk-idUSKBN1GX23R; and Laura Pitel, "Turkish Press Baron
Agrees to Sell Media Arm to Erdogan Ally," *Financial Times*, March 21, 2018, https://
www.ft.com/content/c4d3c3f0-2d2d-11e8-a34a-7e7563b0b0f4.

5. Izzy Finkel, "Istanbul Protest Is—and Is Not—About the Trees," *Salon*, June 5, 2013,
https://www.salon.com/test/2013/06/05/no_this_is_not_just_an_environmental
_protest/.

6. See Andrew Finkel, *Captured News Media: The Case of Turkey* (Washington, DC:
CIMA, 2015), 18, also at http://www.cima.ned.org/wp-content/uploads/2015/10
/CIMA-Captured-News-Media_The-Case-of-Turkey2.pdf.

7. *Bianet*, "7 gazete, 1 genel yayın yönetmeni," June 7, 2013, http://bianet.org/bianet/
siyaset/147327-7-gazete-1-genel-yayin-yonetmeni.

8. If the novel presentation of news and current affairs was a key to the establishment of
private television channels in the 1990s, then a new generation of serials or soaps
arguably has guaranteed those stations' continuing influence. The values propagated
by these series is closely monitored but not always successfully, and the political and
cultural debates that are now conducted on this popular dramatic format are equally
significant, as suggested in Nükhet Sirman and Feyza Akınerdem, "From Seekers of
Truth to Masters of Power: Televised Stories in a Post-truth World," *South Atlantic
Quarterly* 118, no. 1 (January 2019): 129–44, doi: https://doi.org/10.1215/00382876
-7281648.

9. See Andrew Finkel, "Who Guards the Turkish Press? A Perspective on Press Corruption," *Journal of International Affairs* 52, no. 1 (Fall 2000): 147–66.

10. See Mehul Srivastava, Benjamin Harvey, and Ercan Ersoy, "Erdogan's Media Grab
Stymies Expansion by Murdoch, Time Warner," *Bloomberg*, March 3, 2014, https://
www.bloomberg.com/news/articles/2014-03-03/erdogan-thwarts-murdoch-as
-graft-probe-reveals-turkey-media-grab; and Mehul Srivastava and Benjamin Harvey, "The Edifice Complex Driving Turkey's Scandal," *Bloomberg*, January 9, 2014,
https://www.bloomberg.com/news/articles/2014-01-09/in-turkey-erdogans
-construction-projects-draw-corruption-probe.

11. Yavuz Baydar, "Turkish Media Boss Insulted, Reduced to Tears by PM Erdoğan,
Audio Recording Reveals," March 7, 2014 https://yavuzbaydar.wordpress.com/2014
/03/07/turkish-media-boss-insulted-reduced-to-tears-by-pm-erdogan-audio
-recording-reveals/.

12. A curious corollary is that it was all one could do as a foreign correspondent at the
time to overcome the cognitive dissonance of international news desks to focus on
Tayyip Erdoğan and the rise of the AKP (which won the election) rather than on
Kemal Derviş, a World Bank technocrat turned politician (who lost).

13. Tayyip Erdoğan, quoted in *Hürriyet Daily News*, "Turkish President Erdoğan Blasts
'Global Smear Campaign'—Turkey News," October 3, 2018, http://www.hurriyetdai-
lynews.com/president-erdogan-vows-democracy-not-possible-with-media-137491.

14. Terrence McCoy, "Turkey Bans Twitter—and Twitter Explodes," *Washington Post*,
March 21, 2014, https://www.washingtonpost.com/news/morning-mix/wp/2014/03
/21/turkey-bans-twitter-and-twitter-explodes.

15. Agence France-Presse, "Turkey's Anti-Twitter Leader Erdoğan Sends His First
Tweet," *Guardian*, February 10, 2015, https://www.theguardian.com/world/2015/feb
/10/turkeys-anti-twitter-leader-erdogan-sends-his-first-tweet.

16. Recep Tayyip Erdoğan, tweet, Twitter, October 2018, 11:19 a.m., https://twitter.com
/RTErdogan/status/1051130307905241088.
17. See, for example, George J. Stigler, "The Theory of Economic Regulation," *Bell Jour-nal of Economics and Management Science* 2, no. 1 (Spring 1971): 3–21.
18. Brankica Petković and Trbovc Jovana Mihajlović, *Media Integrity Matters: Reclaim-ing Public Service Values in Media and Journalism* (Ljubljana, Slovenia: Peace Institute, Institute for Contemporary Social and Political Studies, 2015).
19. Paul J. Davies, "Fortis Takes an Economic, Not Political Gamble," *Financial Times*, April 12, 2005, https://www.ft.com/content/8f0baf9a-ab44-11d9-893c-00000e2511c8.
20. There may have been policy differences as well. Often cited is Gülenist opposition to the government's (albeit short-lived) attempt to reach a political compromise with Kurdish nationalists.
21. Mark Lowen, "Turkey's Erdogan Battles 'Parallel State,' " *BBC News*, December 17, 2014, https://www.bbc.com/news/world-europe-30492348.
22. Murat Yetkín, "New Raid on Media Adds to Political Confusion in Turkey," *Hur-riyet Daily News*, December 15, 2014, https://www.hurriyetdailynews.com/opinion
/murat-yetkin/new-raid-on-media-adds-to-political-confusion-in-turkey-75628.
23. *Karar*, "Kamuoyuna ve okurlarımıza zaruri bir açıklama," November 12, 2018.
24. Ozgun Ozcer, "*Cumhuriyet*: A Press Freedom Case Degenerates Into a Boardroom Takeover," Index on Censorship, October 12, 2018, https://www.indexoncensorship
.org/2018/10/cumhuriyet-press-freedom-boardroom/.
25. Benedict Anderson, *Imagined Communities: Reflections on the Origin and Spread of Nationalism* (New York: Verso, 1983).
26. See James Creedon, "Erdogan: 'Social Media Is the Worst Menace to Society,' " *France 24 News*, March 16, 2013, https://www.france24.com/en/20130603-turkey
-twitter-social-media-menace-erdogan-sarkozy-london-goldman-sachs-parallel
-diplomacy.
27. This point is made in Burcu Karakaş, *Yalan Dunya: Reytingler, tıklar ve şimdi reklamlalar!* (Istanbul: P24 Medya Kitaplığı, 2016).
28. Haber Merkezi, "Amnesty International: Osman Kavala and Yiğit Aksakoğlu Must Be Released," *Bianet*, February 21, 2019, http://bianet.org/english/human-rights
/205722-amnesty-international-osman-kavala-and-yigit-aksakoglu-must-be
-released.
29. Efe Kerem Sözeri, "Trolls, Bots, and Shutdowns: This Is How Turkey Manipulates Public Opinion," *Ahval*, November 15, 2017, https://ahvalnews.com/freedoms/trolls
-bots-and-shutdowns-how-turkey-manipulates-public-opinion.
30. For a particularly egregious example of this doublespeak, see an analysis of for-eign bias in the coverage of the election in 2018 produced by the research depart-ment of the Turkish state-operated English-language broadcasting service. The detailed argument of how Western media willfully undermined Turkish eco-nomic credibility is contradicted by the report's cover—a still photo of an inter-view President Erdoğan gave to Bloomberg Television in London in May 2018, during which the lira plummeted in real time as he criticized the independence of his own central bank. See Tarek Cherkaoui, "Representation of Politics or Politics of Representation: Patterns of Western Mainstream Media Coverage During Turkey's 2018 Election," TRT World Research Centre, June 2018, https://
researchcentre.trtworld.com/images/files/reports/PatternsOfWesternMainstream

MediaCoverageDuringTurkey2018Elections.pdf. See also Constantine Courcou-
las and Netty Idayu Ismail, "Lira Falls to New Record as Erdogan Plan Spooks
Investors," *Bloomberg News*, May 15, 2018, at https://www.bloomberg.com/news
/articles/2018-05-15/lira-falls-as-erdogan-intent-to-sway-money-policy-irks
-traders.

31. The restriction of *Wikipedia* went into effect in April 2017 and was not lifted until
    January 15, 2019. See "Block of *Wikipedia* in Turkey," *Wikipedia*, April 4, 2020,
    https://en.m.wikipedia.org/wiki/Block_of_Wikipedia_in_Turkey.

32. *Bianet*, "Report: Turkey Banned 130,000 Web Addresses in 2019," July 3, 2020,
    https://bianet.org/english/media/226856-report-turkey-banned-130-000-web
    -addresses-in-2019.

33. *Ahval*, "Turkish Opposition Daily Has Advertising Cut for Story on Erdoğan Spokes-
    man," May 22, 2020, https://ahvalnews.com/cumhuriyet/turkish-opposition-daily
    -has-advertising-cut-story-erdogan-spokesman.

34. For official statistics, see https://www.icisleri.gov.tr/1-ocak-31-aralik-2018-yili
    -icerisinde-yurutulen-operasyonlar to cite official statistics.

35. *Bloomberg HT*, "Sosyal medyadan 'dolar kuru manipülasyonu'a Ssoruşturma,"
    August 13, 2018, https://www.bloomberght.com/haberler/haber/2147359-sosyal
    -medyadan-dolar-kuru-manipulasyonuna-sorusturma. Television and internet sites
    were also ordered to remove the "ticker" at the bottom of the screens showing the
    devaluation of the currency in real time.

36. Akın Doğan, "Self-Regulation in Internet Media: Problems and Possibilities," in
    Media Self-Regulation in Turkey: Challenges, Opportunities, Suggestions, ed. Yase-
    min Çongar (Istanbul: P24 Media Library, 2018), 218.

37. Freedom House, *Freedom of the Press 2015* (Washington, DC: Freedom House,
    2015), 14, https://freedomhouse.org/sites/default/files/FreedomofthePress_2015_
    FINAL.pdf.

38. The website expressioninterrupted.com monitors and provides updates on journal-
    ists in detention and is based on open sources. The list it provides is generally
    much longer than the one provided by the Committee to Protect Journalists.

39. The legal status of these defendants is not static. Ünker has been released from deten-
    tion, and Altan (though still in prison as of 2020) is being retried on lesser charges.
    See Julian Borger, "Journalist Pelin Ünker Sentenced to Jail in Turkey Over Para-
    dise Papers Investigation," *Guardian*, January 9, 2019, https://www.theguardian.com
    /news/2019/jan/09/journalist-pelin-unker-sentenced-to-jail-in-turkey-over
    -paradise-papers-investigation.

40. One media organization began the wholesale dismissal of staff when the new Istan-
    bul municipality cut off a reported 10 million Turkish lira monthly advertising
    income (more than U.S.$1.75 million, a staggering sum that apparently was paid at
    the same rate before the lira was devalued in 2018).

Chapter Ten

A LOUD SILENCE

RAJU NARISETTI

For most of the seventy-two years that India has been an independent country and the world's largest functioning democracy, it has been lauded as a bastion of free, independent media. Not only is India's free press—loud, argumentative, and cantankerous—perceived as vibrant in its journalism, but in recent years it has also been held up as the rare antidote to global declines in circulation and readership of newspapers, with increases routinely reported by various media industry groups in that country.[1]

The number of newspaper readers in India is estimated to have *increased* by 38 percent between 2014 and 2017, to reach 407 million, and yet that is still only one-third of the nation's growing and relatively young population: in 2020, the average Indian's age is a mere twenty-nine years.[2] Meanwhile, India is also home to one in every three illiterate people on earth, holding out the promise amid large-scale literacy campaigns that tens of millions more potential newspaper readers could emerge in years to come.

The number of registered newspapers and magazines in English and all other Indian languages is astonishingly high, at 105,000, and has increased each passing year, remarkable even for a country of 1.2 billion people. There are 13,000 registered daily, English-language newspapers in India, compared to around 1,300 dailies in the United States, though many of the registered newspapers in India are not published regularly, and some not at all.[3]

India also has upward of 180 million households with televisions and 800 licensed satellite stations, half of them news based. Add to that an estimated 462 million Internet users, and you often get a picture of India as a brightly shining journalistic beacon, with significant upside to come for mainstream media, including and especially newspapers.[4]

Yet in practice and underneath the surface, over the past few years India's press freedoms have been quietly eroding at an alarming pace, often because of an elected national government with a rare single-party majority in Parliament, an administration that in mid-2019 handily won a second, five-year mandate.[5]

This version of "media capture" is unconventional in the sense that it is mostly invisible in its stranglehold and yet both pervasive and persistent in the desired outcome.

India's captured mainstream media have steadily lost their freedom and the ability to inform and reflect the broader interests of the country and, thus, to be able to hold power to account, a key purpose of any Fourth Estate. India's media to a large extent are now captured by the government, corporations, and bureaucrats—a potent triumvirate.

This capture is only privately acknowledged by mainstream media editors and owners in India, who are often unwilling to provoke more drastic action from a popular and increasingly intolerant nationalist government—a government that wields considerable advertising clout of its own, while having a cozy and commanding relationship with corporate advertisers, who remain the revenue backbone of the vast majority of India's media.[6]

Attempts to control media in India are not new. Individual politicians, especially those in power, routinely try to, primarily through their personal connections to newspaper owners and editors. They occasionally have resorted to the power of their office—cutting off access, holding back paid advertising from their ministry, which is a significant loss to media because India's government has been a historically constant, major advertiser in news media, particularly in print. And there was a brief two-year period starting in 1975 when then prime minister Indira Gandhi used the pretext of a "national emergency" to formally restrict Indian media's ability to report and write on many issues.[7]

Such attempts to muzzle haven't been made just by politicians. Major private advertisers have also routinely tried to control Indian media as well, using their disproportionate, advertising-led clout in a country where reader revenue still remains a negligible fraction of most media businesses. And many publishers have offered preferential deals, so-called private treaties, to key advertisers that seek guaranteed ad revenue to their newspapers, but such deals usually come with unwritten offers of significant soft-peddling of any adverse coverage of that advertiser and its owners in those very newspapers benefitting from the ads.[8]

Even against this troubling backdrop, there is a growing consensus inside and outside of India's media ecosystem that the past seven years have shown a significant acceleration in the national government's attempts to capture media rather than just merely influence or shape them.

Led by an unusually large "media-monitoring cell" in the Information and Broadcasting Ministry, which provides analysis to powerful bureaucrats in the Prime Minister's Office (PMO), the New Delhi–based national government has maintained detailed dossiers on media coverage of Prime Minister Narendra Modi and Amit Shah, president of the ruling Bharatiya Janata Party (BJP) and a powerful cabinet minister.[9]

Editors and newspaper owners are typically confronted with bulging folders prepared by the nearly two-hundred-person strong monitoring cell, focused primarily on India's many twenty-four-hour news channels but also tracking every article and headline in mainstream print media and increasingly on digital news sites. This analysis, people familiar with the work say, often groups the most pliant media outlets as "reliable" in terms of their tilt and volume of coverage of Modi but targets those not considered "reliable" to get them to fall in line.

Bureaucrats in the PMO have not been reticent in making implicit and explicit demands by phone or through in-person summons, but never in writing, when editors and newspaper owners are confronted with these folders in meetings that seek to soften coverage that is deemed personally negative of both party leaders or reflecting poorly on Modi's governance.[10]

Because this kind of "media capture" is relatively new in India and distinct from old-fashioned censorship or a visible tilt and bias at a media house, this chapter attempts to illustrate the still evolving nature of what the Modi government has attempted with consistent and growing success in effectively capturing media's output, especially in mainstream television and newspaper media.

There still remain ongoing and significant examples of power holders' use of intimidation and even physical violence against media, which may imply that not all media are fully captured in India. Although that is indeed the case and one can point to some independent and critical voices, such journalism is increasingly confined to narrow slivers of the internet and social media, with limited reach and impact and increasingly drowned by nationalist skepticism as mainstream media quietly devolve into the voice of the Modi government.[11]

India's ruling administrations typically enjoy significant direct leverage: the government, directly and through a vast, so-called public-sector industry, is consistently among the largest advertisers in India's print media. There is also historic indirect leverage—most media companies in India are small pieces of large industrial/business conglomerates that in turn need to be on the right side of various government approvals, business policy, and regulations in a country where industry is still significantly regulated by various government actions.[12]

Although there is some transparency and a level playing field in direct government advertising in media through the Bureau of Outreach and Communication in the Information and Broadcasting Ministry, the ability to influence the release of campaigns or to sign-off on payments due to media companies often provides significant unstated leverage to the government and departmental bureaucrats.

Typically, as the country heads into national elections every five years, India's ruling administrations often dramatically increase advertising rates that they will pay media for government ads, which is another way to try and leverage their influence in media at a critical time.

For example, the Congress Party–led government hiked the rates that the Ministry of Information and Broadcasting set for ads in print newspapers by 13 percent in 2013, although amid rising unrest over corruption it was voted out in the elections that ensued. The BJP, which then swept into power in 2014, announced a 25 percent increase in rates in January 2019, just months before national elections, where it won an overwhelming majority in the Lok Sabha, the key house of India's Parliament.[13]

The Modi PMO's willingness to effectively stifle Indian journalism has by many accounts been unprecedented in India's modern history. And there is increasingly also anecdotal evidence that this behavior is being imitated and fully embraced across India's many state governments, several of which are also ruled by Modi's BJP. For example, in just the month of September 2019 the police in the large and populous northern state of Uttar Pradesh, ruled by the BJP, filed legal cases against eight journalists, all of whom had tried to expose the government's administrative failures, caste discrimination, as well as mounting law-and-order issues in the state.[14]

Similar tactics were also being embraced by powerful regional parties, many in nominal political opposition to the BJP but equally willing to follow this brazen Modi playbook to suppress critical and investigative journalism. Complicating matters has been a surge, which coincided with proliferation of television channels, of media brands being owned directly by regional party politicians across the ideological spectrum, something that could yet happen at the national level, much as it happened in Hungary in 2019 with the ruling FIDESZ Party, whose members control nearly 90 percent of that country's media.[15]

The BJP's actions in India have resulted in growing self-censorship and an unwillingness to pursue and stick with watchdog journalism, unprecedented even for a country with a long history of politicians equating any overtly critical journalism with negative and even unpatriotic views of India.[16]

In India, it is not uncommon for most journalism done by foreign media brands covering that country, most notably the *New York Times*, the BBC, and the *Economist* but also increasingly the *Washington Post* and al-Jazeera, to be dubbed in social media by many BJP followers as being deliberately "anti-Indian."

What is new in recent years are the growing attempts by the Modi government, the ruling BJP, and their sophisticated communication campaigns to imply that any criticism of Modi in the public sphere borders on being "antinational," which expands the attacks on domestic media and plays into the already fervent nationalism at the core of the BJP's electoral success.[17]

Undergirding such social media campaigns is the fact that trust in India's media has continued to erode as "play for pay" scandals periodically surface—only to sink, without any repercussions from within an ostensibly self-governing media industry, thus reinforcing to the outside world what have become enduring, derisive social media hashtags targeting the industry, such as "#presstitutes."[18]

To some extent, this deterioration in press freedoms and attempts to capture media haven't gone unnoticed, but that notice occurs mostly outside India.

India ranked a lowly 142 out of 180 countries in the Press Freedom Index for 2020 compiled by Reporters Without Borders, down from 140 in 2019 and 133 in 2016. And despite India's being the only consistently stable democracy in the region, the ranking puts it below war-ravaged Afghanistan at 122, Sri Lanka at 127, and Nepal at 112 in 2020. Only historically unstable Pakistan at 145 and Bangladesh at 151 have consistently remained worse than India in the same press freedom rankings of countries in the subcontinent.[19]

Meanwhile, with seven journalists killed in 2018 alone, India has also become deadly for those practicing journalism. The alarming rise in violence against media in many regional states has gone mostly unpunished once the headlines die down. In 2018 alone, there were at least twenty-seven recorded incidents of attacks on thirty-three journalists. At least ten journalists were arrested, and six others were temporarily detained, and there were another seventeen instances of threats and harassment.[20]

THE BEGINNING OF THE END

The roots of today's increasingly captured media in India lie deep and go back a couple of decades to the seemingly innocuous newspaper business practices of India's largest media company, the Bennett Coleman & Company Ltd. (BCCL), founded in 1838, whose flagship newspapers include the *Times of India*, the largest-selling newspaper in India, and the *Economic Times*, the market-leading business newspaper.

Early to recognize the highly value-conscious, middle-class urban Indian household as key to its commercial success, BCCL embarked on a strategy of "invitation price," offering new newspaper readers a sharply discounted cover price for its newspapers, starting in Delhi in 1994, as part of an ambitious national expansion strategy for its flagship paper, the *Times of India*.

Today, this permanent "predatory pricing" typically offers an all-color, thirty-six- to forty-eight-page, multisection, broadsheet daily newspaper for an average cover price of around four and a half rupees (six U.S. cents). When the paper is bundled with a regional language or business newspaper from the same media house (the *Times of India* is bundled with the *Navbharat Times* in Hindi or the *Economic Times*), the combined price rarely exceeds seven rupees, or about ten U.S. cents. This relatively cheap cover price is then significantly discounted for home delivery through multiple "trade schemes," such as six-months-free deals for renewal, which further reduce the actual cost to the consumer.

Meanwhile, there is a long-standing tradition in Indian households of stacking up daily household newspapers after they are read, which are then bought each month by neighborhood, door-to-door roving paper recyclers. Newspaper is typically sold for ten to twelve rupees per kilogram, with a month's worth of newspaper equivalent to about eight to ten kilograms in weight. In essence, the household revenue from recycled newspapers in a month more or less covers a hefty portion of the discounted monthly subscription cost of that newspaper, thus making it almost "free" to subscribe to in that household. This explains, to some extent, the many multinewspaper households in India and the continuing growth in circulation.[21]

This "invitation pricing" approach dramatically increased circulation and the reach of BCCL newspapers, cementing that company's market leadership and catching rivals with not-so-deep pockets permanently flatfooted. BCCL's pricing strategy forced all newspaper companies in India to keep their prices competitive, and, as a result, there has been no meaningful price escalation for newspapers in India for decades, even as newsprint, ink, and staffing costs have continued to rise.

It is estimated that just ink, newsprint (India imports a majority of the paper used by newspaper distributors), and distribution costs of a daily newspaper run at 200 to 300 percent more than the current daily cover price of any newspaper in India.

Today, one can't buy a cup of tea from a street vendor in a major city in India for the cover price one pays for a newspaper, and a single popular Wills Red cigarette retails for ten rupees, or 250 percent more than a national newspaper in the same kiosk.

This industry-wide cap on newspaper subscription prices has over time created a very unhealthy, near 100 percent dependence on advertising for all media companies.

As a result, media houses have long had cozy relationships with ad agencies and advertisers in corporate India as well as with many "public-sector" enterprises—state-controlled banks, the Life Insurance Corp., tourism boards, the railways, government-run industrial and mining companies—all of whom are significant advertisers in print. These "commercial" advertisers on occasion hold journalism captive, threatening to pull their ads if a top executive disapproves of certain stories or believes there is a pattern of "negative" coverage against that firm.

But because newspapers have remained cost effective—in terms of their wide reach and engagement in both urban pockets and heartland India—many of the news brands were in the past usually able to "manage" such requests without becoming entirely captive to advertisers, even if the occasional big spender was successful in getting toned-down coverage or the quiet dropping of follow-up stories.

India media houses are also notoriously bad at chasing stories that their rivals break, which allows for advertisers to put pressure on one newsroom to squelch a story without worrying about other newsrooms jumping on it. That practice is coupled with a long-standing, informal "we don't really cover each other" pact among owners and editors that has prevailed across most major newsrooms and with the very little attention given by dwindling media critics to why one-off stories about big companies or CEOs simply seem to fall off the pages of a newspaper. Readers are none the wiser about what might have happened.

Meanwhile, successive governments, both at the state level and at the country level in India's capital New Delhi, have also become significant advertisers in newspapers in India, spending tens of millions of rupees in ad campaigns that ostensibly promote government projects and welfare programs but in practice are mostly campaigns—replete with pictures of those currently in power—intended to bolster the ruling party.

Government data show that the BJP government's ad spending in the four and a half years of its first term, which began in 2014, was on average $170 million annually, a dramatic escalation from the amount spent by the previous Congress Party government, on average $71 million annually from 2004 to 2013.[22]

These figures don't included spending by state governments, where it is not uncommon for a powerful state chief minister on occasion to pull or temporarily withhold advertising from a newspaper as a way to signal disapproval for a specific article. Or in some cases government funds for election ad campaigns are diverted to select news brands, including in the state of Delhi, the home to a majority of media companies in India.[23]

For decades, when the Congress Party and the Nehru–Gandhi dynasty governed India, there were powerful regional leaders who were not micromanaged or did not necessarily behave in lock-step fashion with the national party, especially when it came to exerting influence on media. As a result, many newspaper companies became adept at managing the occasional dispute, be it in Delhi or in a particular state capital, and were confident in their ability to continue to attract much-needed government advertising through the media owners' personal connections to government officials or through paid middlemen who typically funneled money back to the politicians and bureaucrats who were in charge of large advertising campaigns.

To be sure, the Modi government wasn't responsible for giving birth to the desire for media capture in India. Over the many decades of independent India, well-connected individual politicians and cabinet ministers, particularly from the Congress Party, have continued to exert significant influence on certain media houses, though a large part of that influence, unlike in the BJP efforts, came from personal relationships with both newspaper owners as well as with top editors rather than via explicit threats over ad budgets.

"If you look at mainstream, big English newspapers, the rot first began to set in with the kowtowing to corporate advertisers" in the past ten to fifteen years, says Bobby Ghosh, a former editor of the *Hindustan Times*, a nationally circulated English newspaper, in an interview by the author. "Psychologically and in practical ways, that excessive dependency on advertisers opened the door. It began to destroy the fire wall between editorial and advertising. And through that opening, all kinds of genies have now rushed in."

THE TURNING POINT OF NATIONAL ELECTIONS, 2014

Heading into the pivotal election in 2014 that saw the BJP sweep into power as a dominant, single-party majority in terms of Parliament seats, India's media remained both vibrant and polarized, starting with widespread coverage of the massive corruption scandals of the ruling Congress Party coalition as well as deep, visible skepticism of the secular credentials of Modi and his openly Hindu nationalist party, the BJP.

"Sections of the media may have been unfair to some people in BJP when they were in the opposition, but many sections were also very anti-Congress in the run-up to the elections, where it was increasingly clear Modi would likely become the Prime Minister. So, "it mostly balanced it out," recalls Rohini Singh, a consulting editor of the online news site the *Wire* and a reporter with a track record of antiestablishment journalism in the mainstream media, in an interview by the author.

But within a short period after the BJP came into power, it became apparent to journalists that coverage of the government, in particular Modi, was being formally tracked by the government in a manner that remains unprecedented in India's modern history.

"Never had a PMO monitor what journalists do to the extent it happens now," says Singh. "No PM has ever set up a 200-member team to monitor what journalists do, how many times you take Modi's name. The result is that this government is far more heavy-handed than any previous governments I have dealt with."

Observers of the interplay between Indian politics and journalism note that although the Gandhi family also practiced personality-centric politics and was sensitive to "family" coverage, Modi has brought to Delhi a de facto presidential form of governing, where not only is the power fully centralized in the PMO, but the notion that other individual power centers, including powerful cabinet ministers and chief ministers of BJP-run states, can exist independent of Modi has also been actively discouraged and mostly eliminated.

As a result, there has been an acute emphasis within the PMO on how Modi is covered in media, with any criticism of the government writ large considered unwanted criticism of the Indian government.

Indeed, one editor at a national English newspaper, who did not want to be named for fear of personal reprisals, recalled getting a phone call from a top bureaucrat who suggested that the occasional negative articles on the government in the paper were unwarranted but if published should definitely not run under headlines referring to the government as the "Modi govt." Instead, this editor was told, headlines should refer to the nominal coalition headed by Modi, the National Democratic Alliance (NDA), and use the "NDA govt" label. However, the same bureaucrat also said that the newspaper was welcome to use "Modi govt" on "positive" stories, the editor recalled.

"The BJP, as a ruling party, is different from previous governments because they are quite shameless in their willingness to exert pressure," says Mrinal Pande, a veteran editor of Hindi-language newspapers, in an interview with the author. Pande says media owners in India's northern heartland, a politically vital belt for the BJP, have completely abandoned any pretext of balanced coverage in pursuit of both continued government advertising and access to the ruling party's leaders.

"With this government, it is their attitude that is different," says Ghosh, the former *Hindustan Times* editor. "They, particularly Modi, are relatively untutored in the gentle ways of doing business in Delhi. They bring a brute force in politics to Delhi, with any concession seen as a sign of weakness. There is no attempt to first have a conversation. No attempt at persuasion. And they command gestures of supplication. In the past, these kinds of levers—threatening phone calls and hints of consequences—would be a last resort. Now these people go nuclear immediately no matter how small the goal. Once, these kinds of levers would mostly be used to try to hush up big corruption stories. Now it is applied for much smaller things. That is the big change from before, to this BJP government."

Ghosh's tenure as editor of the *Hindustan Times* ended abruptly in September 2018, just sixteen months into the job, following what is widely believed to have been Modi's personal intervention with the newspaper's owner, something that the various parties involved have publicly refuted, even amid multiple news reports about the saga.[24]

"Governments that come with huge mandates, they forgot they don't have mandate to 'fix' media or demand positive coverage," says Singh. "It is a problem with right-wing parties and governments all over the world, not peculiar to India. But this is a government that does not like to be questioned. And I can't think of a single newsroom in India that has not fallen in line. I know of at least six beat reporters whose beats were changed by their editors because a very powerful minister had an issue with how they were covering his then portfolio."

As a result of this power exerted by the PMO, major decisions by the government have gone for extended periods without investigative and critical examination in the media.

Independent observers typically cite the Modi government's abrupt "demonetization" announcement in November 2016, declaring the cancellation of nearly 86 percent of India's paper currency under the pretext of curbing "black money," as a prime example of how the coverage of the aftermath of a story at many newspapers is directly influenced by the government.[25]

"Everyone was in agreement that demonetization unexpectedly hit everyone—be it housewives, the milkman, farmers—but none of the newspapers really took this up as a major crusade or dug into how there was something wrong with how it was executed, and the clear political motives behind the decision," complains Pande.

Although India's media did capture the travails of bank ATMs running out of cash and other visual financial distress, there wasn't the kind of critical, investigative journalism—including in the business press—of a move that is now widely seen as having been rather ineffective in curbing "black money," the original reason Modi offered for the demonetization policy.

Since then it has become harder for business and economics journalists to do even routine stories, such as ones that question how India's gross domestic product calculations are done, says Singh. "This is a government that does not like to be questioned on anything."

Similarly, when the Modi government said in September 2016 that it had carried out so-called surgical strikes across the Pakistan-controlled "Line of Control," a much-disputed border between the two warring nations, "newspapers such as *Dainik Jagran* [India's most-circulated newspaper, with multiple Hindi editions] were very jingoistic and came out chests beating on their front pages. It was almost as if the Information and Broadcasting Ministry sat in a newsroom and dictated what kind of story to publish," recalls Pande. "There [is] an unquestioning veil of silence in Hindi media when it comes to the Modi government claims."[26]

The same scenario played out in February 2019 when a convoy of India's paramilitary was targeted by a suicide truck bomber in Jammu and Kashmir state, killing forty. India blamed neighboring Pakistan and launched an air raid, dropping bombs in Balakot, to overt nationalistic applause from mainstream media, especially television.

An investigation by the Polis Project, an independent nonprofit that monitors media, into the Indian media's reporting on the Pulwama attack found that "many reports were contradictory, biased, incendiary and uncorroborated. News organizations such as India Today, NDTV, News 18, the Indian Express, First Post, Mumbai Mirror, ANI and others routinely attributed their information to anonymous 'government sources,' 'forensic experts,' 'police officers' and 'intelligence officers.' No independent investigations were conducted, and serious questions about intelligence failures were left unanswered," the Polis study concluded, implicating most of India's media, including those that are running on the past fumes of being independent of any government in power.[27]

THE THRIVING GOVERNMENT-BUSINESS NEXUS

What has also been strikingly different this time around—editors and media executives privately say—is the willingness of the BJP as well as of powerful bureaucrats in the PMO to directly persuade corporate advertisers either to threaten media companies with repercussions or simply to pull their corporate advertising from newspapers after critical stories on Modi appear in them.

"They speak to big advertisers and put pressure on them to not advertise and to withhold ads, and such requests, coming directly from the PMO, matter a lot to corporates," says Singh. "Big corporates are friends of everyone in power. And this BJP government does it far more than any other government that I have seen, and far more than regional parties where such commercial strong-arming is more common."[28]

Ghosh recalls ad sales people coming to him to complain about the impact of news coverage. "Advertisers would call and say, 'You are writing antigovernment stories, and we are under pressure to pull ads,' or, in anticipation of such pressure, they would decide 'we better pull ads.' The Indian private sector is completely and utterly spineless" when it comes to fears about being perceived as not supporting the BJP government, Ghosh maintains.

In addition, some media executives say, a desire not to antagonize the ruling administration is more pronounced with this government because all the government policy and regulatory decisions come directly out of the PMO and not from various cabinet ministers, as was commonplace in previous Congress governments. As a result, most CEOs are left to read the tea leaves, and government departments with big ad budgets also end up fearful and think that the PMO might be upset because the departments' ads are prominently running in newspapers that had a critical front-page story of a Modi government initiative.

One former media executive recalls being summoned in 2018 by the head of a large public-sector undertaking headquartered in Mumbai, who explicitly demanded that a series of negative stories be quietly expunged from the newspaper's website, or the chieftain would end a large advertising contract. This media executive, who has since joined another media con-glomerate and did not want to be named, says public-sector bosses have been increasingly emboldened by what they see as a clear endorsement of the blatant arm-twisting of media emanating all the way from the top of the BJP government, the PMO itself.[29]

The BJP's demand for absolute fealty to Modi is also having ripple effects on media's historic ability to hang on to government advertising.

"Ad sales people would tell me that in the 'old' days, even if the Congress Party was upset at the center, you could go to the Congress government in, say, [the state of] Andhra Pradesh, and they would have autonomy to con-tinue the state's ad campaigns," notes Ghosh. "In the Narendra Modi era, it is all top down. Nobody at state level can override the center. For example, we would do a tough story, and there would be immediate reaction in Delhi. But the ad sales guy from Lucknow [in the large, BJP-ruled state of Uttar Pradesh (UP)] would also call, saying, 'I am getting pressure from UP Tourism on their ad campaign' even if a story had nothing to do with UP."

DEEPLY COMPLICIT MEDIA OWNERS

India's news industry is controlled mostly by large business families with significant cross-media and cross-industry holdings, which has long put them at the mercy of successive governments in a country where business success—or failure—is still mostly happening at the intersection of poli-tics, policy, and regulation coming out of Delhi.[30]

And in an era of slowly diminishing profitability in India's news busi-ness as advertising starts to shift to digital, as it is doing elsewhere in the world, the value of owning a newspaper is increasingly skewed toward either helping protect the business owners in their other businesses by potentially giving them a loud, visible platform or being used to peddle influence in return for favorable regulatory policies.

"If you own a big newspaper in India, you can aspire to one of two things—you can aspire to have influence or aspire to access," notes Ghosh. "But you have to surrender influence to get access. And too many Indian newspaper owners aspire for access. Owners have not changed, but owners have changed the direction in which they genuflect. You don't need to nec-essarily buy them out yet. . . . [Y]ou can get the same effect with other means now, and the BJP has perfected that."[31]

Most media owners have other business interests and, as a result, have "secret dependencies on the government, so they are pretty reluctant to step out of line, beyond a point," says Pande, who has worked as the top editor for family-controlled media houses.

"In the Hindi heartland of India, media capture is only strengthening as time goes on," says Pande. "We have always had problems with a few conglomerates owning media, and in Hindi they are all family-owned enterprises that have other business interests like textiles, trading, infrastructure building, with [the] same cross-family directors sitting on their media and nonmedia boards. This means that the grip of the family is pretty firm on what goes into newspapers, how certain stories are featured, and what headlines are written. And if you start working at any of these papers as an editor, you are expected to take it for granted that the family will be quite dominant and [that] the firewall between editorial and business, and these days the government, will be nonexistent."

Indeed, a research study on concentration of ownership in India's Hindi newspapers in 2014 noted that "the emergence of these two Hindi newspapers (family-owned *Dainik Jagran* and *Dainak Bhaskar*) as the indisputable leaders has not only created an environment of monopoly in the future, but it has very adversely affected the existing newspapers i.e. *Rajasthan Patrika* (Rajasthan), *Lokmat* (Maharashtra), *Dainik Tribune*, (Haryana), *Ranchi Samachar* (Jharkhand), *Amar Ujala* (Uttar Pradesh), *Jansatta* (Delhi), *Rashtriya Sahara* (Uttar Pradesh). [The] Indian Readership Survey shows that every year, the readership of small newspapers is diminishing and slowly pushing them on (to) the verge of extinction."[32]

The inability to diversify news revenues beyond advertising has also put India's newspaper owners in a bind. For instance, most of India's media brands have set up for-profit events businesses, where sponsors, typically the same media advertisers, also pay large amounts to be associated with the theme of the event. But in a regulatory-rich world, the desire to have the truly powerful—that is, India's ministers—attend and speak at the many competing newspaper-run events has given the Modi government an even longer lever to keep newsroom owners and editors in line.[33]

Modi and his cabinet ministers are said to have refused to attend well-publicized media company events at the last minute in order to extract significant and permanent shifts in future news coverage as concessions from media conglomerates such as BCCL.[34]

"For a *Hindustan Times*, it matters more that Rahul Gandhi [leader of the Congress Party] comes for their annual Leadership Summit than for their newsroom to dig into land scams or telecom scams involving the extended Gandhi family," says Singh. "For Bennett [BCCL], that the PM comes to a money-making *Economic Times* event is way more important than some big investigative story they can do on [Modi confidante and cabinet minister] Amit Shah."

In effect, the self-imposed inability to increase reader revenue through realistic newspaper cover prices, for example, has led to new revenue-generating events at media companies, where the dependency on government functionaries and CEOs has deepened well beyond their traditional clout. And newsroom coverage of the other activities and policies of such event attendees is increasingly tempered to facilitate continued patronage.[35]

Pande asks: When Modi remains the "big catch" for media-brand events, why would any major newsroom make a big deal in its news coverage of the fact that as prime minister Modi has not held even one formal press conference in his first five years in office?

JOURNALISM OF MISSING COURAGE

It is not uncommon these days for journalists and editors to talk privately about a pervasive sense of intimidation in India, something a few generations of journalists there have not encountered since the end of a brief national emergency in the mid-1970s under then prime minister Indira Gandhi.[36]

"When well-meaning people within the government tell you privately that the govt is tapping your phones, you wonder, 'Are you looking at pictures of my family on my phone?,'" says Singh. "And, yes, I have felt unsafe over my work, for the first time" in the BJP regime.

Social media in India have also created a culture of intimidation because lists of journalists dubbed "anti-India" are routinely circulated by BJP supporters, who also frequently tag Modi's Twitter handle in their tweets.

Sadanand Dhume, an op-ed columnist for the *Wall Street Journal*, tweeted about these new phenomena in India: "When Congress was in power in India, I wrote countless articles criticizing it. Party supporters didn't like it, and some of them would get personal in their responses. But nobody ever appealed to the government authority to shut me down."[37]

"Long before Donald Trump was saying 'fake news,' people in India were saying 'libtards' and 'presstitutes,' but it is part of the same violent rhetoric and pathology," says Ghosh, who says he was quite shocked at this widespread antipathy toward journalists when he moved to India to become editor of the *Hindustan Times* in May 2016.[38]

In fact, a now widely used Twitter hashtag in India, #presstitutes, was first used there in April 2015 by a retired general, V. K. Singh, then a minister in the national BJP cabinet, thus helping legitimize what has since become widespread antimedia sentiment as well as personal trolling and malicious abuse of journalists on social media. Amid silence from the PM and the BJP over that initial tweet, Minister Singh defended his labeling: "I apologize if the 90% felt bad. I used the word for the 10% and they deserve that word."[39]

Many journalists in India see the killing of journalist turned activist Gauri Lankesh in September 2017 as a visceral turning point that highlighted how successful the Modi government had become at creating an antimedia sentiment across the country.[40]

An editor at *Lankesh Patrike*, a relatively obscure weekly in the south Indian Kannada language that was owned by her father, Gauri Lankesh also published her own small weekly magazine, *Gauri Lankesh Patrike*, and was known for being a staunch critic of right-wing Hindu extremism. She was shot and killed outside her home in a Bangalore suburb.

"The Gauri Lankesh killing was a shock," says Ghosh. "The killing was bad enough, but the absolute lack of sympathy, empathy, or interest among the political elite was a rude shock. On social media, BJP activists openly celebrated her death. It wasn't as bad as [President Rodrigo] Duterte in the Philippines attacking opponents, but in the Indian context it came as a shock to me as to how little people seem to care about these issues."

It also didn't go unnoticed among journalists and others in India that PM Modi's Twitter account was following some of the people who seemed to be lauding the Lankesh killing, in particular Nikhil Dadhich, a self-proclaimed Hindu nationalist. Dadhich was only one of eighteen hundred Twitter users that Modi, who has a growing following of more than 50 million on Twitter, was following back in 2018.

Dadhich wrote on Twitter in Hindi: "One bitch dies a dog's death all the puppies cry in the same tune." In response to criticism of this tweet, Modi's party issued the official statement that the PM had more pressing matters than to respond to questions about who he followed on Twitter and why.[41]

"Our PM [still] personally follows some of the vilest people on Twitter who are issuing rape threats and sexual violence threats to women journalists," notes Singh.

In mid-2018, a Special Investigation Team probing the Lankesh murder said that it had detained two suspects and that one of them had confessed to the murder, claiming he was told to kill someone to save his religion and that he did not know who the victim was going to be. The case is ongoing.[42]

Meanwhile, the Committee to Protect Journalists database shows that since 1992 fifty-one journalists have been killed in India, with near-record number of deaths annually in 2017 and 2018. Out of the thirty-five journalists specifically targeted for murder in India, thirty-three "were murdered with impunity," according to the Committee to Protect Journalists. A majority of these killings remain unresolved.[43]

WHITHER INDIA'S SELF-REGULATED JOURNALISM WATCHDOGS

India has long had, at least on paper, media self-regulation in the form of the Press Council of India and the Editors Guild, bodies that have successfully lobbied to avoid direct government regulation of media by claiming they can be effective in self-regulating. But both bodies have been woefully inadequate at protecting newsrooms and journalists from external influences and pressures.

"There is an inner buckling of spines that is very worrisome," says Pande, who resigned from the Editors Guild in 2019 over what she says is its reluctance and inordinate delay in responding to serious sexual harassment and assault charges against at least one editor who was a member of the guild.[44]

Singh says it is unreasonable, given the lack of external support, to expect individual journalists in major newsrooms in India to battle against pressures coming from both their own editors and media owners. "The onus is more on editors than [on] media owners to ensure free and fair journalism," says Singh. "We journalists have bills to pay, children to worry about.

But the responsibility of doing a story that is factually correct and has checks and balances falls entirely now [more] on the committed individual journalist than [on] the news organization. The editors have done a pretty bad job at self-regulating over the years."

Even Ghosh notes how difficult it is for individual journalists to continue to stand up to their own bosses in India. "I always had [the] luxury of knowing I could stand up for my principles. I had a good contract. I assumed things would end badly. And if they did, I could get on a plane and leave India," says Ghosh, an American citizen of Indian origin. "I had no family in India, and there was nobody in danger of physical harm. I had these luxuries. I would like to think [that even] if I didn't, like most Indian journalists don't, I would have made [the] same decisions. But I don't know if I would have. And I don't think we can automatically expect those living and working in India as journalists to take stands every day."

Even as some journalists see rays of hope among small, digital newsrooms with young journalists willing to challenge the status quo on social media, veterans remain pessimistic about the vast majority of India's mainstream media.

"Among top editors that I have worked with, I see a great desire to be a friend of a powerful person, to be invited to dinners and lunches, get a government award and, if you are really ambitious, a seat in Parliament," says Singh. "So if you are A's lapdog, it doesn't take too long to become B's lapdog. That worries me. And if I look at where they are headed in mainstream media newsrooms, I see no hope there."

Another intimidation tactic in India in recent years has been the growing use of defamation lawsuits, which initially coincided with the first term of the BJP government. Led by the industrialist Anil Ambani, such defamation suits have become the favorite legal weapon of choice to harass and intimidate journalists as well as news organizations. From January 2018 into early 2019, Anil Ambani–owned companies alone filed twenty-nine defamation suits—twenty-one of which were against media organizations and journalists, including international news organizations such as *Bloomberg* and the *Financial Times* as well as a wide range of Indian publications, such as the *Economic Times*, the *Financial Express*, the *Week*, the *Tribune*, the *Wire*, the *Hindu*, and NDTV.

The filing is typically followed by asking the media organization to immediately publish an unconditional apology and a complete retraction;

remove the published article from all online access; and cease and desist from publishing similar articles, all "within twenty-four hours of the receipt of this notice." The court filings also routinely seek tens of millions of dollars from the news organization in alleged damages and typically name individual journalists, masthead editors, and publishers as defendants.

At least twenty-six of these cases were civil suits filed in the Ahmedabad City and Civil Sessions Court, claiming damages under India's Code of Civil Procedure of 1908. Ahmedabad has become a preferred destination for filing these defamation suits because Gujarat state laws, unlike the laws in most other states, cap court filing fees at seventy-five thousand rupees (U.S.$1,200), no matter how high the value of damages claimed in the suit.[45]

For most news organizations, these suits are a nuisance, though with significant costs incurred to respond to and try to quash them. For individual journalists, the burdens are significantly higher because Indian courts routinely see nontimely responses as a reason to issue an arrest warrant and other, more draconian ex parte fiats. Although these cases may eventually never amount to anything in terms of final verdicts and get dismissed, they are intended to engage news organizations in a battle of attrition, with crony lower-court systems stacked against them and India's highest courts too backlogged to be effective in a timely fashion.

With no pushback from India's politicians or lawmakers over such deliberate intimidation—these lawsuits are often over a media outlet's assertion of alleged kickbacks in shady government contracts—the legal system has thus become a contributing factor in silencing news media from continuing to investigate corruption and crony capitalism in India.

A DARK WAY FORWARD

Although the Modi-led BJP government has been markedly different in its approach to controlling media from previous administrations, one with little signs of softening, some hope that India's periodic and mostly free elections will eventually bring a new regime that will then ease up on its media.

Indeed, India's Congress Party devoted a section of its Elections Manifesto in 2019 to "media and freedom of media," saying it "firmly believes that the media must be free and self-regulated." Without offering any specifics, the Congress Party said it will "amend" the Press Council of India

Act of 1978 to "strengthen the system of self-regulation of journalists, uphold editorial independence and guard against government interference." The party also promised it would "pass a law to preserve the freedom of the Internet" and another law to "curb monopolies in the media, cross-ownership of different segments of the media."[46]

The BJP's competing manifesto in 2019 made no mention of media in a forty-page list of electoral promises.[47] Meanwhile, the Congress Party ended up getting crushed in the 2019 elections, becoming a pale shadow of its former self as a national party.

Also, not everyone is hopeful that a change in the government in a future election may automatically reverse the trend of power holders' capture of India's media.

"To me, the question is, 'What happens when and if the Modi government goes away?,' " asks Ghosh. "But I am no longer sure if a new government is going to treat media any differently, as they are all learning how to really handle the media from the BJP and are also very angry with the media for being [intentionally or forcibly] unfair to them, when the BJP was in power." Adds Singh: "Even if it is a new government, I don't know which party wants a free and fair media anymore. They want it when they are in the opposition, not when they are in power."

All of which raises the chilling possibility that in the second Modi term, which runs through 2024, India could end up going the way of Turkey and Hungary with respect to press freedoms, engendering an even more pliant media ownership or fully owned media as ruling-party politicians stop fearing electoral consequences from their media-capturing tactics.

Although the Modi BJP government is seen as largely behind the growing capture of India's mainstream media, a significant part of the culpability clearly falls on media owners and editors and their own continuing practices. The business practices of large newspaper media companies have created the financial leverage that governments can successfully use to capture media by controlling advertising revenues.

Meanwhile, the massive reader subsidy—with minuscule paid subscriptions—has also resulted in readers' significant devaluation of news content in India. As historically cheap pricing models in the news industry perpetuate the perception of low-to-no-value news content, the challenge in India remains one of how to break free from the chokehold of advertisers—both private and government.

This perception of lack of value in news content has become a major barrier to creating viable digital subscriptions for journalism in India, which could be one potential step toward lessening the influence of advertisers.

Some media brands have made nascent attempts to dip their toes in reader revenue, a trend that, to some, offers glimmers of hope for independent media in India to potentially survive and perhaps thrive.

"First and foremost, we are working very hard to try to get more capital into the space—capital that does not have strings attached when it comes to editorial policy," says Nishant Lalwani, managing director at Luminate, in an interview by the author. Luminate is part of the Omidyar Group and has invested in some of India's emerging, for-profit digital media brands. "The other solution set, which we have been actively promoting, is trying to increase the sustainability of organizations and try[ing] to increase the trust factor in organizations, which are highly linked. We are helping reorient the value proposition away from advertisers and back to readers and the audience. And doing what we can to bolster best practices. This is very much relevant to India, where you can monetize middle-class Indians to sufficiently support membership news organizations, such as the *Ken*."

The *Ken* is a tech-focused independent digital news startup that offers just one in-depth article a day to its subscribers and in 2019 claimed about ten thousand paying members.[48]

Although the rise in startup digital media news brands in recent years in India offers some green shoots, in 2018–2019 there were also growing signs that fledgling newsrooms are being pressured to fall in line by means of more conventional strong-arm tactics used in countries such as Turkey.

The early years of these Modi pressure tactics appeared to have focused extensively on mass-market television and newspapers, but the same tactics are starting to be applied to small, relatively independent digital media news operations, such as the *Quint*, whose owners faced raids by India's Income Tax Department in 2018, what some observers saw as a chilling message to those media owners who might balk at falling in line.[49]

The mostly ineffective Editors Guild of India did call out the government through a press statement, which is about the only form of public action that this particular self-regulatory body is increasingly known for in Indian journalism. "While the tax administration is within its rights to make inquiries in compliance with the relevant laws, it should not exercise those powers in a way that could be seen as an intimidation of the government's critics," the guild opined but promised no other follow-up action to protect against such selective targeting by the Modi government.[50]

Although tax raids tend to be somewhat public, selectively putting pressure on individual digital brands continues under the current administration. "We know of a top cabinet minister [who] spoke personally to top donors and said 'don't fund them [digital news outlets],'" says Singh, who writes for the *Wire*, an ad-free, digital-only, nonprofit news site that began in 2015 and has received initial funds from media foundations and individual contributors.

But she holds out hope. "There is a population willing to pay for a media that is committed to readers [more] than to the political establishment," says Singh. "I really think those digital newsrooms are the future. I don't know how scalable they are, but I see *Quint, Scroll*, the *Wire*, and *Caravan* as somewhat hopeful signs," she noted, citing some of the smallest albeit independent media companies.[51]

Ghosh, now based in London working for an international media company following his short-lived stint in India, is urging those who care about press freedom to focus on India's independent digital outlets.[52]

"If I were to advise people on how best to help safeguard journalism in India, it would be to focus on the canary in the coal mine, the one or two independent voices, such as the *Wire*," Ghosh urges. Putting Maria Ressa of *Rappler* on the cover of *Time* magazine as one of its Person of the Year selections in 2018, he says, could potentially have dissuaded the Duterte government in the Philippines from trying to shut the *Rappler* site down entirely.[53] "Trying to reform or protect all of Indian journalism is simply not going to work. Pick one or two independent voices and make it clear that any attempt to interfere with them would be heard globally."

For those looking for how the media might behave in the Modi government's second five-year term, which began mid-2019, the continuing signs of the results of a captured mainstream media are alarming.

After his win in 2014, Modi made a triumphant visit in September to the United States, holding a large public meeting in New York's Madison Square Garden, near the United Nations. An estimated nineteen thousand fans, mostly Indian immigrants, vastly outnumbered outside protestors, who nonetheless got air time on Indian television. This coverage included a widely seen viral video that showed one well-known Indian television journalist, Rajdeep Sardesai, interviewing some of Modi's critics on air before being roughed up by Modi supporters.

Now, fast forward to September 2019, when Modi made yet another triumphant visit to the United States, this time to Houston, Texas, where the crowd in the local stadium was estimated to be around fifty thousand fans and those on stage included President Donald Trump.

This time the protests against Modi were much more organized and larger, just outside the stadium where Modi spoke. But almost all Indian media focused on the Modi show, and the few references to any protests appeared to cast the protestors as fake or decidedly anti-Indian. This skewed coverage prompted Pamela Philipose, the public editor of the *Wire*, to see the Houston event as a clear tipping point: "By ignoring this section of opinion, by reporting with nationalist filters, by cocooning audiences in layers of triumphalist reportage, the 'patriotic' media was in fact doing the country a huge disservice. They [India's audiences] were being denied the whole picture."[54]

NOTES

1. *Economic Times*, "Indian Media May Touch Rs 2 Lakh Crore by 2020: Report," March 5, 2018, https://economictimes.indiatimes.com/industry/media/entertain ment/media/indian-media-may-touch-rs-2-lakh-crore-by-2020-report /articleshow/63165021.cms.

2. *Media and Entertainment Industry*, "India Brand Equity Foundation," March 2019, https://www.ibef.org/industry/media-entertainment-india.aspx; *BBC News*, "India Media-Profile," March 9, 2017, https://www.bbc.com/news/world-south-asia -12557390.

3. Saket Shukla, Akshay Sachthey, and Debottam Chattopadhyay, "India: Media & Entertainment: The Good, the Bad, and the Uncertain," *Mondaq*, September 26, 2018, http://www.mondaq.com/india/x/739826/broadcasting+film+television+rad io/Media+Entertainment+The+Good+The+Bad+And+The+Uncertain; "Govern ment of India Registered Newspapers and Periodicals," *Data.gov.in*, https://data .gov.in/resources/all-india-number-registered-newspapers-and-periodicals -language-2001-2013-14.

4. Noshir Kaka, Anu Madgavkar, Alok Kshirsagar, Rajat Gupta, James Manyika, Kushe Bahl, and Shishir Gupta, *Digital India: Technology to Transform a Connected Nation*, McKinsey Global Institute Report, March 2019, https://www.mckinsey.com /business-functions/digital-mckinsey/our-insights/digital-india-technology-to -transform-a-connected-nation?.

5. Prasun Sonwalkar, "From By-line to Bottom-line: Trust Deficit in World's Largest Democracy," *Journalism* 20, no. 1 (2019), https://journals.sagepub.com/doi/full/10 .1177/1464884918809270.

6. *Quint*, "Free Speech in India 2018: The State Rolls On," April 1, 2019, https://www.thequint.com/news/india/free-speech-in-india-2018-the-state-rolls-on.

7. Hardev Sanotra, "As Anil Ambani's Rafale Deal Soars, His News Agency Is Being Run to the Ground," *Wire*, March 25, 2019, https://thewire.in/media/as-anil-ambanis-rafale-deal-soars-his-news-agency-ians-is-being-run-to-the-ground.

8. Ken Aulettam, "Citizens Jain," *New Yorker*, October 1, 2012, https://www.newyorker.com/magazine/2012/10/08/citizens-jain.

9. Punya Prasun Bajpai, "A 200-Member Government Team Is Watching How the Media Covers Modi, Amit Shah," *Wire*, August 10, 2018, https://thewire.in/media/narendra-modi-amit-shah-media-watch-punya-prasun-bajpai.

10. Anuj Srivas, "*Hindustan Times* Editor's Exit Preceded by Meeting Between Modi, Newspaper Owner," *Wire*, September 25, 2017, https://thewire.in/media/hindustan-times-bobby-ghosh-*narendra*-modi-shobhana-bhartia/amp/.

11. Paranjoy Guha Thakurata, "Media Ownership in India, an Overview," *Hoot*, June 30, 2012, http://asu.thehoot.org/resources/media-ownership/media-ownership-in-india-an-overview-6048.

12. Saiprasad Bejgam, "Who Owns/Runs Indian Media?," *Medium*, May 13, 2015, https://medium.com/three-much/who-owns-runs-indian-media-eb6c5cfbf9e7; Krista Mahr and Sumit Chaterjee, "Indian Media Fret as Conglomerate Buys Up Major News Channel," Reuters, August 2, 2014, https://www.reuters.com/article/india-media/indian-media-fret-as-conglomerate-buys-up-major-news-channel-idINKBN0G301920140803.

13. *Times of India*, "Govt Hikes Ad Rates for Print Media by 25%," January 8, 2019, http://timesofindia.indiatimes.com/articleshow/67446148.cms?.

14. Anoo Bhuyan, "UP Police Goes After 8 Journalists," *Wire*, September 19, 2019, https://thewire.in/rights/uttar-pradesh-police-journalists.

15. Aditya Thakur, "Top 7 Indian Channels That Are Owned by Politicians," *Hill Post*, August 21, 2013, http://hillpost.in/2013/08/top-7-indian-channels-that-are-owned-by-politicians/95166/; Patrick Kingsley, "Orban and His Allies Cement Control of Hungary's News Media," *New York Times*, November 29, 2018, https://www.nytimes.com/2018/11/29/world/europe/hungary-orban-media.html.

16. *Economist*, "Propaganda in India: Straight to Television," June 12, 2013, https://www.economist.com/banyan/2013/06/12/straight-to-television.

17. Ishita Mishra, "Pro-BJP or Anti-BJP: Inside the Modi-Shah Media Tracking 'War Rooms,'" *Wire*, August 11, 2018, https://thewire.in/politics/narendra-modi-amit-shah-bjp-india-media; Derek O'Brien, "Surviving TV Channels Who Are Government Mouthpieces," NDTV, July 2, 2017, https://www.ndtv.com/opinion/surviving-anchors-who-are-gau-rakshaks-in-suits-1719588; Nalin Mehta, "Who Owns the News and Why Politicians, Real Estate, Chit Funds, and Large Corporations Now Have Deep Stakes in the Majority of the News TV Business in Most Indian States," *Outlook India*, May 16, 2015, https://www.outlookindia.com/website/story/who-owns-the-news-and-why/294350.

18. *Wikipedia*, "Presstitutes," n.d., https://en.wikipedia.org/wiki/Presstitute; Harinder Baweja, " 'Presstitutes' and 'Prostitutes': The Language Our Netas Use," *Hindustan Times*, July 20, 2016, https://www.hindustantimes.com/analysis/presstitutes-and-prostitutes-the-language-our-netas-use/story-4sotjBK2tLpg3Prf4RKz9O.html;

Indian Express, "General V K Singh Presses on Presstitute Again," April 8, 2015, https://indianexpress.com/article/india/india-others/general-v-k-singh-presses-on-presstitute-again/.

19. Reporters Without Borders, "2020 World Press Freedom Index," April 2020, https://rsf.org/en/india.

20. Zeenat Saberin, "The Perils of Being a Journalist in Modi's India," Al-Jazeera, June 14, 2018, https://www.aljazeera.com/indepth/features/perils-journalist-modis-india-180614103115577.html.

21. Navin Singh Khadka, "Why India Is a World Leader in Waste Paper," *BBC News*, March 12, 2019, https://www.bbc.com/news/world-asia-india-46641059.

22. Dheeraj Mishra, "Modi Government Has Already Spent Double What the UPA Did on Publicity," *Wire*, October 29, 2018, https://thewire.in/government/modi-bjp-government-publicity-advertisement.

23. Anish Dayal, "Inside Law: Political Ads in India," *Wall Street Journal*, September 2, 2013, https://blogs.wsj.com/indiarealtime/2013/09/02/inside-law-political-advertising-in-india/.

24. *Outlook India*, "Editor of *Hindustan Times* Resigns," September 11, 2017, https://www.outlookindia.com/website/story/hindustan-times-editor-in-chief-bobby-ghosh-resigns-to-help-in-transition/301562.

25. Namita Dharia and Nishita Trisal, "Demonetization: Critical Responses to India's Cash(less) Experiment," Society for Cultural Anthropology, September 27, 2017, https://culanth.org/fieldsights/series/demonetization-critical-responses-to-indias-cash-less-experiment.

26. See also Ilyas Khan, "India's Surgical Strikes in Kashmir: Truth or Illusion?," *BBC News*, October 3, 2016, https://www.bbc.com/news/world-asia-india-37702790.

27. Suchitra Vijaya and Vasundhara Sirnate Drennan, "After Pulwama, Indian Media Proves It Is BJP's Propaganda Machine," *Washington Post*, March 4, 2019, https://www.washingtonpost.com/opinions/2019/03/04/after-pulwama-indian-media-proves-it-is-bjps-propaganda-machine/?.

28. See also Krishn Kaushik, "The Big Five: The Media Companies That the Modi Government Must Scrutinise to Fulfill Its Promise of Ending Crony Capitalism," *Caravan*, January 18, 2016, https://caravanmagazine.in/vantage/the-big-five-the-media-companies-that-the-modi-government-must-scrutinise-to-fulfill-its-promise-of-ending-crony-capitalism.

29. Kaushik, "The Big Five."

30. Dev Vrat Singh, "Media Concentration and Diversity in Media," Center for Mass Communication, Central University of Jharkhand, 2014, https://www.academia.edu/9211080/Media_Concentration_and_Diversity_in_Media_Study_of_Indian_media_ownership_patterns_in_the_context_of_diversity_debate.

31. See also *Wire*, "Stories on Amit Shah's Assets, Smriti Irani's 'Degree' Vanish from TOI, DNA," July 30, 2017, https://thewire.in/media/amit-shah-assets-smriti-irani-degrees-toi-et-outlook.

32. Singh, "Media Concentration and Diversity in Media."

33. Gaurav Laghate, "Events Industry to Cross Rs 10,000 Crore by FY21: Report," *Economic Times*, September 11, 2017, https://economictimes.indiatimes.com/articleshow/60454703.cms?.

34. Raju Gopalakrishnan, "Indian Journalists Say They [Are] Intimidated, Ostracized If They Criticize Modi and the BJP," Reuters, April 26, 2018, https://www.reuters.com/article/us-india-politics-media-analysis/indian-journalists-say-they-intimidated-ostracized-if-they-criticize-modi-and-the-bjp-idUSKBN1HX1F4.

35. Vanita Kohli-Khandekar, *The Indian Media Business* (New York: Sage, 2010).

36. Gopalakrishnan, "Indian Journalists Say They [Are] Intimidated."

37. Sadanand Dhume, tweet, Twitter, April 19, 2019, https://twitter.com/dhume/status/1119266017241456641.

38. K. K. Sruthjith, "Sanjoy Narayan Is Leaving *Hindustan Times*, Bobby Ghosh to Be Named Editor-in-Chief," *Huffington Post*, May 2, 2016, https://www.huffingtonpost.in/2016/05/02/sanjoy-narayan-bobby-ghos_n_9819416.html.

39. *Indian Express*, "General V K Singh Presses on Presstitute Again."

40. Siddharth Deb, "The Killing of Gauri Lankesh," *Columbia Journalism Review*, Winter 2018, https://www.cjr.org/special_report/gauri-lankesh-killing.php.

41. *India Today*, "#BlockNarendraModi: PM Following Twitter Trolls Abusing Gauri Lankesh Prompts Hashtag in Protest," September 7, 2017, https://www.indiatoday.in/india/story/blocknarendramodi-pm-following-twitter-trolls-abusing-gauri-lankesh-prompts-hashtag-in-protest-1039662-2017-09-07.

42. Deb, "The Killing of Gauri Lankesh."

43. Committee to Project Journalists, India, "Getting Away with Murder," October 29, 2018, https://cpj.org/asia/india/.

44. See also *News Central 24x7*, "Mrinal Pande and Mythili Bhusnurmath Quit Editors Guild Following Continued Membership of MJ Akbar, Tarun Tejpal," November 20, 2018, https://newscentral24x7.com/mrinal-pande-and-mythili-bhusnurmath-quit-editors-guild-following-continued-membership-of-mj-akbar-tarun-tejpal/.

45. Vijayta Lalwani, "Anil Ambani's Defamation Blitz: 28 Cases Filed by Reliance Group in Ahmedabad Courts This Year," *Scroll*, November 25, 2018, https://scroll.in/article/903119/anil-ambanis-defamation-blitz-28-cases-filed-by-reliance-group-in-ahmedabad-courts-this-year.

46. Indian National Congress, "Manifesto 2019," April 2019, https://manifesto.inc.in/en/.

47. Bharatiya Janata Party, "Manifesto 2019," April 2019, https://www.bjp.org/en/manifesto2019.

48. Rohin Dharmakumar, "What Product-Market Fit in Subscription Journalism Looks Like," *Ken*, January 1, 2019, https://the-ken.com/blog/what-product-market-fit-in-subscription-journalism-looks-like/.

49. NDTV, "Editors Guild of India Condemns Raids at Raghav Bahl's Home, Office," October 11, 2018, https://www.ndtv.com/india-news/raghav-bahl-editors-guild-of-india-condemns-raids-at-quint-founder-raghav-bahls-noida-home-office-1930420.

50. Editors Guild, quoted in NDTV, "Editors Guild of India Condemns Raids at Raghav Bahl's Home, Office."

51. See also Sanya Dhingra, "The Omidyar Network: 'Committed to a Free Media,' Via Two Indian Companies Too," *Print*, November 7, 2017, https://theprint.in/report/omidyar-network-two-indian-companies/14889/.

52. See also Lakshmi Chaudhry, "Can the Digital Revolution Save Indian Journalism?," *Columbia Journalism Review*, Fall–Winter 2016, https://www.cjr.org/special_report/india_digital_revolution_startups_scoopwhoop_wire_times.php.

53. Karl Vick, "The Guardians and the War on Truth," *Time*, December 11, 2018, http://time.com/person-of-the-year-2018-the-guardians/.

54. Pamela Philipose, "The Back Story: Modi Media Coverage from Madison Square Garden to Houston," *Wire*, September 28, 2019, https://thewire.in/media/back-story-modi-media-coverage-madison-square-garden-houston.

Chapter Eleven

THE CAPTURE OF BRITAIN'S FERAL BEAST

MARY FITZGERALD, JAMES CUSICK, AND PETER GEOGHEGAN

The *Evening Standard* is a newspaper distributed free of charge to millions of commuters across London. It is an effective monopoly: the only free paper made available across the capital's transit routes every weekday afternoon. It claims to reach 1.5 million readers every day. It is owned by Russian oligarchs. And until recently it was edited by the former British finance minister George Osborne.

Before Brexit upended British politics in the summer of 2016, George Osborne—a Conservative and one of the key architects of the failed "Remain" campaign—was tipped as the next prime minister. But after the surprise European Union (EU) referendum result, it was Theresa May who took the top job; Osborne was dismissed as chancellor of the Exchequer and—with no experience in journalism—was controversially appointed editor of the *Evening Standard*.

What happened next, according to insiders at the *Standard*, was decisive for the increasingly frail internal structure that once divided advertising from independent editorial content at the flagship London paper. The story of Osborne's tenure at the *Standard* highlights a number of serious concerns with the U.K. media ecosystem, including the dangers of concentrated ownership and media capture. It also flags the need for alternative media models and new approaches.

In May 2018, *openDemocracy* revealed that in a project led by Osborne and provisionally titled "London 2020," the *Standard* promised "money can't buy" editorial coverage in its news and comment pages to a number of major firms, including Uber and Google. This coverage would effectively be sponsored content that would not be branded as such. Readers would be unaware that the stories were part of a wider £3 million sponsorship package that would help boost diminishing revenues at the *Standard*. Millions of readers across London would be fed positive news about the giant multinational firms "partnering" with the *Standard*, with no idea that the firms themselves were paying for this "news."[1]

Why does all this matter? Because it has become relatively easy—and cheap—to buy influence over what citizens read, hear, and see in the U.K. media, as in the media of much of the rest of the world. Of course, special interests have always attempted to capture the press: Britain is no different in this regard. But collapsing print and subscription revenues and digital media models present myriad new opportunities for a wider set of players to have a go—at a far lower price tag. In the past, a press baron had to own a newspaper and run an expensive operation to advance his business or political agendas; now ever more aggressive forms of "sponsored content" or "native advertising" give many more advertisers or other institutional funders a slice of the action. With the media industry suffering huge financial losses and structural disruption, the barriers to purchasing influence are far lower. Many outlets have fought to maintain the wall between journalism and advertising—"church and state"—and have so far succeeded. But at many other outlets, the separation is disintegrating.

According to one leading agency sales executive who spoke to *openDemocracy* on condition of anonymity: "It's a given that straight ads no longer work, so we bend and blur. As the advertising industry guru, David Ogilvy, said: 'There's no need for advertisements to look like advertisements.' Now they don't. But unlike Ogilvy, I think the public would resent knowing they are being tricked. So best not to always tell them."[2]

HOW THE "CASH FOR COLUMN INCHES" SCANDAL BREWED

We work at *openDemocracy*, a global nonprofit web publication headquartered in London. We were leaked early details of the "London 2020" deal and of the promises that had been made to Google, Uber, and others about positive coverage. The story particularly caught our attention because Uber had been ruled "unfit" to operate in London after a string of controversies about its working practices, and the firm was preparing an imminent court appeal against the decision to cancel its license.

George Osborne, the *Standard*'s editor at the time, also happens to draw £650,000 a year for a part-time job with the fund managers BlackRock, which holds a £500 million stake in Uber—a conflict of interest that he has repeatedly failed to declare in public statements about the firm's activity.

Google's decision to involve itself in the controversial paid-for news deal was also remarkable. For a number of years, Google has been trying to cozy up to European publishers, many of whom are furious about how its search advertising business is draining their own ad revenues. Google has also found itself fighting the EU about individuals' rights to have references to them excluded from search results and about whether publishers should be obliged to automatically check the copyright of everything they put online.[3] In July 2018, the European Commission handed Google a massive €4.34 billion fine for breaking EU antitrust laws in forcing Android device makers to preinstall the Chrome browser, among other things.[4]

As part of its European public-relations (PR) effort, Google has put €150 million into its Europe-wide Digital News Initiative, which bankrolls a number of media initiatives with a stated aim of "combating misinformation and disinformation" and "helping consumers distinguish fact from fiction online." The irony that the London 2020 deal appeared to be offering Google positive editorial coverage—leaving readers unable to distinguish between news and advertising—was not lost on us.

In British media organizations, it has traditionally been expected that journalists and advertising sales teams will not attempt to influence each other. This principle is often called a "church–state divide." It is the subject of a self-regulated set of rules overseen by the U.K. Advertising Standards Authority. The basic idea is that when a member of the public sees published material, be it on the printed page or on a website, advertising must not be presented as editorial content.

The Google/Uber deal apparently wasn't the first time that the *Evening Standard* crossed the line separating church and state. In 2017, before Osborne became editor, the paper landed a lucrative deal with the Swiss agrichemical giant Syngenta. Osborne's predecessor chaired public debates on the future of food supplies for London, and related puff pieces for Syngenta's business agenda appeared in news pages—some not marked as paid-for news. There was, not surprisingly, no mention of the multi-billion-dollar lawsuit that Syngenta faced across thirteen U.S states. Nor was mention made of the Brexit context that might have made a deal with the *Standard* so attractive to Syngenta: the EU has some of the world's strictest regulations on the use of genetically modified organisms for food; once outside of the EU, the United Kingdom would come under intense pressure to relax these rules in order to secure lucrative trade deals with the United States and other countries.[5] Syngenta and other agribusiness firms have been engaging in expensive lobbying to push for this outcome.[6]

The Syngenta story attracted relatively little notice. However, the Google–Uber story (and in particular Osborne's involvement in it) eventually caught fire in the U.K. media. To boost coverage of *openDemocracy*'s scoop, we decided to offer a major U.K. newspaper the opportunity to run the story exclusively with us before other outlets had the chance to pick it up. The paper in question has a number of important commercial sponsorship relationships. Its news desk turned us down.

We also offered two well-known politicians the chance to comment on the story before we published. The first declined, citing the importance of an upcoming by-election for the London parliamentary seat of Lewisham. Put simply, the politician's team was unwilling to risk the ire of London's dominant local newspaper. The second political figure declined because of an upcoming legal case involving Uber. The firm subsequently won its challenge against Transport for London's decision to revoke its license to operate in London.

Nevertheless, when we published the London 2020 story, it went viral—and prominent politicians and media figures were soon speaking out. Tom Watson, deputy leader of the Labour Party, tweeted: "This is cash for column inches and amounts to a corporate fake news factory on a grand scale." Caroline Lucas, leader of the Green Party, called on the *Standard* to "come clean" about its "commercial agenda." George Monbiot, an influential columnist at the *Guardian*, said, "There is a word for this—corruption." Another leading columnist, Jenni Russell, writing in center-right *Times*, said that Osborne "should resign."

Instead of apologizing or explaining, however, Osborne had his executives issue denials and then hunted for those responsible for the leak.

Insiders described the atmosphere as "febrile." The project's launch date was pushed back.

A month later the project materialized under the banner "Future London." The names and logos of all the companies involved were clearly labeled. Interestingly, Google and Uber were joined as partners by a relatively unknown company called Babylon. The health-care firm sponsoring Future London's health initiative has declared that its aim is to create a "new dimension in healthcare" through the "wide use of data and technology." Babylon's CEO previously headed a company criticized for delivering inadequate patient care at a National Health Service hospital that it managed until 2015. Another partner in the project, Source London, is owned by Bolloré Group, a French conglomerate that has sought to suppress criticism of its operations by suing dozens of journalists.[7] The *Standard* has subsequently published countless sympathetic news stories about Uber that are not labeled as sponsored, including a positive two-page interview with Uber CEO Dara Khosrowshahi right after the launch of Future London. The paper denied the coverage was connected to the Future London project.

In an editorial accompanying the launch of Future London, the *Evening Standard* said: "Working with businesses as advertisers and sponsors is what enables us to employ world-class journalists, and provide almost two million of you every day with a great newspaper—entirely for free."

THE "PRIZATION" OF NEWS

The London 2020 story was a disturbing example of corporate influence in the British media, but it was far from unique. The *Standard* is published by ESI Media, which is owned by the Moscow-based oligarch Alexander Lebedev and run in London by his son Evgeny. ESI Media also includes the diminished online remnant of the once-influential newspaper the *Independent* (Lebedev closed the print operation and dramatically scaled back expenditure in 2016) and a barely watched local television channel London Live. Inside the *Independent*, young reporters—who refer to themselves as "the crèche" in a nod to their relative inexperience—have told *openDemocracy* that it is not unusual for advertising sales executives to walk directly to their desks and order the way a story should be covered.

Lebedev, who bought the *Standard* from the owners of the *Daily Mail* in 2009, ended the retail sale of the loss-making paper and turned it into a free sheet distributed across London's rail and underground stations. Without direct sales revenue, advertising became the sole source of income, a change that altered the internal balance of power.

Throughout his years as chancellor, from 2010 after the global financial crash right up to Brexit in 2016, George Osborne was obsessed with reducing the United Kingdom's budget deficit. He deployed tough austerity measures that have had far-reaching consequences for some of the most vulnerable people across Britain but have brought no meaningful reforms of the banking and finance sector that had caused the financial crash in 2008 and subsequent economic slump. Given this track record, he may not have been overly concerned that he was siding with advertising finance and effectively intensifying the "PRization" of the product he was in charge of.

But this pattern of PRization in the U.K. media is not confined to ESI Media and Osborne's editorship of the *Standard*.[8] In 2015, one of the United Kingdom's best-known political commentators, Peter Oborne, published a long resignation letter from his position as chief political correspondent of the *Daily Telegraph*, a leading conservative broadsheet. He alleged the *Telegraph* had suppressed investigations into HSBC, a major advertiser with the paper, and that this type of editorial "protection" extended to a number of its other big advertising clients, including supermarket giant Tesco.[9] The revelations prompted a number of journalists working at other media outlets to make allegations—both privately and publicly—of similar types of editorial interference or enhancement.

Buzzfeed, for example, was forced to clarify its policy after allegations that it had deleted two articles unfavorable to advertisers.[10] And the *Guardian* revealed that HSBC had stopped buying its advertising space when it reported on the "Swissleaks" investigation that was deeply damaging to the bank.[11]

The *Telegraph* issued firm denials of Oborne's allegations, although an analysis by researchers at King's College London backed up his claims.[12] Internal sources confirmed that in the wake of the scandal some *Telegraph* executives were less willing to spike stories unfavorable to advertisers, and the paper publicly committed to new guidelines for employees to reinforce the independence of editorial from advertising. However, within a few months the same internal sources were reporting that operations were back to "business as usual."

In the wake of the *Telegraph* story, *openDemocracy* launched a pan-European survey of journalists to investigate the scale of commercial capture at media outlets across Europe, alongside project partners Index on Censorship, Reporters Without Borders, King's College London, and the European Federation of Journalists.[13] More than two hundred journalists from thirty-seven European countries responded. The majority of the respondents were based in the United Kingdom, and the findings were striking:

- Thirty-eight percent (70 people out of the 186 who answered) said reporters in their newsroom had been instructed not to criticize a company or person with commercial or investment ties to their employer.
- One-third (62 out of 186) said their news outlet is "less critical of commercial partners."
- Twenty-nine percent (54 out of 186) said that a line editor had altered the focus or tone of stories when individuals or organizations with a commercial relationship to their employer were affected.
- Sixty-two percent (93 out of 151) felt there has been an increase in the influence of PR, advertisers, and/or other commercial interests at the media outlet they work for.
- Forty-one percent (62 out of 151) said that reporters in their newsroom have been offered money or other benefits by a company or third party simply to cover a story.
- Only 15 percent (22 out of 151) said that those benefits had been disclosed in the resulting article.

The survey responses paint an overall picture of growing concerns about media capture and PRization in newsrooms. The once rigorously policed "church–state" divide appears to be under ever-increasing pressure, with PR officers and private companies holding ever-greater sway in the news media. Private responses suggest that press freedom is a flattering myth. Evidence in the public domain points the same way.

SAUDI-SPONSORED WAR REPORTING

Advertiser- or sponsor-led capture might be more expected in certain niches of journalism—lifestyle, health and beauty, and technology, for instance.

But *openDemocracy*'s survey showed that commercial capture cuts across a range of subject areas. A little more than half of the respondents to the survey said that they cover politics; one-third work on arts and culture desks; one-tenth cover sport.

Nor is "capture" unique to domestic reporting. Last year amid rumors of financial difficulties and renewed attempts to offload ESI Media's loss-making TV station, the owner of the *Evening Standard*, Alexander Lebedev, sold an unconfirmed 50 percent of the online *Independent* newspaper to a Saudi investor, Sultan Muhammad Abuljadayel. The sale left Lebedev and the other co-owner of the digital title, Justin Byam Shaw, as minority shareholders.

At first, any worry over potential Saudi influence at the *Independent* and indeed over the influence of Saudi cash in other parts of the ESI group appeared unjustified. In May 2018, however, the *Standard* published a series of Saudi-friendly articles by its defense editor on the conflict in Yemen, where the Saudis back the formal state government against the Houthi rebellion. Although the reporting was careful to acknowledge the allegations made by human rights nongovernmental organizations regarding war crimes committed by the Saudis, it took a noticeably pro-Saudi line.

Around the same time, Evgeny Lebedev posted on Instagram a sequence of photographs and comments about a trip he made to Yemen accompanied by the celebrated war photographer Don McCullin. *openDemocracy* has established that the military officials protecting Lebedev were from Saudi special forces and that the aircraft used to transport him around Yemen was part of the Saudi military fleet. Saudi "capture" or simply a proprietor using available military to protect himself, as many journalists do when reporting from war zones? Readers of the *Standard* were given no information to help them decide.

"FERAL" PRESS—BUT CONCENTRATED OWNERSHIP

Although British news outlets have long held up the putative separation of advertisement and editorial as a primary virtue, this has somewhat paradoxically often gone hand-in-hand with a wry celebration of the "feral" character of the United Kingdom's press. The British media's reputation as untamable is often adduced in industry circles as a sign of its enduring independence. To many, the idea of a "captured" Fourth Estate feels impossible in the country that created the Magna Carta and parliamentary rule and is home to so many boisterous tabloids. Yet just a few organizations control a huge amount of the British media.

Analysis by the Media Reform Coalition in 2019 shows that 83 percent of the national newspaper market is dominated by just three companies: News Corporation, owned by Rupert Murdoch; Associated Newspapers, owned by Jonathan Harmsworth, the fourth viscount Rothermere; and Reach, founded in 2018 by a merger of Trinity Mirror and Express Newspapers. This figure is up from 71 percent in 2015. When online readers are included, just five companies (News UK, Daily Mail Group, Reach, Guardian News & Media, and Telegraph Media Group) dominate nearly four-fifths of the market.[14]

Sky—once under the effective control of Murdoch but bought by Comcast in 2018—is the United Kingdom's most profitable commercial broadcaster, dominating the pay-TV market. Among commercial free-to-air broadcasters, ITV remains a major player, with Channel 5 now in the hands of Viacom, the U.S. communications giant. Channel 4 remains an important public-service broadcaster, funded through profit-making operations. Two companies hold nearly 40 percent of commercial analogue radio licenses and control two-thirds of all of the United Kingdom's digital stations.

The BBC—state funded but not state controlled—remains the United Kingdom's largest broadcaster, although some feel its independence is under increasing threat.[15] Recent governments have tried to limit its power by cutting the near-obligatory license fee by which the British public funds its Broadcasting Corporation. In the last round of license-fee negotiations, George Osborne—then still running the nation's finances—gave Murdoch details of the agreed funding curbs before he told the BBC's own bosses about them.

In this context, the Media Reform Coalition asked, "What does it mean to have a 'free' media when the nation's TV channels, news outlets, radio stations, search engines and social media platforms are owned by a handful of giant corporations? What does it mean to have 'independent media' when many of our most influential media organisations are controlled by individuals and Boards that are so closely connected with vested interests?"[16]

"IT'S *THE SUN* WOT WON IT"?

In April 1992, a headline in the Murdoch-owned tabloid declared, "It's *The Sun* wot won it." It followed the unexpected Conservative victory in that year's general election, although Murdoch himself has always dismissed the boast as more fun than fact. But how far was the narrow outcome of the Brexit referendum in 2016 influenced by Murdoch titles and the unambiguously anti-EU rhetoric of Rothermere's *Daily Mail*?

The latter, along with the less widely read *Daily Express*, has waged a twenty-year campaign vilifying and "othering" immigrants, popularizing phrases such as "bogus asylum seekers," and demanding an end to EU "red tape" and "rule by Brussels." Many have since asked if a more diverse, plural U.K. media market would have created the conditions for a different referendum result.

Of course, media capture is nothing new. The early part of the twentieth century is often described as the era of press "barons," when Lord Beaverbrook owned the *Daily Express* and the first Viscount Rothermere owned the *Daily Mail*, both high-circulation newspapers. These men were as much interested in directing the policy of governments as they were in improving their profits—and neither objective obstructed the other.

Stanley Baldwin, Conservative prime minister three times between 1923 and 1937, was regularly at boiling point over Beaverbrook and Rothermere's efforts to dictate policy. He called newspapers "engines of propaganda" and believed their two lordships were interested only in "power without responsibility—the prerogative of the harlot throughout the ages."[17]

That newspapers were a tool of power and political influence, a source of wealth for owners, and also a source of information for those who bought them was never in question. Along with newspaper sales, advertising revenue helped give press barons in Britain and elsewhere more than enough authority to challenge political leaders. The journalists they employed were certainly powerful, too, and readers did not expect them to simply trot out the government line. But their power was nevertheless conditional.

Self-censorship and knowing one's place cannot have been far from the minds of reporters and editors whose overlord happened to be a Beaverbrook or a Rothermere. Fleet Street, the traditional home of British journalism, became, as the historian Piers Brendon has pointed out, a "Yes Man's Land," a place where "sickening scenes of subserviency" were often observed.[18]

Murdoch bought the *Sun* in 1969 and the *Times* in 1981. Often regarded as the man who both saved and destroyed Fleet Street, Murdoch may have been lauded as a revolutionary, but there is nothing new in a newspaper owner influencing governments or advancing his own power and wealth. He is merely part of a British tradition going back through Beaverbrook and Rothermere and defined by concentrated power and ownership—which remains so today.

EDITORIAL INDEPENDENCE, GOING CHEAP

As newspaper profits have been hit by the onset of digital media, the cost of buying influence—or "capture'—in the U.K. media has dropped. Uber and Google are believed to have committed only £500,000 each over two years to the controversial *Evening Standard* scheme—chump change for these multinational giants, both with much to gain from influencing the public conversation.

"Enders Analysis" predicted that U.K. print advertising turnover would fall from £1.5 billion ($1.9 billion) in 2011 to £533 million ($689 million) by 2019. The growth in digital media does not come even close to compensating for this fall: online revenue going to U.K. publishers (not to Google and Facebook) stood at £117 million ($151 million) in 2011 and is forecast to grow to only £227 million ($293 million) in the next two years.[19]

Alongside the concentration of ownership, there is a similar concentration of valued brands whose ongoing advertising contracts—traditional, branded, and covertly deployed—provide badly needed revenues to the beleaguered news-publishing industry. And as advertising revenues plummet, the power of the brands that are still willing to be "in the game" (and are therefore badly needed) looks only set to grow.

In the PowerPoint presentation drawn up by ESI Media to attract partners to London 2020, there was a wide range of promises, including exclusive research, bespoke social media, public debates, badged "wraparounds," and special eight-page sections for each division of London 2020. The relationship being created here—aside from the controversial assurance of "money-can't-buy" news and comment—goes beyond the normal one of advertiser and publisher to an unquestioning subservience where a newspaper in a tough, deteriorating market simply cannot afford to lose such clients.

Data from Nielsen Research show the scale of the problem. In 2015, the total advertising spend on U.K. publishers from the top two hundred ad buyers was £677 million. By 2017, it was down to £511 million. Over the three years from 2015 to 2018, ad incomes fell by more than a fifth at the *Daily Express, Financial Times, Daily Star, Daily Mirror, Sunday People, Sun, Daily Telegraph*, and *Times*, with even higher losses, more than 30 percent, for the *Sunday Telegraph, Sunday Express, Guardian, Sunday Mirror*, and *Observer*, which is published by Guardian News & Media.[20]

Yet large advertisers continue to use print. The remaining big spenders include discount supermarkets, internet media, key retailers, car manufacturers, banks, and—increasing their percentage reach—gambling companies, whose influence remains substantial despite their omnipresence in expensive ad slots connected to televised sporting events.

Jonathan Hardy, a media academic at the University of East London, has suggested that newspapers' ongoing failure to raise enough revenue directly from consumers has meant an even greater reliance on key advertisers such as those listed earlier, giving those advertisers even greater power.[21] And with the separation principle—the divide between advertising and editorial content—disintegrating, this increasing reliance is changing the shape of the industry.

With traditional advertising sometimes dismissed as no longer efficient or attractive enough and prone, in the industry jargon, to "evasion" by consumers, sponsored content and native advertising grew to £509 million in the United Kingdom in 2014—giving it a 22 percent share of all display-ad spending. And its share is continuing to rise. Total spending on native advertising in Europe is expected to rise from €5.2 billion in 2015 to €13.2 billion by 2020.[22]

This forecast is in line with an international survey carried out in 2017 by the International Center for Journalists (ICFJ), working with Georgetown University. The ICFJ survey was conducted across 130 countries and showed that although most news organizations still depend on advertising (70 percent), revenue from sponsored content comes second (44 percent)—ahead of subscriptions, content sales, philanthropic contributions, state funding, and crowdsourcing.[23]

Hardy suggests that the rise of native advertising reflects not only new opportunities but also shifts in governing values across established media. Although he avoids asking directly if well-integrated shape-shifting content is a form of media capture, he nevertheless asks: "Is sponsored content an acceptable trade-off in order to finance high-cost newsgathering and reporting?" Answering his own question, he suggests that sponsored content favors "resource-rich commercial sources, friendly coverage, best-selling stories and soft news."[24]

This recipe and ingredients list aptly sum up a large part of the output of the new "dream factories" now producing tailored sponsored material in dedicated departments at the *Guardian*, the *Times*, the *Daily Telegraph*, and, of course, Osborne's *Evening Standard*.

So is friendly, best-selling, soft news, all lightly branded, a worrying form of capture in the United Kingdom? Although the Advertising Standards Authority has been "active," there is "a low adherence to rules and a strong incentive to evade them."[25]

Hardy's Branded Content Research Network aims to encourage dialogue between academia and the ad industry. He says that in the United Kingdom there remains a lack of agreement about consistent signposting of sponsored content for consumers. If allowed to continue, this lack of agreement risks media capture both by default and by a lack of regulatory or industry or political momentum. Moreover, research shows that an alarmingly large proportion of readers often do not recognize branded content as such even when it is labeled.[26]

EDITORIAL INDEPENDENCE?

Guardian Labs, which runs content funding for Guardian News & Media, has one of the clearest sets of guidelines in the industry about how content has been commissioned and produced and who has funded it. Guardian Labs says *one of three labels* will appear on its paid-for content: "supported by" or "paid content/paid for by" or "advertiser content/from our advertisers."

However, a former commissioning editor at the *Guardian* told *openDemocracy* that "supported by" is a "gray area for many writers." The *Guardian* maintains that "supported by" content is still "editorially independent content" because the editor in chief has the final say over whether a funding deal is accepted and that the commissioning editor is not obliged to accept ideas from the funder. Guardian News & Media says it does not show copy to funders for approval.

"Supported by" is also used to mark content that has been produced with funding from a larger global foundation. Guardian News & Media has received money from the Bill and Melinda Gates Foundation (for its Global Development site), from the Rockefeller Foundation (for its Cities Project), and from the Skoll Foundation (for climate and environment reporting).

"This is a sensitive area for many contributors and staff writers," one former section head told *openDemocracy*, "and it can lead to self-censorship because the question of critical funding for the paper is always hovering in the background. So you ask: 'Do I really want to piss off a major funder?'"[27]

OpenDemocracy is no stranger to this dilemma. Funded by a combination of philanthropy, voluntary reader contributions, and editorial partnerships, we strive to maintain our independence through a decentralized fund-raising model and the maintenance of a range of income sources, all of which are made public. There have been only a few occasions since its foundation in 2001 when *openDemocracy* has lost funding due to "pissing off" a funder, either deliberately or unintentionally. But it is definitely true that the decision to publish weighs far more heavily in these rare cases and that the material involved is intensely scrutinized. This dilemma is a reflection of the financial precarity felt across the industry.

WHAT ARE THE ALTERNATIVES?

Digital disruption has had other effects on the media landscape. The past fifteen years has seen the emergence of a range of journalism startups in the United Kingdom. Well-established new media players such as *Vice*, *Buzzfeed*, and the *Huffington Post* have U.K. divisions, and—much like the online divisions of newspapers—are funded predominantly by advertising, augmented by advertorial and other curated content, leading to similar capture issues.

Meanwhile, alternative approaches to sustainable journalism startups have also grown, particularly among outfits dedicated to investigative and public-interest journalism. Most operate on a mixed funding model, with income coming from grants, subscribers, sales, events, syndication, and other revenue streams. In conjunction with the global rise of "stakeholder media," many seek a more democratic form of media ownership and a more active response to media capture. The Slovakian newspaper *Dennik N*, for example, was established in 2015 after forty-five journalists at one of the most widely read broadsheets, *Dennik SME*, left in protest at a local oligarch's takeover of the latter newspaper. Half of the business at *Dennik N*—which has grown into a significant player in the Slovak media—is owned by the reporters.

In the United Kingdom, such initiatives are rarer, and those that exist are generally in a less-advanced state of development. The fact that legacy media remain dominant—despite declining revenue—perhaps reflects a long-standing British suspicion of alternative media models. The prevailing notion of the British "free press" has often produced unease around models of media ownership that explicitly empower stakeholder groups. Conversely, until recently there has been far less unease about the outsized share of the U.K. media market enjoyed by a small number of owners and the attendant issues of media capture. However, this is beginning to change.

Although the United Kingdom has yet to see an alternative outlet of the size and heft of the French online investigative journal *Mediapart*, new media startups operating on radically different funding models have appeared and are growing in reach and influence. One of the coauthors of this chapter, Peter Geoghegan, was part of the small team that launched the *Ferret* as a digital investigative platform in Scotland in the summer of 2015. The *Ferret* is a cooperative: every subscriber automatically becomes a member, with an equal stake in the business. Both readers and journalist members are represented on the company's board and as such have a direct say in the organization's focus and direction. The *Ferret*—which emerged in direct response to the retrenchment of local media in Scotland—is funded by a variety of sources, including subscriptions, crowdfunding, grants, training, and events. As of March 2019, the *Ferret* had more than thirteen hundred subscribers paying between £3 a month and £100 a year for full content access, thus funding journalism that appears online only, often gets national media pickup, and has won a number of awards.[28]

The *Ferret* is not unique in the United Kingdom. The *Bristol Cable*, which emerged around the same time, describes itself as a "pioneering media cooperative" and has two thousand members. It publishes online and also produces a free quarterly print magazine. Like the *Ferret*, the *Bristol Cable* publishes transparency reports that detail all incomings and outgoings.

Although these cooperatives rely on subscriptions to get both members and funding for journalism, they also increasingly have attracted donor grants. The *Ferret*, for example, has received grant funding from Google's Digital News Initiative, Luminate (formerly the Omidyar Network), and other entities. Other important and impactful journalism projects such as the Bureau of Investigative Journalism, which among other things has devised the brilliant Bureau Local initiative to address problem of local news "deserts," are more heavily reliant on philanthropy to support their work, reflecting a slow but growing awareness among U.K. and European donors that journalism is a "public good" that requires support.

But this growth in philanthropic funding also raises the possibility of alternative media outlets also being "captured" by donors rather than by advertisers. There is also a less-recognized issue that new, subscriber-funded journalism projects often grapple with: readers and members are liable to withdraw their financial backing when news outlets publish stories that they disagree with—for example, articles that are critical of politicians or political parties that the readers/members support, no matter how well sourced those articles are. This withdrawal of membership support can lead to self-censorship among journalists in small outlets that are reliant on subscriptions.

Stakeholder media and the alternative funding models that often underpin them have been identified as a possible solution to the crisis of paying for journalism.[29] In the United Kingdom, the Media Fund is an embryonic cooperative specifically designed to support alternative media outlets and to allow the public to donate to a broad sweep of news organizations. Many of the outlets listed in this section are members of the Media Fund, and there is generally more skill sharing and collaboration among organizations in this sector. But there are clear challenges, too. Stakeholder media risk furthering the development of "echo chambers," with like-minded readers seeking out and supporting like-minded media outlets. There are also important questions about just how scalable these new models can be. The *Ferret*, for example, has achieved slow and steady growth but was for a long time heavily dependent on a largely unpaid core team of journalists and a relatively small active community. Turning a largely passive online readership into an active community requires intensive engagement, particularly through events that can be time-consuming and often require journalists to take time away from actual journalism.

As in the United States, in the United Kingdom there are a growing number of "reporting deserts." Even the BBC has recognized this problem, hiring hundreds of local democracy reporters to work for regional and local newspapers paid for by the license fee. This step, however, has done little to build sustainable local media in the United Kingdom. At the same time, the prospects of replacing outlets that employ thousands—even tens of thousands—of journalists with small-scale startups is still remote. Many such startups have significant gaps in both professional skills and industry experience. In addition, daily news coverage costs a great deal of money, so it is not surprising that all of the outlets reviewed here do little, if any, of it. Instead, they focus on niche issues or communities or both.

Alternative funding models and stakeholder media are not a panacea and come with their own risks of capture, but they do offer the possibility of high-quality investigative journalism that can feed into the wider news ecosystem, especially about issues of public interest, at a time when budgets for such journalism at larger commercial outfits are being dramatically cut or disappearing altogether. More investment in these models is urgently needed so that they can produce more public-interest journalism, challenge the hegemony of the large players, and experiment with new models of sustainability.

SHOW US THE MONEY

So how "captured" is Britain's "feral press" now, and how much more captured might it be tomorrow? There are some reasons not to fear the worst. Our investigation into the *Evening Standard*'s London 2020 campaign found that some companies did reject the offer of paid-for positive news and comment. A Starbucks U.K. executive called the project "PR death," suggesting that perhaps a sensitivity exists, even in big companies, to the idea that Britain's media are there to be "captured" or at least that there's some doubt that media capture is an effective promotional strategy.

It is also encouraging that the *Guardian* did not bow to HSBC's pressure when it was preparing to publish the Swissleaks reporting. But the fact that a giant bank such as HSBC was successful in muting criticism of its

operation in the pages of the *Daily Telegraph* and tried to use its commercial muscle to do so in the *Guardian* as well (a charge HSBC denies) is a
matter of serious concern. For obvious reasons, it is very rare that journalists are willing to blow the whistle on their employers or for executives
in turn to blow it on valuable commercial relationships. So confidential
surveys such as the one we did at *openDemocracy* offer limited insight. It is
impossible to assess the scale of the problem.

This chapter has attempted to broadly outline the most dominant forms
of commercial capture of the media in the United Kingdom, which is linked
primarily to ownership concentration, intense financial pressures on publishers, and the evolving nature of advertising and sponsorship relationships. And the obvious connecting thread here is money, or lack of it.
Guardian News & Media, for example, has the backing of a long-standing
endowment, the Scott Trust, which has long offered a cushion unavailable
to most of the *Guardian's* competitors.

Whereas publishers' advertising revenues have nosedived, platforms such
as Google and Facebook (neither of them domiciled in the United Kingdom
for tax purposes) continue to be extremely profitable. Google is increasingly
part of the capture problem, not only through its controversial partnership
with the *Evening Standard* but also through its Digital News Initiative,
which funds numerous established and alternative media outlets. Martin
Moore has written persuasively about the complexity of the problems posed
by Facebook, Google, and other large platforms and how the traditional
solutions open to governments—legislation, regulation, and taxation—will
not be sufficient.[30]

Nevertheless, a more active engagement by government and regulators
would make a difference. A tax on the social media and advertising giants
that call themselves platforms rather than publishers, used to subsidize the
production of high-quality, truly independent, public-interest journalism,
would be a good start. Given growing public awareness of the power of Facebook in particular and its consequences for democracy, there is certainly a
political opportunity for this taxation.

In a landmark article, James Deane, the director of policy and research
at the BBC's media-development arm, argues that "the fight to support independent media is being lost" due to the slow response of donors both to
"the problem of money" and to the threats of "shrinking civic space." He

argues for a new global fund, with resources that "very substantially exceed" existing allocations to media assistance. There are now efforts, spearheaded by Luminate and other partners, to try and build such a fund.[31]

Philanthropy in the United Kingdom is alive and well, with large donors giving £1.83 billion in 2016 to causes as diverse as scientific research and donkey sanctuaries. But only a tiny fraction of these donations currently goes to supporting media. Progressive European institutional donors, shocked by the rapid growth of authoritarian populism across the continent, which is often bolstered by nakedly racist or xenophobic political movements, are beginning to wake up to the importance of independent media as a vital pillar of civil society and to the reality that there is currently no business model that sustains it. New pooled funds have been set up to tackle disinformation, "fake news," and xenophobic propaganda. However, progress has been slow; this slowness is an inbuilt feature of institutional philanthropy but is ill afforded at this critical moment.

Of course, philanthropy is not the only answer—and comes with its own set of problems. There is still a question over which donors will be willing to support independent media without seeking to influence what topics are covered or how and which will seek a more active role in shaping editorial strategy, thus risking another form of capture. The American Press Institute's work looking at the ethical issues raised by growing reliance on philanthropic funding sources for journalism—including concerns around editorial independence and self-censorship of stories that might relate to donors or potential donors—could prove instructive for U.K. media outlets, where the culture of receiving donations is far less developed than it is in the United States.

The inconvenient truth remains that until a broader base of public appetite for "uncaptured" news exists, the proposition for voluntary reader or member-supported models still looks precarious. The growth in public interest in and support for the alternative media models described in this chapter is encouraging, but the news sector needs a game-changing level of investment to fully explore its potential. That is likely to mean more than donors and investors supporting individual outlets, particularly in outlets' experiments in sustainability. It's likely to mean removing some of the key barriers to entry and scale that currently exist: for example, providing secure, open-source tech that independent media outlets can share; equipping media outlets that fulfill certain "independence" and "public-interest" criteria with back-office, operational, legal, and security expertise; providing them also with business-development expertise that reduces rather than adds to the workload of smaller outlets that have a proven track record in public-interest journalism and are seeking to grow their operations and achieve sustainability.

In February 2019, the U.K. government published a report on how to protect high-quality journalism. The *Cairncross Review* recommended that public funds should be used to save local journalism and called for a public investigation into the dominance of Facebook and Google in the advertising marketplace.[32] There were encouraging aspects to the report, but successive U.K. governments, particularly now that they are riven with divisions over Brexit, have demonstrated little appetite for bold and creative solutions to the myriad democratic challenges the country faces.

Brexit itself has been a reflection of how badly we need media plurality and more resources committed to public-interest reporting and investigations. The deeply troubling story of how the pro-Brexit campaign was funded—and by whom—was for a long time largely ignored by most established media outlets, with the exception of Carole Cadwalladr in the *Observer,* our colleagues at *openDemocracy,* and a small network of freelance and citizen journalists. As a result of this work, in 2018—two years after the Brexit vote—the architects of the Leave campaign were finally hit with record fines, but this response was two years too late. Britain urgently needs a stronger, more independent Fourth Estate to hold both corporate and political power to account. And as the Brexit experience shows, the consequences of inaction can reach far beyond the shores of the United Kingdom.

NOTES

1. Cusick (2018).
2. In cases where we do not provide source citations for quotations or other specific information, they come from confidential sources and were relayed directly to us.
3. Court of Justice of the European Union (2014).
4. European Commission (2018).
5. Dickhut (2018).
6. Cusick and Boros (2018a).
7. Fitzgerald and Bychawski (2018).
8. Davies (2008).
9. Oborne (2015).

10. Castillo (2015).
11. Ponsford and Turvill (2015).
12. Ramsay (2015).
13. Fitzgerald (2017).
14. Media Reform Coalition (2019).
15. Cohen (2018).
16. Media Reform Coalition (2019).
17. Perkins (2006).
18. Brendon (2007).
19. *Business Insider* (2017).
20. Nielsen Research.
21. Hardy (2017a).
22. *Business Insider* (2017).
23. International Center for Journalism (2017).
24. Hardy (2017a).
25. Hardy (2017b).
26. Amazeen and Muddiman (2018).
27. Cusick and Boros (2018b).
28. See also Geoghegan (2017).
29. Hunter and Van Wassenhove (2010).
30. Moore (2016), (2018).
31. Deane (2018).
32. Cairncross (2019).

REFERENCES

Amazeen, Michelle A., and Ashley R. Muddiman. 2018. "Saving Media or Trading on Trust?" *Digital Journalism* 6 (2): 176–95. https://doi.10.1080/21670811.2017.1293488.
Brendon, Piers. 2007. *The Decline and Fall of the British Empire, 1781–1997*. London: Jonathan Cape.
Business Insider. 2017. "Enders Analysis." February 16. http://uk.businessinsider.com /enders-analyis-graph-slow-death-british-newspapers-2017-2?r=US&IR=T.
Cairncross, Frances. 2019. *The Cairncross Review: A Sustainable Future for Journalism*. London: Assets. https://assets.publishing.service.gov.uk/government/uploads /system/uploads/attachment_data/file/779882/021919_DCMS_Cairncross _Review_.pdf.
Castillo, Michelle. 2015. "After Removing Article Critical of Dove, *BuzzFeed* Says It Wants to Avoid Publishing 'Hot Takes.' " *Buzzfeed*, April 10. https://www.adweek .com/digital/after-removing-article-critical-dove-buzzfeed-says-it-wants-avoid -publishing-hot-takes-164001/.
Cohen, Nik. 2018. "How the BBC Lost the Plot on Brexit." *New York Review of Books Daily*, July 12. https://www.nybooks.com/daily/2018/07/12/how-the-bbc-lost-the-plot -on-brexit/.
Court of Justice of the European Union. 2014. Judgment in Case C-131/12: *Google Spain SL, Google Inc. v Agencia Española de Protección de Datos (AEPD), Mario Costeja*

González. http://curia.europa.eu/juris/document/document_print.jsf?doclang=EN
&docid=152065.

Cusick, James. 2018. "George Osborne's *London Evening Standard* Sells Its Editorial
Independence to Uber, Google, and Others—for £3 Million." *openDemocracy,*
May 30. https://www.opendemocracy.net/uk/james-cusick/george-osborne-s
-london-evening-standard-promises-positive-news-coverage-to-uber-goo.

Cusick, James, and Crina Boros. 2018a. "How a GM Giant Bought Control of What Millions of Londoners Read." *openDemocracy,* February 8. https://www.opendemoc
racy.net/james-cusick-crina-boros/how-gm-giant-bought-control-of-what-mill
ions-of-londoners-read.

——. 2018b. "The Secrets of 'Black Ops' Advertising. Who Is Paying for Our News?"
openDemocracy, February 8. https://www.opendemocracy.net/james-cusick-crina
-boros/blurred-lines-and-black-ops-disappearing-divide-between-uk-news-and
-adverti.

Davies, Nick. 2008. *Flat Earth News: An Award-Winning Reporter Exposes Falsehood,
Distortion, and Propaganda in the Global Media.* London: Chatto and Windus.

Deane, James. 2018. "Is It Time for a Global Fund for Free and Independent Media?"
BBC Media Action Insight Blog, July 3. http://www.bbc.co.uk/blogs/mediaaction
insight/entries/1d207ec1-0502-4329-b458-87bc1c111c40.

Dickhut, Sarah M. 2018. "The Future of GMOs in the UK Post-Brexit." *Filewrapper,* February 15. https://www.ipmvs.com/filewrapper/the-future-of-gmos-in-the-uk-post
-brexit.

European Commission. 2018. "Antitrust: Commission Fines Google €4.34 Billion for
Illegal Practices Regarding Android Mobile Devices to Strengthen Dominance of
Google's Search Engine." Press release, July 18. http://europa.eu/rapid/press-release
_IP-18-4581_en.htm.

Fitzgerald, Mary. 2017. "Why We're Launching openMedia." *openDemocracy,*
November 29. https://opendemocracy.net/openmedia/mary-fitzgerald/welcome
-to-openmedia.

Fitzgerald, Mary, and Adam Bychawski. 2018. "George Osborne's *Evening Standard*
Launches Delayed 'Money-Can't-Buy' Campaign—with More Controversial Partners." *openDemocracy,* July 12. https://www.opendemocracy.net/uk/mary-fitzgerald
-adam-bychawski/george-osborne-s-evening-standard-launches-delayed-money
-can-t-buy.

Geoghegan, Peter. 2017. "Data Journalism in a Cold Climate: The Case of the *Ferret.*"
In *Data Journalism: Past, Present, and Future,* ed. John Mair, Richard Lance Keeble,
Megan Lucero, and Martin Moore, 81–88. Bury St. Edmonds, U.K.: Abramis.

Hardy, Jonathan. 2017a. "Resourcing a Viable Digital Journalism." In *Routledge Companion to Digital Journalism Studies,* ed. Bob Franklin and Scott A. Eldridge II,
155–165. London: Routledge.

——. 2017b. "Sponsored Content Is Compromising Media Integrity." *openDemocracy,*
April 12. https://www.opendemocracy.net/jonathan-hardy/sponsored-content-is
-blurring-line-between-advertising-and-editorial.

Hunter, Mark Lee, and Luk N. Van Wassenhove. 2010. *Disruptive News Technologies:
Stakeholder Media and the Future of Watchdog Journalism Business Models.* Fon-
tainebleau, France: INSEAD Business School.

International Center for Journalism (ICFJ). 2017. *Report: The State of Technology in Global Newsrooms*. Washington, DC: ICFJ. https://www.icfj.org/sites/default/files /2018-04/ICFJTechSurveyFINAL.pdf.

Media Reform Coalition. 2019. *Who Owns the UK Media?* London: Media Reform Coalition. http://www.mediareform.org.uk/who-owns-the-uk-media.

Moore, Martin. 2016. "Tech Giants and Civic Power." Centre for the Study of Media, Communication, and Power, King's College London.

———. 2018. *Democracy Hacked: Political Turmoil and Information Warfare in the Digital Age*. London: One World.

Oborne, Peter. 2015. "Why I Have Resigned from the *Telegraph*." *openDemocracy*, February 17. https://opendemocracy.net/ourkingdom/peter-oborne/why-i-have -resigned-from-telegraph.

Perkins, Anne. 2006. *Baldwin*. Volume 7 in *The British Prime Ministers of the 20th Century*. London: Haus.

Ponsford, Dominic, and William Turvill. 2015. "HSBC—the Bank 'You Cannot Afford to Offend'—Stops Advertising with *The Guardian*." *Press Gazette*, February 18. https://www.pressgazette.co.uk/hsbc-advertiser-you-cannot-afford-offend-stops -advertising-guardian.

Ramsay, Gordon. 2015. "Was Peter Oborne Right about the *Telegraph*'s Coverage of the HSBC Scandal?" *Policy Wonkers*, February 18. https://blogs.kcl.ac.uk/policywonkers /was-peter-oborne-right-about-the-telegraphs-coverage-of-the-hsbc-scandal/.

PART III

Solutions

Chapter Twelve

A GLOBAL STRATEGY FOR COMBATING MEDIA CAPTURE

MARK M. NELSON

Plagued by a failing business model and a regulatory environment that has been outpaced by technological change, independent media around the world are struggling to survive. The media's weak economic position has made the news and information business vulnerable to takeover and control from predatory business tycoons and politicians, who conspire with each other to manipulate public opinion. This type of privately owned, regime-collusive media is becoming the dominant model in a growing number of countries around the globe.

Media capture presents one of the biggest and most complex challenges facing the global community. Capture inhibits the media from their Fourth Estate functions of providing increased accountability, government monitoring, and feedback from citizens. Instead of producing a vital public good—high-quality, relevant, and verifiable news and information—captured media produce propaganda, distractions, and scandal that serve the interests and ambitions of a select group of powerful elites. Such media are feeding a global wave of authoritarianism and democratic backsliding.

Economic and political incentives for media capture are enormous, and competition to capture the media—long focused on television, radio, and print—has now turned with equal vigor to the internet. Influence-driven investors seem as determined to control internet service providers as they are to control the news, indicating that they see enormous potential in tracking people's online behaviors or shutting down the internet.

Examples abound of how the internet is becoming an instrument of capture. In South Africa, the wealthy Gupta family used digital platforms to flood the information space with propaganda in favor of former president Jacob Zuma, with whom the family was closely tied in corrupt dealings.[1] In Bulgaria, the dramatic rise of antidemocratic messages in local media from 2013 to 2016 originated largely from Bulgarian news sites and other digital media owned by local pro-Russian businesspeople.[2] China's giant telecommunications companies and data-driven multinationals are not just capturing media and shaping global discourse but also "seeking to build out the infrastructure of the evolving global information ecosystem itself, targeting not simply media-related products but the mechanisms that determine what kinds of products are produced in the first place."[3]

The internet, which has been described as a complex domain of "competing forces and constraints,"[4] is becoming the key battleground for the major forces shaping our global future. According to Sarah Oh, "These forces are comprised of [sic] powerful businesses, states, politicians, criminal enterprises, advocacy groups . . . [and] compete in part on the shifting ground of the technological and physical infrastructure of the internet, where some players wield more power than others with an ability to mold the terrain in their favor. Authoritarian states aware of what is at stake in the evolution of the internet are beginning to engage in long-term and well-resourced efforts to undermine the democratic rights of citizens."[5] Even more worrying, as audiences move from traditional media to internet-based media, media capture is no longer a purely national problem. By allowing nondemocratic forces and corporate giants to operate globally, largely unregulated digital media platforms are posing new challenges to social cohesion, democratic governance, and global security.[6]

Authoritarian leaders—from Vladimir Putin in Russia to Tayyip Erdoğan in Turkey, Viktor Orbán in Hungary, Rodrigo Duterte in the Philippines, and Donald Trump in the United States—focus obsessively on controlling the media, both digital and traditional. The empirical evidence suggests that the obsession is well founded and that the benefits are quantifiable: according to one well-known study of the Fujimori regime in Peru, the cost of bribing the media was ten times larger than bribing judges or legislators.[7] Once embedded in an unhealthy political system, the collusive behavior between politicians and media is, not surprisingly, notoriously difficult to eliminate. A growing body of data and analysis suggests that capture of the media is associated with a host of other economic and political problems: bolstering income inequality, undermining international trade and political cooperation, and increasing global conflict. At the country level, with the help of a subservient media, a relatively small group is able to manipulate not only budgets and spending but also regulations, taxes, trade, and natural-resource extraction.[8]

Although attempts to influence the media are nothing new, previous models of authoritarian control of the media have relied mostly on censorship, government manipulation of advertising markets, and other repressive tactics. In many captured environments today, governments can often rely on a large part of privately owned media to willingly do the governments' bidding. And for such media owners, it matters little to them if they make a profit in the media business because the profits are realized in other industries that receive highly valuable tax, regulatory, and tariff concessions from the government. Growing evidence suggests that regimes such as China, Russia, Turkey, and Hungary are actively engaged in redistribution of economic benefits to buy support from and to manipulate both public and private institutions, including the media. Making sure that the media are in friendly hands does away with the need for a massive censorship bureaucracy and can even create the impression of press freedom, pluralism, and independence.[9]

The purpose of this chapter is to review briefly the characteristics of media capture and consider some of the possible pathways to abating it. This chapter shows that although media capture in the global South is today mainly a phenomenon of traditional media, the explosive growth of the internet and social media platforms is rapidly changing the nature of the problem. It argues that governments have a role and responsibility to enact policies to prevent media capture. At the same time, the most important forces in pushing governments toward democratic media systems are civil society organizations and coalitions, both at the country as well as at the regional and global levels. Finally, the chapter proposes a strategy for combating media capture with global, regional, and country-level elements.

The extent of media capture across the world is poorly understood, mainly because of a lack of global data and transparency on media ownership. A growing number of studies suggest that capture is widespread and becoming a dominant model of media ownership, particularly in developing and emerging-market countries:

- One of the most revealing data sets showing the deeply embedded nature of media capture is an eleven-country survey carried out by the Organized Crime and Corruption Reporting Project. That survey uses investigative journalistic methods to trace the ownership of all the major media companies and internet service providers in the eleven countries. The news media survey, consisting of 530 enterprises, showed that 41 percent of the companies in those countries are operating with a nontransparent ownership structure, 27 percent are owned by political operators, and 10 percent are owned by people with links to organized crime. The ownership of internet service providers is allocated in an almost identical pattern.[10]

- Similarly, the Media Ownership Monitor—which measures ten dimensions of media-ownership pluralism, competition, regulatory quality, and funding transparency—had as of late 2019 carried out in-depth studies of twenty-one countries across the world. It shows that an overwhelming majority of the countries studied are in the problematic red or yellow zones of the traffic light assessment system, with serious challenges to the structure of ownership and competition in the media sector, to governments' regulatory capacity and policies, and, as a result, to the production of unbiased news and information.[11]

- Another set of indicators of the extent of media capture emerge from the Media Pluralism Monitor, which tracks five broad dimensions of media pluralism in thirty European countries (the European Union plus Turkey and Montenegro). The 2017 study shows only three countries with "low" levels of overall risk. The market-plurality indicators, one of the key subcategories of the monitor, articulate a set of media-market features that help define media capture, looking at the transparency of ownership, media-ownership concentration, the structure of competition within the media market, and commercial and owner influence over editorial content. A separate group of indicators of political independence, equally important to defining media capture, also shows most countries in the yellow and red zones. In both measures, the highest risks appear in the eastern and southeastern zones of Europe, where authoritarianism has been on the rise.[12]

- At the global level, the V-Dem Institute report for 2019 demonstrated that media indicators—measuring elements such as media autonomy, freedom of expression, availability of alternative sources of information, and the rule of law—have undergone conspicuous declines compared to other democracy metrics over the past decade. In figure 12.1, the areas that saw the most significant declines are shown in the southeast sector of the graph (i.e., below the diagonal line), and, of those, the ones depicted in bold black typeface are the media indicators in decline. "Recent research has provided strong evidence that voters make poor choices if they lack accurate and independent information. Thus, manipulation of the media reduces the effectiveness of elections and limits citizens in the exercise of their fundamental rights."[13]

None of the indicators detailed in the previous bulleted material is a perfect proxy for media capture, especially when defined as a system of private media ownership that colludes with political leaders. To understand that type of collusion—which distinguishes media capture from old-style government or corporate censorship or media bias—we would need a deeper understanding of the motives of both media owners and political leaders and the nature of their collusion. Yet even without that deeper knowledge, these indicators point out clear weaknesses in the competitive environment for media, unhealthy patterns of ownership and political behavior, and undesirable outcomes for democratic media systems. They are thus a useful guide for shaping media polices aimed at deterring capture.

POLICY PARALYSIS

Whereas authoritarians have a clear understanding of the value of captured media to their aims, their democratic opponents are much less organized or confident of their media policies and approaches. Media capture is thriving in this atmosphere of policy paralysis. No countries are immune to the scourge of media capture, but emerging democracies and developing countries in particular face daunting obstacles to formulating an effective strategy against it. Few governments—even those willing to address the problem—have the policy expertise or political resolve to implement appropriate countervailing measures. Most concerning of all is that the same forces that have captured the media are usually in control of the *policy process*, keeping any prospects for change caught in a maze of uncertainty and inertia.

Part of the problem is a loss of faith in media regulation. Many defenders of media freedom have argued that *all* government interventions in the media sector are harmful. They have rightly pointed out that few

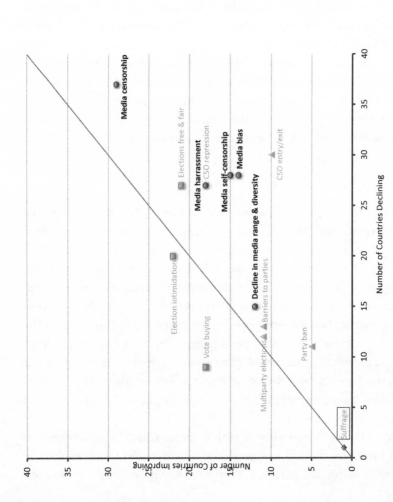

Number of countries with substantial and significant changes in democracy indicators 2008-2018
(V-Dem, 2019)

- ▲ Freedom of Association
- ■ Clean Election Index
- ● **Freedom of Expression & Alternative Sources of Information**
- ◆ Core Elections Indicators

FIGURE 12.1. Decline in media sector indicators suggests backsliding in other measures of democracy.
Source: Lührmann et al. 2019.

governments have the capacity to implement the complex array of polices that both defend freedom of expression but also maintain open, healthy competition in the media markets. Much of the regulation that has been put in place—social media taxes in Uganda, blogger taxes in Tanzania, blocks on sites with more than five thousand followers in Egypt—are meant to stifle speech and were put in place against strong public opposition. And the attempts to transform state-controlled public broadcasters into independent public-service media have rarely created truly independent voices that produce high-quality journalism.[14]

Yet for most of the modern era democratic societies have understood the need for government interventions in the news media environment to ensure that it produces positive outcomes for society. In a background paper for a meeting in 2012 on the role of the social media platforms in the U.S. news media, the Open Markets Institute reviewed the history of regulation of media markets going back to the U.S. Constitution and the founding of the American republic. The review shows not only that there are "ceaseless private initiative and innovation" in the news business but also that "even before the Declaration of Independence, Americans used government both to promote the building of technologically sophisticated infrastructures to distribute the news and to directly address threats to the free press posed by either private monopolists or by government actors."[15] Through a detailed history of media regulation and a timeline of laws and regulatory policies, the study shows that government regulation was the response repeatedly used to maintain a free and open media market that served public interests. These media regulations—covering both content and competition issues—stretch across American history, from the first major technological revolutions instigated by the creation of railroad and telegraph networks to the invention of radio and television and the establishment of the Federal Communications Commission in 1934. Only in relatively recent times— starting in the late 1970s and continuing with today's unprecedentedly large corporate giants who control the internet—has antitrust policy moved away from its focus on widely distributed competition and benefits to society. Today's regulatory focus is on price and efficiency, particularly geared toward large industries.[16]

It has also been in this current period, marked by rapid globalization and the spread of the internet and mobile phone technologies, that the American model of media regulation—or, perhaps more accurately, the increasing lack thereof—has had the strongest influence internationally. For countries emerging from the Soviet bloc in the 1990s, for example, the explosive increase in media freedom was not matched by a parallel increase in strong media laws and institutions. As a result, governments in the formerly communist parts of Europe did too little to develop independent media regulatory systems, to put public-service media on stable footing, or to manage the private monopolies and merchants of social conflict that were to emerge.[17]

The current environment has also paralyzed policy makers in the United States and the European Union, who for many decades led the world in maintaining open democratic systems and competitive media markets. Unsure how to manage the collapse of the business model for independent news, the growing concentration of media ownership, and the rise of giant data-driven monopolies such as Google, Facebook, and Amazon, they have erred on the side of doing nothing. One author declared "the death of media regulation in the age of the internet."[18] Others, including the Federal Communications Commission, have taken a wait-and-see approach. "While it is evident that older regulatory classifications fail to reflect the dynamic and multi-faceted character of new media, it is unknown what might be adopted in their place."[19]

The European Union's failure to adopt a unified media policy among its twenty-seven members is both a reflection of policy paralysis and an indicator of the complexity of the current media environment.[20] As a result, among its members are both the world's most well-governed media systems in northwestern Europe and systems rapidly descending into full-fledged media capture in eastern and southeastern Europe.

A similar failure of regional policy characterizes a deeply fragmented Asia. Although Japan and South Korea have created well-governed media environments, they have had little influence spreading their systems regionally. More countries (such as Vietnam and Cambodia) are following China's ironhanded censorship than taking a more liberal path. A small number of Asian countries such as Indonesia and Malaysia are struggling against the tide to develop the independent institutions necessary to foster quality journalism.

Engaging in efforts to ensure that developing countries and emerging democracies build the media-governance capacities needed for the rapidly changing media environment is also not a top priority for international donors or private funders of media-development initiatives. Media-development assistance has focused for the most part on journalist training and other sector-level technocratic interventions. The more expensive, politically charged, and difficult policy reforms—that is, developing governments' technical capacity to ensure a fair and open media marketplace, ensuring transparency of ownership, breaking up media conglomerates and monopolies, and reforming state broadcasters—fall by the wayside. The numbers tell it all. Total spending by international donors for media development accounts for about $450 million annually—or just 0.3 percent of the $150 billion in annual overseas development assistance as measured by the Organization for Economic Cooperation and Development (OECD).[21]

A STRATEGY FOR IMPROVED MEDIA GOVERNANCE

So how should country actors, regional institutions, and the international community go about addressing the problem of media capture? To be sure, a global strategy will have many interlocking components. It will require strengthening not only laws and regulations at the country level but also a more complex array of institutions and social behaviors that cut across national borders. Although many of the most egregious manifestations of media capture are currently happening at the country level, a growing set of problems will require engagement and action at the regional and global levels, particularly on digital media and platforms. Because opponents of media reform are highly motivated and usually involve powerful political and economic forces, successful strategies for such reform usually require a broad political movement that convinces citizens and political allies to support major changes in policy.

The key player in this process is almost invariably civil society. In a regime where media owners and political forces are aligned to assert their power, civil society organizations can band together, develop alternative ways of informing the public, and build coalitions that have the potential to rebalance a captured political structure. Several notable examples of this type of political action have emerged, particularly in Latin America. "By bringing in critical and deliberative politics, citizen activism has been a counterpoint to power hierarchies and spearheaded important innovations in contemporary media governance."[22]

The literature on international development and governance is increasingly recognizing the key role of civil society in dealing with highly political governance failures such as media capture. The World Bank's *World Development Report* for 2017 points out that many well-known development problems, even those with obvious solutions, fail to be resolved not because of the lack of a technical solution but because they threaten the political status quo. Those who would benefit from reforms lack power, and those with power see the change process as a zero-sum game. Tackling political gridlock, overcoming entrenched interests, and stopping corruption require not only changes in the incentives of actors to pursue reform but also a shift in power or a shift in the preferences and beliefs of those with power. Open multistakeholder debates about laws and reforms can produce changes in both incentives and beliefs, and they can empower actors outside elite circles.[23]

The economists Shantayanan Deverajan and Stuti Khemani suggest that in addition to an engaged society, efforts to increase transparency among all elements in a complex system can also be critical and transformative. They argue that knowledge provided to citizens to build their capacity to choose and sanction leaders, especially when civil society organizations build broad-based movements, can be a powerful force for reform. Outside actors such as international donors can reinforce these movements by insisting on transparency in their engagements and financial arrangements with governments and by providing a platform for including all interested country-level stakeholders in the deliberations.[24]

Another key lesson from such literature is the importance of multicountry, regional approaches. Civil society organizations that operate or associate with like-minded allies across borders often benefit from knowledge gained in other countries, and multicountry alliances can help protect isolated movements in hostile countries from government crackdowns. Media-reform movements in Latin America have relied heavily on these cross-border networks, and the inter-American system for the protection of human rights has successfully created a multilayered set of laws, norms, and standards that have helped nudge laggard governments toward better policies. The evidence suggests that regional approaches deserve a higher level of support from international donors. Although not a substitute for building local media-reform movements, transnational networks "contribute to the organizational and strategic goals of local media movements by plugging them into global communities of practice, funding programs, raising their visibility and legitimacy, bolstering discursive frames, and engaging in moral persuasion with governments, media owners and others."[25]

TWO EXAMPLES

In West Africa, civil society organizations focused on media issues are working strategically not only to pressure governments but also to help government agents address problems in the media space. They advocate for media reforms nationally, but they also see regional institutions and approaches as beneficial to their cause. At a meeting in May 2018, the Media Foundation for West Africa in Accra, Ghana, brought together delegates from sixteen national partner organizations. These groups reported to the other delegates on their key country-level challenges and on their strategies for improving the media environment. This highly effective organization is leading a strategy to build a set of norms and standards at the regional level by engaging with the fifteen-country Economic Community of West African States, which has signaled its openness to developing a framework of minimum standards to strengthen independent media at the regional level.

Another example, where the focus on media capture has at times been more explicit, is the media-reform movement in Ukraine. Reform advocates there developed a series of detailed objectives for the media environment focusing on creating an independent public-broadcasting system, reforming commune- and state-owned media, and making a series of transparency reforms aimed at private media ownership, including full disclosure of sometimes hidden owners and the source of their financial resources. The six goals are elaborated by a series of more specific subobjectives to ensure that laws or specific regulations are adopted where needed.[26]

For all its valuable content, the Ukrainian approach is probably even more notable for its method: the reformers are focusing on building political will and consensus around the reform program. The reforms are promoted by a large coalition of civil society organizations—eighty-three organizations and twenty-two expert groups—who are working together to explain the reform plans to the public and legislators and to integrate the media reforms into a broader set of governance and public-policy measures. "Building wide public awareness is important," said Taras Shevchenko, founder of Ukraine's Center for Democracy and Rule of Law and a leader of the reform movement. He argues that successful reforms of media require support from activists on other issues such as access to information, transparency, and public-sector governance.[27]

EXPANDING VOICE IN INTERNET GOVERNANCE

So how do countries with weak institutions and poor governance cope with the age of the internet?

Whereas in the United States and western Europe more than half of people get news daily from the internet or social media platforms such as Facebook and Twitter, the internet is still a less important player in the news environments of the developing world. According to data from a thirty-eight-country survey conducted by the Pew Research Center in 2018, traditional media remain the major news providers for developing and lower-income countries. For more than half of the people in the twenty-five countries in the survey with per capita gross domestic product lower than $25,000 a year, the internet and social media are a source of news less than once a month. In the poorest six countries in the survey, more than 60 percent of respondents said they *never* use the internet or social media to access news.[28]

For such countries, finding a way to improve governance of existing media and stimulating a more open country dialogue about the role of media in society may be the best ways to prepare for fruitful participation in global internet governance. Although the governance issues for traditional media are quite different from those for internet media—the transformative power of the internet is its access to global knowledge—the democratic principles that define an open national media system can be useful guideposts for both traditional media and global internet governance.

In Ghana, for example, National Media Commission chair Nana Kwasi Gyan-Apenteng worked to build a network of independent regulators across West Africa. The institutional capacity and practices that go into creating real independence are a challenge for the regulators in many countries, he says, and international cooperation draws attention to national strengths and weaknesses. Such networks are particularly helpful for smaller countries. Mr. Gyan-Apenteng points to Niger, one of the poorest countries in

West Africa, which in recent years established a reasonably well-governed regulatory framework for the media, whereas the much larger, richer, and highly tech-savvy Nigeria suffers from corruption and political capture of its regulatory environment. As the media move more into the digital realm, national regulators are barely coping with the transition. "The regulations we want are enabling, to protect the population from exploitation," Mr. Gyan Apenteng says. "But on the digital side, we are struggling. Our governments, our various governmental bodies, do not know how to proceed."[29]

For now, the big companies and the highly developed governments of North America, Europe, and Asia dominate internet governance. This (im) balance of power is evident at the Internet Governance Forum (IGF), one of the few places where civil society organizations, governments, and internet companies come together to discuss policy issues. At the IGF in Geneva at the end of 2017, about half of the 411 governmental representatives came from rich, industrialized countries of the OECD. Another large block of representatives came from countries such as China (twenty-five) Egypt (nine), Iran (five), Turkey (four), Cuba (four), and Vietnam (three), who advocate for "internet sovereignty" and other restrictive policies aimed at closing the global free flow of knowledge and information. Global civil society organizations consider the forum an important place to defend basic rights and democratic norms, but organizations and governments from the global South are poorly represented (Ghana had one official delegate, for example) and rarely even try to influence the agenda or outcomes of the meetings.[30]

This participation of democratically oriented developing countries is important because the internet-governance community has a weak understanding of the problems that developing countries face in their media environments. Facebook rarely has representatives in the countries where its platform is increasingly influencing the political environment, even during elections. At the same time, Facebook has been linked to violence and ethnic strife in a growing list of countries, from Germany to Myanmar, the Philippines, Libya, Sri Lanka, and India.[31]

In such contexts, building media-policy literacy in civil society is critical. International civil society organizations such as Article 19, International Media Support, and the National Endowment for Democracy are helping digital experts from the global South engage in global internet debates. They also support traditional media-development experts to build their knowledge on internet-governance issues. Another group of activists developed the Democratic Principles for an Open Internet, which are designed mainly for citizens and civil society organizations in fragile and emerging democracies. These principles outline the crucial elements of internet governance that affect the least-represented people in the global debate about how the internet is designed and controlled.[32]

One of the enduring lessons of international development policy is that if you put enough development experts, economists, lawyers, and accountants in a room, they will come up with the "perfect blueprint" to solve any public-policy problem. A second lesson is that such blueprints almost never work. Indeed, the challenge of media governance at this time of rapid change and uncertainty is that the problem is less about the technical details for how the media environment is structured and organized and more about the *process* for generating public debate and engagement on the questions.

This is particularly true now, when even the experts admit that they do not have all the answers. As media enterprises experiment with new revenue models, and as social media companies grow exponentially and soak up most of the growth in advertising sales, calls for regulation are multiplying. But what should be the key elements of media governance in an age of media capture, spreading authoritarianism and disinformation, and social media platforms that know no boundaries?

The current environment is creating conditions for a much-needed public debate about the news and information environment. From Russian meddling in the U.S. elections in 2016 and 2020 to widespread public concerns about how Facebook and Google are using private data, these issues are now front-page news across the world. Debates about improving media governance are also widespread in developing countries.

Although the details of how media markets will be structured across the world will undoubtedly differ from country to country or region to region, a set of democratic principles and policy objectives are becoming clearer and more widely held. Table 12.1 outlines key elements of this emerging consensus. Many of these core ideas are already articulated in the founding documents and constitutions of nations. Freedom of expression and the rights of people to receive and impart information were also core principles in the establishment of the United Nations in 1945 and the Universal Declaration of Human Rights of 1948. At the regional level, the Inter-American Commission on Human Rights, the African Commission on Human and People's Rights, and the Organization for Security and Cooperation in Europe have established monitoring mechanisms to reinforce such international norms and standards. Asia and the Arab world, however, are lacking such regional institutions to defend core democratic principles and values.

MEDIA-REFORM TARGETS FOR UKRAINE

1. Public broadcasting is independent.
2. State and communal publications are free from government interference.
3. Media ownership is open and transparent.
4. European standards for audiovisual regulation are adopted.
5. Citizens get free and impartial information during elections.
6. Guarantees for media freedom and protection of human rights are strengthened.

In this time of uncertainty and rapid change in the global media system, a growing chorus of activists are returning to such core principles and using them to guide the debate about policy. These principles include reaffirming the need in our societies for an independent news media that produce a diversity of views and help create an informed and engaged citizenry. Yet the unfinished debate about the balance between freedom of the media and other societal goals and expectations—such as fairness and acting in the public interest—still needs to be conducted as an open, democratic exchange.

The devastating shortcomings of current media governance are sure to be exposed in this debate, such as the lack of transparency in the ownership of media houses and the eroding of professional ethics, norms, and standards in the media profession. Many of the needed reforms will require new laws, regulations, and practices—at both the national and the international level—aimed at preserving freedom of expression and fair competition in the media space. By generating debate about these topics, activists will serve the critical purpose of building stronger media-policy literacy as stakeholders in the system.

International players—donors and media-development program implementers—can play a supportive role in this period of transition. In addition to training journalists, they should do more to support policy reform, knowledge gathering, and coalition building. They can also support the creation of regional institutions that, in Latin America at least, have been critical to strengthening freedom of expression and quality journalism.

It would be folly to expect that a problem as far-reaching and complex as media capture will be solved overnight, but growing numbers of the world's citizens are now paying attention to this problem. It will fall largely at the feet of global civil society and enlightened governments to take advantage of this moment of opportunity and to get engaged in the tough politics of reform. The media capturers are armed for this battle. It is now time for democratic actors to steal the initiative to forge a constructive environment and sustainable financial system for news media in our societies.

NOTES

1. Wasserman and Benequista (2017), 6.
2. Human and Social Studies Foundation (2017), 6.
3. Kalathil (2017).
4. Deibert and Rohozinski (2012), 18.
5. Oh (2017), 1.
6. See Nelson (2016).
7. McMillan and Zoido (2004).
8. For scholarship on the broader economic and social impact of media capture, see the following three sources: Corneo (2005); Lublinski, Meuter, and Nelson (2015); Petrova (2008).
9. Huang (2009), 2.
10. Organized Crime and Corruption Reporting Project n.d. The eleven countries covered by the survey are Czech Republic, Slovakia, Slovenia, Serbia, Hungary, Bosnia-Herzegovina, Macedonia, Romania, Bulgaria, Moldova, and Ukraine.
11. Media Ownership Monitor n.d. The twenty-one countries are Albania, Argentina, Brazil, Cambodia, Columbia, Egypt, Ghana, India, Lebanon, Mexico, Mongolia, Morocco, Pakistan, Peru, Philippines, Serbia, Sri Lanka, Tanzania, Tunisia, Turkey, and Ukraine.
12. Brogi et al. (2017).
13. Lührmann et al. (2019), 18–19. Figure 12.1 is also adapted from this source.
14. Abbott (2016).
15. Open Markets Institute (2018), 2.
16. Open Markets Institute (2018), 8–9. See also Corn-Revere (2011).

17. The Media Sustainability Index (2018) for Europe and Eurasia shows that only three of the twenty-one countries studied have moved into the "Near Sustainability" range of the business-management dimensions of the index. The index can be seen in IREX (2018).
18. Mitra (2001).
19. Corn-Revere (2011), 17.
20. Llorens and Costache (2014).
21. Myers and Angaya Juma (2018).
22. Segura and Waisbord (2016), 185.
23. World Bank (2017).
24. Devarajan and Khemani (2016).
25. Segura and Waisbord (2016), 143.
26. Ukraine Reform Coalition (2018).
27. Taras Shevchenko, interview by the author, October 12, (2017), Washington, DC.
28. Mitchell et al. (2018).
29. Nana Kwasi Gyan-Apenteng, interview by the author, May 3, (2018), Accra, Ghana.
30. For a list of attendees at the IGF in (2017), see IGF n.d.
31. For evidence and links to examples of Facebook as a vector for violence, regional instability, and threats to democratic governance, see Ingram (2018).
32. The Democratic Principles for an Open Internet can be found in Open Internet for Democracy (2020).

REFERENCES

Abbott, Susan. 2016. *Rethinking Public Service Broadcasting's Place in International Media Development*. Washington, DC: Center for International Media Assistance. https://www.cima.ned.org/wp-content/uploads/2016/02/CIMA_2016_Public_Service_Broadcasting.pdf.

Brogi, Elda, Konstantina Bania, Iva Nenadic, Alina Ostling, and Pier Luigi Parcu. 2017. *Monitoring Media Pluralism in Europe: Application of the Media Pluralism Monitor 2016 in the European Union, Montenegro, and Turkey*. Florence, Italy: European University Institute. http://cmpf.eui.eu/media-pluralism-monitor/mpm-2016-results/.

Corneo, Giacomo. 2005. "Media Capture in a Democracy: The Role of Wealth Concentration." *Journal of Public Economics* 90 (1–2): 37–58.

Corn-Revere, Robert. 2011. "United States Media Policy and the Global Information Revolution." Working Paper no. 26, Plataforma Democratica and Konrad Adenauer Stiftung. http://www.plataformademocratica.org/Arquivos/Plataforma_Democratica_Working_Paper_26_English.pdf.

Deibert, Ronald, and Rafal Rohozinski. 2012. "Liberation vs. Control: The Future of Cyberspace." In *Liberation Technology: Social Media and the Struggle for Democracy*, ed. Larry Diamond and Marc F. Plattner, 18–32. Baltimore: Johns Hopkins University Press.

Devarajan, Shantayanan, and Stuti Khemani. 2016. "If Politics Is the Problem, How Can External Actors Be Part of the Solution?" World Bank Policy Research Working Paper no. 7761. https://openknowledge.worldbank.org/handle/10986/24842.

Huang, Haifeng. 2009. "Essays on News Media, Governance, and Political Control in Authoritarian States." PhD diss., Duke University.

Human and Social Studies Foundation. 2017. "Summary of Report on the Study of Anti-democratic Propaganda in Bulgaria." Sophia, April. https://hssfoundation.org/wp-content/uploads/2017/04/SUMMARY_Bulgaria-and-Russian-propagandaI_EN.pdf.

Ingram, Matthew. 2018. "Facebook Now Linked to Violence in the Philippines, Libya, Germany, Myanmar, and India." *Columbia Journalism Review*, September 5. https://www.cjr.org/the_media_today/facebook-linked-to-violence.php.

Internet Governance Forum (IGF). N.d. "IGF 2017 Onsite Participants." Table. https://www.intgovforum.org/multilingual/igf-2017-onsite-participants.

IREX. 2018. *Media Sustainability Index 2018: The Development of Sustainable Independent Media in Europe and Eurasia.* Washington, DC: IREX. https://www.irex.org/sites/default/files/pdf/media-sustainability-index-europe-eurasia-2018-full.pdf.

Kalathil, Shanthi (director, International Forum for Democratic Studies, National Endowment for Democracy). 2017. Testimony before U.S.-China Economic and Security Review Commission, Washington DC, *Hearing on Information Controls, Global Media Influence, and Cyber Warfare Strategy*, May 4. https://www.uscc.gov/sites/default/files/transcripts/May%20Final%20Transcript.pdf.

Llorens, Carles, and Andrea Madlina Costache. 2014. "European Union Media Policy and Independent Regulatory Authorities: A New Tool to Protect European Media Pluralism?" *Journal of Information Policy* 4: 396–420.

Lublinski, Jan, Sacha Meuter, and Mark Nelson. 2015. "Considering the Dark Side of the Media." Deutsche Welle Akademie Discussion Paper. https://www.dw.com/downloads/28543632/considering-the-dark-side-of-the-media-pdf.

Lührmann, Anna, Lisa Gastaldi, Sandra Grahn, Staffan I. Lindberg, Laura Maxwell, Valeriya Mechkova, Richard Morgan, Natalia Stepanova, and Shreeya Pillai. 2019. *Democracy Facing Global Challenges: V-Dem Annual Democracy Report 2019.* Gothenburg, Sweden: V-Dem Institute, University of Gothenburg. https://www.v-dem.net/media/filer_public/99/de/99dedd73-f8bc-484c-8b91-44ba601b6e6b/v-dem_democracy_report_2019.pdf.

McMillan, John, and Pablo Zoido. 2004. "How to Subvert Democracy: Montesinos in Peru." *Journal of Economic Perspectives* 18:69–92.

Media Ownership Monitor. N.d. "Country Projects." https://www.mom-rsf.org/.

Mitchell, Amy, Katie Simmons, Katerina Eva Matsa, and Laura Silver. 2018. *Publics Globally Want Unbiased News Coverage but Are Divided on Whether Their News Media Deliver.* Pew Research Center, online report, January 11. http://assets.pewresearch.org/wp-content/uploads/sites/2/2018/01/09131309/Publics-Globally-Want-Unbiased-News-Coverage-but-Are-Divided-on-Whether-Their-News-Media-Deliver_Full-Report-and-Topline-UPDATED.pdf.

Mitra, Steve. 2001. "The Death of Media Regulation in the Age of the Internet." *NYU Journal of Legislation and Public Policy* 4 (2): 415–38. http://www.nyujlpp.org/wp-content/uploads/2012/11/Steve-Mitra-The-Death-of-Media-Regulation-in-the-Age-of-the-Internet.pdf.

Myers, Mary, and Linet Angaya Juma. 2018. *Defending Independent Media: A Comprehensive Analysis of Aid Flows.* Washington, DC: Center for International Media

Assistance. https://www.cima.ned.org/wp-content/uploads/2018/06/CIMA-Aid Data-Report_web_150ppi_rev.pdf.

Nelson, Mark M. 2016. "What Is to Be Done? Options for Combatting the Menace of Media Capture." In *In the Service of Power: Media Capture and the Threat to Democracy*, ed. Anya Schiffrin, 143–62. Washington DC: Center for International Media Assistance.

Oh, Sarah. 2017. *Advocating for Openness: Nine Ways Civil Society Groups Have Mobilized to Defend Internet Freedom*. Washington, DC: Center for International Media Assistance. https://www.cima.ned.org/publication/advocating-openness-nine-ways -civil-society-groups-mobilized-defend-internet-freedom/.

Open Internet for Democracy. 2020. "Democratic Principles for an Open Internet." https://openinternet.global/read-principles.

Open Markets Institute. 2018. "America's Free Press and Monopoly: The Historical Role of Competition Policy in Protecting Independent Journalism in America." Discussion paper, June. https://static1.squarespace.com/static/5e449c8c3ef68d752f3e70dc/t /5ea9fddc9d36302f95e273b8/1588198890990/Americas-Free-Press-and-Monopoly -PDF-1.pdf.

Organized Crime and Corruption Reporting Project (OCCRP). N.d. "OCCRP Media Ownership Project." Resource Centre on Media Freedom in Europe. https://www .rcmediafreedom.eu/Tools/Monitoring-tools/OCCRP-Media-ownership-project.

Petrova, Maria. 2008. "Inequality and Media Capture." *Journal of Public Economics* 92 (1–2): 183–212.

Segura, Maria Soledad, and Silvio Waisbord. 2016. *Media Movements; Civil Society and Media Policy Reform in Latin America*. London: Zed Books.

Ukraine Reform Coalition. 2018. "Media Reform." Online policy document. https://rpr .org.ua/en/groups-rpr/11media-reform/.

Wasserman, Herman, and Nicolas Benequista. 2017. *Pathways to Media Reform in Sub-Saharan Africa*. Washington, DC: Center for International Media Assistance. https://www.cima.ned.org/wp-content/uploads/2017/12/CIMA-Media-Reform-in -SSA_web_150ppi.pdf.

World Bank. 2017. *World Development Report 2017: Governance and the Law*. Washington, DC: World Bank.

Chapter Thirteen

THE HAMSTER WHEEL, TRIUMPHANT

Commercial Models for Journalism Are Not Working; Let's Try Something Else

DEAN STARKMAN AND RYAN CHITTUM

When 80 percent of the public-school teachers of East Palo Alto, California, signed a petition in 2016 calling for the ouster of the town's school superintendent, charging gross mismanagement, the headline in the local paper the next day announced . . .

. . . nothing. The turmoil was not reported until six days later, after some student journalists at nearby Stanford University heard about it.

A few papers in neighboring towns caught up over the next couple days and later followed up to find out what was behind it but found . . .

. . . nothing. No one followed the story at all in the three months after the vote, according to the *Washington Post*.

The *Post*'s headline asked a question that its story is unable to answer: "What happens to local news when there is no local media to cover it?"[1]

The East Palo Alto case is an extreme example of a bigger problem. It's not only about no coverage but also about *bad* coverage.

A study in the *Journal of Politics* in 2017 found that coverage of local congressional races in newspapers declined by 19 percent from 2010 to 2014, reporting that "local newspapers over this period published less, and less substantive, political news," even when controlling for the competitiveness of the races.[2]

And when the *New Orleans Times-Picayune* shifted to a "digital-first" business model in 2012, shuttering print editions and ramping up online offerings, the percentage of its sports and entertainment stories spiked, whereas the percentage of hard news plummeted, a benchmark Tulane University study found. Meanwhile, the number of human sources quoted per story declined 31 percent.[3]

The *Washington Post* headline hints at bigger questions: What happens to democracy when its main fact-gathering infrastructure breaks down? What happens when local news, the oxygen of the public sphere, is now so thin that democracy itself gasps for breath?

More than a decade into the digital disruption of the U.S. newspaper industry, it seems a good time to take stock of where we have been and to find a new way forward.

The purpose of this chapter is to force the public to face an uncomfortable fact: The commercial market has tried. And tried. And tried. It has tried, and it has failed to support what Ricardo Gandour calls "stable platforms of journalistic production."[4] A review of the record since the great journalism meltdown began around 2007 shows that all conceivable efforts by journalism outlets to wring profit from the internet have either failed or failed to scale or failed to prove replicable.

The remorseless productivity demands of digital technologies—their efficiency, their very measurability—have proved incompatible with public-interest journalism, which requires many things but one above all: a reporter with time on her or his hands. Digital technology has proved *highly* compatible, however, with Wall Street financial engineering, which has carried production efficiencies to their logical conclusion. In a word, local journalism and to an important extent all journalism have been captured. Journalism has been captured by a technology and internet economics supercharged by Wall Street.

It is not for nothing that the nation's first- and third-largest newspaper companies are ultimately owned by New York vulture funds and that the second largest is, well, Gannett, a pioneer in the financialization of news. And in 2019 Gannett itself became the target of one of the hedge-fund-backed chains as the bottom-feeding frenzy accelerated.

After detailing failed efforts to turn a profit on journalism, let alone public-interest journalism, we propose a public alternative that is not meant as a miracle cure but as a way to provide a stable income stream that would serve as one pillar on which public-interest journalism can be built.

The magic elixir can be found in, of all places, Hungary, better known these days as the point of the populist spear, where most independent media have been lost in the maw of a party-controlled oligarch-owned system. All true. But a progressive policy device passed during the 1990s is helping to keep what's left of Hungary's inspiring, fact-driven, and thoroughly professional free press afloat. We explore here the Hungarian policy measure, a tested and proven form of tax credit, in depth.

In 2010, one of us (Starkman) wrote "The Hamster Wheel," a study/polemic that documented stunning increases in reporter productivity requirements at the *Wall Street Journal* from 2000 to 2008 and warned that the consequences would infantilize reporters, strengthen public relations, and irreparably damage journalism's ability to have a say in setting the public agenda.[5] With journalists chasing stories that could be turned around quickly, the news would become what some institution or another—city hall, Goldman Sachs, the White House—said it was.

The Tulane study—a landmark in documenting the shift from an already depleted print journalism operation to a digitally oriented one—was designed to address the all-important problem of measuring journalism quality. It's the hardest question to study, but really the only one that counts, and we encourage further work in this area. The Tulane study pointed to a precipitous decline in journalism quality following a shift to a digital-ad-based model. And the study indirectly also showed how utterly reliant the model had become on local institutions and their press releases, in particular sports teams and especially high school sports.

It can be argued that no variety of capture is more all-consuming than the Wheel: the need, exacerbated dramatically by the internet, to churn out content to fit the commercial or practical requirements of a media organization. This productivity imperative shuts down public-service journalism before it starts. It makes investigations if not unviable, then, from an economic point of view, irrational. It enhances the value of press releases, tethers news organizations to the agendas set by powerful institutions, and renders access to the powerful (and their supply of quick and easy scoops) ever more imperative. A journalist under constant deadline pressure is an unwilling if not unwitting transmitter of elite discourse. The Wheel makes the press profoundly more vulnerable to an outrage-creation machine such as Donald Trump, who can single-handedly pull massive journalistic resources into a news vortex that he controls. As Monika Bauerlein and Clara Jeffery, the great editorial leaders of *Mother Jones*, put it: "The most important ingredient in investigative reporting is not brilliance, writing flair, or deep familiarity with the subject (though those all help). It's something much simpler—time."[6]

The local journalism meltdown has been the quietest of crises because, as Noam Chomsky reminds us, "you don't know what you don't know." In 2009, Paul Starr warned that the end of the age of newspapers would usher in a golden age of state and local corruption.[7] Has it happened? Who knows? And that's the point. Around the same time, an array of scholars and journalists warned that the crisis of journalism would bring with it a crisis of democracy.

Newspapers have now lost $40 billion in real advertising revenue in the past decade—a 68 percent drop—and the losses continue at a double-digit pace. Newspaper newsrooms have now shed 40 percent of their journalists in the decade. Daily circulation has now plunged by a third.

Journalism, to paraphrase Clay Shirky, has fallen, and it can't get up. The internet is no country for young journalists. We are living the doomsday scenario. The market has failed. There is no cavalry coming to the rescue. Independent checks on state and local corruption *n'existe plus*. Even when commercial internet models work financially, the models incentivize journalism captured on an endlessly spinning hamster wheel of death. And the models *don't* work financially.

Much of the country is a news desert. Many Americans outside of media bubbles on the coasts will live their entire lives without ever meeting an actual, live human reporter, making it all the easier to demonize "the media," while forcing news consumption into the waiting arms of polarizing national partisan media.

Commercial journalism is broken. It is not stunned. It is not resting. It is a dead parrot.

An alternative way forward, we argue, can be found in a country where, in the words of the great Hungarian public intellectual Miklós Haraszti, "media are the ultimate frontiers in defending freedom in society." In Hungary, an alliance of neoliberal capitalism and power-grabbing elites have morphed into a version of a mafia state that has made its first priority the crushing of the free press and the replacement of it with propaganda-spouting state and allied media. Yet it is precisely because the environment for independent media there is so hostile politically and financially that our path offers hope.

But first let's review the record.

FOR-PROFIT JOURNALISM IS NOT WORKING (SAD)

Throughout its free fall, the news industry has made strenuous efforts to make the web work for news. It's true, as we'll see, that some of these efforts were none too bright. But some were and were backed by formidable talent and deep pockets. And they failed anyway.

Cosseted by decades of monopoly profits, the newspaper industry was singularly unprepared when it found itself confronted by a new technology that cut the price of publishing and distributing information effectively to zero, bridging the moat that had long made publishers so invulnerable to new entrants.

Most cities had become one-newspaper towns with the TV-driven decline of afternoon papers in the quarter century or so before the dawn of the Web. Whatever chance newspapers may have had to adapt to the digital threat was diminished by the financialization of the industry, which sent its huge profits to shareholders rather than to investments in technology. Groping attempts to adapt fell short. A skunkworks team at Knight Ridder, for instance, famously developed an iPad prototype nearly two decades before Apple unveiled the tablet computer, but it came to nothing. The *San Jose Mercury News* was wise to the digital shift early but was unable to sustain efforts at innovation. *Washington Post* owner Don Graham had a handshake deal with Mark Zuckerberg in 2005 to invest $6 million for a 10 percent stake in Zuckerberg's social media startup. Zuckerberg begged out of the deal when he got a higher offer, and Graham let him walk away. That 10 percent piece of Facebook, which would go on to help bury the newspaper business, would as of this writing be worth upward of $55 billion.

Journalists report, transcribe, and write more stories more quickly than they did fifteen years ago, while also posting on Twitter, Facebook, and Instagram, recording podcasts and video hits, writing blog items, and taking photos. "The Hamster Wheel" showed how the digital diktat had warped journalistic incentives, causing a rush toward "volume without thought," "news panic," and "a recalibration of the news calculus" away from deeper pieces. The study found that the *Wall Street Journal* published nearly twice as many stories in 2008 as it had eight years earlier—with about 13 percent fewer journalists.[8]

A vicious cycle took hold as advertising declines led to layoffs and print cutbacks, which worsened the quality of the print product, which encouraged readers to drop print, which caused more ad declines, and on and on. As the cycle continues, the economies of scale built in print over the centuries dissolve. In the meantime, digital journalism jobs—often less than civic focused—have replaced fewer than a third of the newspaper jobs lost, and many newspaper jobs have become hamsterized, with reporters churning out content in a desperate and largely failing bid for digital ad revenue. Another study showed that major newspapers' production of longform writing, in which an organization commits significant time, space, and resources to a single story, collapsed. Between 2003 and 2012, the number of stories longer than two thousand words fell 35 percent at the *Wall Street Journal*, 50 percent at the *Washington Post*, and 86 percent at the *Los Angeles Times*. Only the *New York Times* held the line.[9]

The industry fatally failed to grasp until too late that its main competitive advantage was now its information-*production* capacity. Newspapers had massive staffs of reporters and editors gathering and publishing information that no one else could produce. It was an understandable mistake. For years, the industry's most important constituency had been advertisers. Now it was readers.

The Blue Pill: Digital Ads

But there were plenty of consultants around to tell the industry otherwise. Lacking confidence in its own product, the industry fell under the sway of a "future of news consensus" that held that asking readers to pay for content online was a form of old-think by dinosaurs who didn't get it. This consensus said the future lay in assembling as much internet traffic as possible to maximize digital advertising, which necessitated chasing marginal readers by optimizing news content for Google and Facebook without impediments such as paywalls.

By betting the future on digital ad dollars, the industry not only chose the wrong financial horse but also largely ceded distribution of its content to the internet giants. The model inevitably led to the rise of so-called clickbait—the sensationalist, misleading, manipulative, and usually frivolous news content that has reigned for much of the social media era. Felix Salmon, somewhat approvingly, explained the inexorable logic for quantity in a blog post on blogs in 2012:

> The great is rare; the dull quite common. But—and this is the genius of the online format—that doesn't matter, not anymore, and certainly not half as much as it used to. When you're working online, more is more. If you have the cojones to throw up everything, more or less regardless of quality, you'll be rewarded for it—even the bad posts get some traffic, and it's impossible ex ante to know which posts are going to end up getting massive pageviews. The less you worry about quality control at the low end, the more opportunities you get to print stories which will be shared or searched for or just hit some kind of nerve.[10]

The quality argument aside, the bet on digital ads proved a financial loser. And no one can say it was for lack of investment, management strategizing, and sheer, hamster-powered effort.

One of the most systematic—and expensive—attempts to increase digital ad revenue through ramped-up journalistic productivity was made by AOL Inc., an effort detailed in a memo leaked in 2011, "The AOL Way: Content, Product, Media Engineering, and Revenue Management." The much-ridiculed memo instructed journalists to cover a story based first on its traffic potential, then on its revenue potential, and finally on how quickly it could be produced. A lower priority was whether the story was "high-quality content," and no wonder: the memo included productivity requirements of five to ten pieces each and every day.[11]

Patch, a hyperlocal reporting/blogging network later bought by AOL, was another high-profile attempt to make the digital ad model work. It was said to have the potential to replace medium-size newspapers "with a single person," as prominent tech journalist Alex Wilhelm put it in 2010. "Patch is making the choice to hire the exact people that US newspapers can't compete against: driven innovators," he wrote. "Patch is on the warpath, expect it to win."[12] Within three years, AOL had unloaded a majority stake in the site after blowing through some $200 million on the venture. In 2014, Patch's new owner promptly laid off 82 percent of its staff.

Doubling Down

In 2012, Advance Publications dropped a bombshell in New Orleans: it was ending its fabled daily newspaper, the *Times-Picayune*, and replacing it with a "digital-first" newsroom working with a sharply reduced workforce, plus a thrice weekly print edition fed with repurposed content from its website.

Advance downsized to a significantly smaller newsroom focused on funneling "inventory" to its website in a bid for clicks.

The Tulane study by Vicki Mayer is one of the few to track qualitative declines accompanying a shift to a digital-ad-oriented strategy in news. The content analysis was designed to compare the quality of the printed *Times-Picayune* of 2011 with the newspaper of 2013 as well as with the allied digital platforms—website, tablet, and smartphone—then given primary emphasis. The study found "an overall increase in news coverage that is, at the same time, softer and less sourced." It stated that

- More than half of print stories in 2011 were on politics, education, business, and the environment. Only one in five fit those categories online in 2013.
- The percentage of crime stories, which are cheap and easy to do, jumped from 18 percent of the content to 33 percent in the two formats and time periods.
- Overall, sports, entertainment, and other soft news made up made 9 percent of front-page stories in 2011 and 33 percent of the homepage in 2013.

Further, "hardly any of the hard news stories [online or on mobile] could be considered enterprise or analysis stories, signaling that readers of these formats received institutionally or traditionally focused stories with little innovation, historical background, or social context for the news they received."[13] And so on.

Closely held by the Newhouse family, of Condé Nast fame, Advance owns a chain of regional newspapers, including the *Oregonian* in Portland and the *Plain Dealer* in Cleveland, and its strategy across the country has been uniform: slash newsrooms, increase content production, reduce print costs, and squeeze out profits while the value of its assets declines.

After six years, Advance's clicks-based strategy clearly hadn't worked as a sustainable model. In 2015, the *Times-Picayune*, for one, shed an additional 21 percent of its already shrunken news staff.

Indeed, despite corporate protestations, it was never clear that financial sustainability was the goal of the digital model in the first place. An analysis in 2013 led one of us (Chittum) to conclude that Advance's New Orleans strategy "looks like an orderly liquidation," albeit with a digital gloss.[14]

Finally, in 2019 the *Times-Picayune* was bought by a rival, the *Advocate*, based in Baton Rouge, which was forced to lay off another slew of *Times-Picayune* reporters. As the *New York Times* put it at the time: the sale of the iconic brand to an upstart "delivered a stunning verdict on an unpopular and often muddled strategy pursued by its owner," Advance.[15]

No newspaper company deployed a "digital-first" strategy—and rhetoric—more aggressively than Digital First Media (DFM, née Journal Register Company and MediaNews Group). Under CEO John Paton, the company appointed an advisory board of leading digital news thinkers, including Jeff Jarvis, Clay Shirky, Emily Bell, and Jay Rosen, and set off on a free-news "engagement" strategy meant to boost traffic that included opening newsrooms to the public and streaming news meetings online.

"Stop listening to newspaper people," Paton told a gathering of newspaper executives in 2010. "Put the digital people in charge—of everything."[16] In February 2012, he would tell another newspaper convention, "What we know and what we traditionally do has finally found its value in the marketplace and that value is about zero"—a scathing assessment of the futility of paid content and a clarion call for free news.[17]

Seven months later, Digital First filed for bankruptcy protection.

Digital First, by the way, was then and is now controlled by Alden Global Capital LLC, a New York hedge fund run by Heath Freeman, who, Joe Nocera notes, has been accused of using his newspapers to supply cash for other investments, such as a bankrupt Mexican developer accused of fraud and the failing pharmacy chain Fred's.[18]

"There's no long-term strategy other than milking and continuing to cut," writer Ken Doctor told the journalist Julie Reynolds, "Their view is that in 2021, they'll deal with that then. Whatever remnants are there, they'll try to find a buyer."[19]

And in early 2019, Digital First, these days officially known as MNG Enterprises Inc., launched its hostile bid for Gannett, provoking unlikely support among journalists for a chain that was once justly blamed for hollowing out and zombifying local newspapers in America. Just when you think it can't get worse, it does.

Venture Capital Rolls In

Whether "digital first" was in fact a good-faith effort at reorienting the newspaper business for the digital age or a Wall Street ploy to put digital lipstick on a financialized pig is an open question. But no one can question the sincerity of efforts to launch digitally native news startups, many of them backed by hard venture-capital cash and all of them aimed at turning a profit in the digital news business, however news would be defined in this new era.

In the early to middle part of this decade, Silicon Valley money positively flooded into new media news ventures, promising a much-needed dose of disruption. Marc Andreessen, the venture capitalist best known as the guy who invented the internet browser, said in 2014, "I am more bullish about the future of the news industry over the next 20 years than almost anyone I know. You are going to see it grow 10X to 100X from where it is today."[20] That year, his industry and old media giants such as Time Warner poured fully $814 million into media upstarts.[21]

The venture-capitalist funding helped *Mic*, *Mashable*, famously *Buzzfeed*, and others build businesses gearing content to generate viral sharing on Facebook and the digital ad revenue that went with it. After years of impressive growth, the model took a hit in 2016 when Facebook tweaked its algorithms to de-emphasize those businesses' viral style of news. And in recent years, the diminishing returns of internet economics have taken their toll. Big names such as *DNA Info*, *Gigaom*, and *Circa* have shut down, while *Mashable*, *Mic*, and AOL's Patch have mostly flamed out, as has Fusion Media Group, the well-financed multiplatform operation under Univision Communications and aimed at millennials. Nate Silver's data-driven website FiveThirtyEight was reported in 2018 to be losing about $6 million annually on revenue of about $3 million and was shopped to prospective buyers before being shifted among Walt Disney Co. properties from ESPN to ABC. Even a relative success story, *BuzzFeed*, has had major layoffs, and in 2019 it announced another round of two hundred job cuts, including news personnel. Around the same time, telecom giant Verizon Communications Inc.'s media-group unit, which owns *HuffPost*, Yahoo, and AOL, announced another eight hundred or so layoffs. (Gawker Media, one of the most innovative digital publishing firms of them all, is of course gone for nonbusiness reasons and can no longer serve as an exception that proves the rule.)

The deflation of the venture-capital bubble has followed the continued dominance of Facebook and Google in digital advertising, which combined to take an estimated 58 percent of the market in 2018. Even more ominously, the duopoly—despite serious reputational problems for both players—continues to snap up the lion's share of growth in the digital ad market. Their only serious competition is a startup known as Amazon. All others on the scene, including news outlets, are fighting over their crumbs.

Other Ill Effects

The rise of Facebook (and to a much lesser extent of Twitter) as the dominant traffic provider to news sites also supercharged incentives for traffic because organizations must tailor output to mesh with platform algorithms. As Emily Bell and Taylor Owen wrote in 2017, "Decisions made by Facebook, Google, and others now dictate strategy for all news organizations, but especially those with advertising-based models." So besides their being "arguably responsible for a mass defunding of journalistic institutions," what they incentivize "has no correlation with journalistic quality."[22]

And then there's bubblification.

Although local journalism's headcount has sharply declined, national coverage, which by its nature has larger potential audiences, has fared better. The media have long been disproportionately concentrated in New York, Washington, DC, Los Angeles, and other major cities. But digital disruption has created a new "big sort" in blue states on the coasts. A *Politico* analysis in 2017 found that nearly 90 percent of all internet-publishing employees work in a county that Hillary Clinton carried in 2016, and 75 percent of them work in a county that she won by more than 30 percentage points. "Newspaper jobs are far more evenly scattered across the country, including the deep red parts," wrote Jack Shafer and Tucker Doherty. "But as those vanish, it's internet jobs that are driving whatever growth there is in media—and those fall almost entirely in places that are dense, blue and right in the bubble."[23]

All this is helping to further distance conservative-leaning readers from the mainstream press and at least tempting the press to chase a more-liberal readership, potentially further polarizing readers along partisan or ideological lines. And one has to wonder whether the phenomenon has something to do with the general shock that followed the discovery of Trump's—and, for that matter, Bernie Sanders's—popularity outside the media bubble.

And this is to say nothing of the general degradation of public discourse. As Ricardo Gandour observes, "With newsrooms reeling, and staffing decimated, a weakening of the stable platforms threatens to cause general informational impoverishment, a degradation of the entire information ecosystem."[24] We agree, but we think it's safe to say that's already happened.

Local News Is Now Vulture Food

The financialization of the newspaper industry began decades ago, led, as noted, by Gannett, as newspaper companies sold shares to the public and consolidated into chains. But with the crash of newspaper stock prices, private equity has moved in and supercharged this trend.

GateHouse Media—affiliated with the publicly traded New Media Investment Group Inc., which is externally managed and advised by an affiliate of Fortress Investment Group LLC, now part of Japan's SoftBank Group Corp.—was the biggest newspaper owner in the United States in 2018. DFM, controlled by Alden Global, was number three. As of 2016, six of the top ten newspaper chains were owned by investment firms.

A NewsGuild analysis of DFM's tactics at twelve papers between 2012 and 2017 found that the company slashed newsrooms by nearly 70 percent. That was twice the overall national rate of layoffs. At one DFM paper, the *Delaware County Daily Times*, the newsroom losses hit 78 percent.[25]

In a long exposé on GateHouse in 2017, the *American Prospect* found that, along with the usual newsroom job cuts, copyediting had been moved out of town and wages had been frozen for nearly a decade. The company's "wages are so low and working conditions so high-pressured and unpleasant that turnover among layout staff is constant—so mistakes are rampant." The magazine estimated the big private-equity newspaper companies generate profit margins of 15 to 25 percent.[26]

Of course, we do not deny—and have no interest in denying—that there *have* been digital commercial success stories. After enduring years of ridicule, *Buzzfeed* built an impactful and well-respected newsroom that endures despite recent growth struggles. *Business Insider* built a digital-only business and sold a majority share to a legacy-media company near the end of the digital media bubble that valued it at $442 million.

And your authors have long been fervent advocates of paywalls—paying for news—and have noted with no little satisfaction the widespread, if

244

SOLUTIONS

belated, adoption of paywalls across the news industry in the United States and around the world. The success of the *New York Times* paywall in 2011, a take on the already successful paywall at the *Financial Times* and, to a lesser extent, at the *Wall Street Journal*, has been no less gratifying. The *Washington Post*, now owned by Jeff Bezos, also says it is profitable and is increasing its newsroom to eight hundred journalists. That's what we mean by scale.

We hate to say we told you so, so we won't, except in a couple of footnotes (etc.), but we will say it's nice to see that paywall-powered New York Times Co. shares are up 207 percent since January 2011, while digital-ad-powered Demand Media (now called Leaf Group), the ultimate content hamster farm, has faded into obscurity, with shares down 79 percent since it went public that month.

Still, everyone knows by now that the success stories mentioned in the preceding paragraphs are the exceptions that prove the rule. Significantly, the models do not appear replicable, at least for a mass-media publication on a local level.

Digital economics aren't going to support the kind of robust, reporting-heavy journalism we need, particularly at the local and regional level. Period.

LET'S TRY SOMETHING ELSE

For those of us who grew up in the era of commercial-market dominance, giving up on private solutions is not an easy pill to swallow. We remember not just the financial stability of monopoly-like positions in small- and medium-size advertising markets but also the sense of independence that came with the knowledge that the paper's revenues depended not just on a few benefactors, nervous foundation boards, or Facebook algorithm writers, but on hundreds if not thousands of smaller advertisers and tens of thousands of readers. Of course, the commercial system wasn't perfect. Of course, there were conflicts—downtown real estate interests, the local department store, and other big advertisers. And of course it wasn't fair to local businesses, which had to pay through the nose to reach the market—and put up with horrible service to boot.

But for a robust model to drive a robust, scalable, financially autonomous, sustainable, *mass-market* news operation, you could do a lot worse than the commercial private market.

For those of us living in modern-day Hungary, where commercial options are even more constrained by a small market, low incomes, and—mostly—regulatory manipulation and total domination of the advertising market by an authoritarian-leaning government, a robust, financially autonomous, private model looks even better. Viktor Orbán's FIDESZ (Alliance of Young Democrats) Party now has near total control over the media system by almost universal acknowledgment, with only a few remaining pockets of resistance. It is not a coincidence that Hungary's last remaining independent, mass-market daily, *Népszabadság*, was shuttered in 2016 by what is widely understood to have been a behind-the-scenes coup engineered by government-allied oligarchs and their strawmen. It is further not an accident that the most financially stable, independent source of news for the mass market (emphasis on "mass") remains RTL Klub, the leading commercial television station, which is owned by German publishing giant Bertelsmann SE & Co. (For that matter, living in Hungary also puts foreign media ownership in a new light: it can be a saving grace.)

Given all that, it may come as a surprise that it is none other than Hungary that offers a sound alternative for a sustainable funding stream free of both market vagaries and government control. Students of the region, though, will not be surprised.

Antigovernment Feeling Leads to a Funding Innovation

Hungarians' fidelity to free-speech principles is deeply rooted and has proved irrepressible. It helped to drive the failed revolutions of 1848, led by journalist Lajos Kossuth, and 1956, which germinated in Hungarian literary clubs. The country was a center of the samizdat movement in the 1980s, and when communism fell in 1989, parliamentary debate on the problem of guaranteeing freedom of expression and media independence dominated public debate for years, becoming known as the "media wars."

The 1990s, now recalled wistfully by Hungarian liberals, was a tumultuous but hopeful time that saw the country establish one of the more robust and open media systems in central Europe.

As it happens, before his dramatic turn to the right in 1994, Orbán and his FIDESZ Party, along with the SZDSZ (Alliance of Free Democrats), were pushing for the most liberal regulatory regime—full independence for public broadcasting, privatization of broadcast licenses—against a coalition of conservatives and former Communists who made suspicion of independent media a common cause. The media law of 1995 that finally emerged was deeply flawed but contained important progressive elements, most notably a relatively fair distribution of TV and radio licenses and a fairly robust private media sector, as Peter Molnar writes.[27]

Around the same time, a tax-centered provision was making its way through Parliament that, though its proponents didn't know it, would turn out to be an important source of support for free and financially autonomous media. The law grew out of another Hungarian tradition: a long-held suspicion of governments reinforced by decades of communism and a related reliance on self-help and voluntary organizations. Nongovernment organizations (NGOs) predated even the end of communism (invariably called "socialism" in Hungary, even by anti-Communists) and were officially "rehabilitated" by the regime in 1987, receiving direct government support along with tax-exempt status for the nonprofits and deductibility for contributions similar to that enjoyed by 501(c)(3)s in the United States.

In 1991, as part of the parliamentary debate on how to finance the churches, the liberal SZDSZ proposed that taxpayers be authorized to transfer one percent of their personal income tax payment either to churches or to voluntary organizations. The intention was to reform church finances, but the Socialist government added NGOs as possible beneficiaries.

"The government wishes to let taxpayers freely decide on the use of a given part of their personal income tax. The recipients of this share of the personal income tax can be religious, cultural, social, and other civic organizations, but not the political, business and professional advocacy groups," the official proposal read.

The idea took years to pass into law. The Catholic Church was afraid the new mechanism would supplant its direct government funding; some objected that it would give more influence to the rich than to lower-income taxpayers (true enough); some worried it would crowd out private donations (it didn't); others that it would turn NGOs into crass marketers (it did, but so what?).

In any event, in 1996 the government passed Law CXXVI/1996 on the Use of Some Part of the Personal Income Tax in Accordance with the Disposition of Taxpayers. Because of objections by the church, though, the law

was eventually amended to allow taxpayers to make two 1 percent donations: one for NGOs, one for the church.

There were no ticker-tape parades about the law, which had nothing to
do with the press, but public opinion was generally favorable.

Part of the Landscape

Because the law was conceived with noncontroversial charities in mind, it
made qualifying as an eligible "public-benefit" organization or foundation
easy and defined the term expansively to include national and local cultural
institutions (theaters, museums, exhibition halls, community centers; institutions engaged in preventive medicine, health care, social services, education, research, public safety, human rights, environmental protection,
protection of cultural heritage, sports and leisure-time activities for the
youth and the disabled; institutions that provide care for the elderly, children, the poor, the handicapped, national and ethnic minorities, and Hungarian minorities in foreign countries; and so on).

After early scandals involving fraudsters who brought in "one percent"
money to a so-called NGO and then spent it all on salaries and expenses,
tax authorities imposed strict accounting and reporting provisions, and the
problems soon abated.

A study four years after passage found that 94 percent of the adult population had heard of the one percent law and that 90 percent of taxpayers
approved of it. Most people used the law to support an organization to which
they had a local connection or benefitted from personally.

The study indicated that NGOs said that, beyond the money, they found
validation in being included as official beneficiaries while, importantly,
being free of any direct connection to the state: "What is really unique and
unprecedented in the 1% scheme is not that nonprofit organizations can
have access to a separate government fund. More importantly, they can get
this state support through a decision making mechanism which is completely different from the traditional distribution procedures of public
support, and completely independent of government authorities, which usually play a decisive role in the redistribution process."[28]

Today more than thirty-five thousand Hungarian organizations
receive one percent funding, about a quarter of them operating *only* on

that funding. About 60 percent of the total possible amount designated actually *is* designated.[29]

The program grew to take in €70 million in 2008, before the recession and tax cuts lowered the overall take. The number must seem low to Americans, but in a country of 10 million people where per capita income is less than a fourth of that of the United States, it is meaningful. And the one percent system, known in tax lingo as a "percentage tax designation mechanism," has since been copied in Poland, Slovakia, Romania, Lithuania, Italy, and other countries.

Today, the one percent system is noncontroversial. It is part of the social landscape. Every spring before the tax filing, public-benefit organizations, including Central European University, where one of us (Starkman) is affiliated, conduct marketing campaigns to convince taxpayers to designate their one percent to them. The Catholic Church is known as a particularly effective marketer. The biggest hurdles are logistical. Taxpayers fill out separate forms and must post them separately. They need to know the organization's tax ID number. And in 2017 the government provided the option of preparing returns electronically, allowing taxpayers to passively accept the return and do nothing, which automatically leaves the one percent box blank, and the money stays in the Treasury.

Over the years, the roster of eligible NGOs began to include civil rights, refugee support, environmental, and other not so anodyne groups that began to rely on the law as an important funding source.

Why describe a twenty-year-old Hungarian tax law, though? Precisely because it is twenty years old. It works. It works practically. It works politically. It works financially. It provides a funding stream for public-benefit organizations that has allowed the sector to grow and fulfill important and sometimes unpopular needs.

And the one percent law has been tested in ways that Americans can only imagine.

Keeping the Lights On

In 2010, Tamás Bodoky, an investigative reporter for Index.hu, one of Hungary's two largest digital news sites, got into one too many fights with the advertising side over what he could and couldn't cover. In this case, the story was about a real estate magnate's corrupt ties to a publicly funded football stadium deal. But this was hardly the first feud, and Bodoky quit. "I didn't want to fight with my own publisher, my own boss, anymore," he said.[30]

After an ambitious effort to raise €1 million for a news startup failed, he started a site on his own, Atlatszo.hu, with the help of two friends: Csaba Tordai, a constitutional lawyer ("I was sued all the time," Bodoky explained), and Ákos Maróy, a technology activist and denizen of the Budapest hacker scene. Bodoky set up a Wikileaks-like leaks portal and went to work.

The launch of Atlatszo coincided with the ascension of Viktor Orbán's FIDESZ Party government, which promptly began its now infamous assault on liberal democratic norms and institutions, packing the country's Supreme Court with loyalists, dismantling government financial oversight and white-collar crime enforcement, and, crucially, launching a takeover of the country's diverse but vulnerable independent media.

The infamous Media Law of 2010 consolidated regulatory control under party loyalists, turned public broadcasting into a state propaganda service, and, among other things, stripped journalists of the right to protect sources from government interference.

Within weeks, Atlatszo published a story disclosing that an important local financial brokerage had been hacked and had failed to disclose the incident to regulators or customers. Hungarian police soon raided Bodoky's Budapest apartment, demanding his source. When he refused, police seized his hard drive (which, unfortunately for authorities, was encrypted). Tordai challenged the police ruling, and within six months the country's High Court, which still retained vestiges of independence, found for Atlatszo. The precedent-setting case forced the government to rewrite part of the media law to include new media protections.

With the fledgling Atlatszo suddenly famous, Bodoky started a crowd-sourced fund-raising drive, and within six months he had raised three million Hungarian forints ($10,000), which in Hungary is real money and, in any event, wildly exceeded Bodoky's expectations.

Still, Bodoky needed another funding source. Although the one percent law seemed like a promising option, it was available only to official Hungarian foundations or associations, which require time, expense, and effort to set up. So Bodoky struck a bargain with friends who ran the Asimov Foundation, a tiny group of Hungarian techies and hackers, in which Atlatszo would use its rising prominence and social-networking prowess to ask taxpayers to make their one percent designation to Atlatszo through

Asimov. In the first year of the bargain, 2014, Atlatszo took in 5.3 million forints in designations, or $21,000, to go with the 27.2 million forints ($94,000) received in microdonations. Bodoky began to hire staff.

Meanwhile, Orbán's crackdown on civil society and the press quickened. In the spring of 2014, the country's largest independent business news site, Origo.hu, reported on lavish travel spending by a close Orbán aide. The site's owner, Magyar Telekom, a unit of Deutsche Telekom, which has close ties to the government, promptly fired the site's editor in chief, prompting the resignation of the bulk of its staff and public demonstrations. The government rolled out a punitive advertising tax that targeted a single news outlet, RTL Klub, which had been broadcasting hard-hitting investigation into government spending and corruption. And government agents raided three NGOs that distributed grants from Norway and other northern European countries to thirteen Hungarian civil society groups, including the Asimov Foundation.

Attacked by the Government and Thriving

Exposed to nasty pro-government attacks, the Asimov leaders thought better of their ties to Atlatszo, and the news organization was forced to set up its own foundation. Since then, Atlatszo's one percent funding has grown dramatically and is now one of three main pillars of the organization's funding base, along with memberships (crowdfunding) and foundation grants. One percent designations quadrupled to 23 million forints in 2017, or about $90,000, and remained at that level in 2018. Meanwhile, microdonations doubled from 2014, climbing about 12 percent in 2018 to 49.9 million forints, or about $170,000. Bodoky attributes slowing growth to competition from new independent news startups.

One percent donations in 2018 made up about 23 percent of the operation's funding of $400,000, helping to wean the organization from foundation support. Open Society Foundation (OSF) grants dropped dramatically to 14 million forints ($48,000) in 2018, from 48 million forints ($188,000) in 2017.

About 0.6 percent of Atlatszo's funding in 2017, it should be noted, came from ads.

Bodoky hopes one day to dispense altogether with philanthropic funding, and well he might. The government spent €100 million on a "Stop

Soros" campaign, an advertising blitz against George Soros, who funds many of the NGOs in Hungary, including OSF. In recent years, the government pushed through the Law on the Transparency of Organizations Funded from Abroad, which requires NGOs receiving foreign funding to register with authorities. In 2018, it introduced a bill that aimed to close NGOs that help migrants. Later that year, OSF closed its Budapest headquarters and moved to Berlin.

Today, Atlatszo has a staff of nine full-time employees, bolstered by a platoon of subcontracted and volunteer video journalists as well as legal and IT experts. It boasts a camera-drone project that has filmed oligarchs' estates, an independent blogging platform, the Tor-based leaking platform, an "FOI [freedom of information] request generator" for the public, a crowdsourced "bribe tracker," and other innovative features such as a legal program to sue the government to release public information.

Atlatszo's springtime one percent marketing campaign is witty and sophisticated. It includes an explanatory video on how to fill out the tax form to designate the one percent, an ad showing a FIDESZ Pac-Man gobbling up industry after industry while racking up a score of "99," after which a slogan appears: "Give us 1% and we'll find out where the other 99 are going!"

About 3,700 people make donations to Atlatszo, while 3,500 taxpayers designate one percent to the operation. It's impossible to know if they are the same people because the government doesn't share the names of one percent contributors, and most contributors of any kind are anonymous. "This is a very paranoid country," Bodoky said. Atlatszo donors whose names are known get free tote bags, refrigerator magnets, and coffee mugs ("Keep calm and support Atlatszo").

Bodoky says one percent funding helps fend off charges by government allies that because Atlatszo relies on OSF grants, it is a "foreign" agent. The funding "brings us legitimacy," he said. "We can say we have a local constituency and local resources. It's very important."

And it's hard to overstate the importance of Atlatszo and other independent investigative sites to Hungary's struggling democracy.

Exposing Corruption and Creating a Counternarrative

In February 2018, the European Union's Anti-Fraud Office, known by its French acronym OLAF (Office européen de lutte antifraude), issued a blistering report that found "serious irregularities" in EU-funded work contracted to Orbán's son-in-law, István Tiborcz. The long-awaited report—some believed it would never see the light of day—rocked the political establishment and sent the Orbán government scrambling. The report cited in particular a series of tainted construction contracts to Tiborcz and his company.

What is notable about the OLAF report is that virtually all of the information in it had been uncovered by Hungarian investigative news sites, led by Atlatszo.

Atlatszo first introduced the public to Tiborcz's rapidly rising wealth in 2012 with a story about a rigged public-land deal. A story in 2013 zeroed in on the lighting contracts at the center of the OLAF report under the scathing headline: "The Dowry of István Tiborcz." After a drumbeat of smaller stories, a piece in 2014 pulled together the big picture of the Orbán family's gaming of more than a dozen contracts in cities around Hungary.

Although the prime minister announces zero tolerance for corruption, his family members receive billions of public contracts with special competitive conditions: his son-in-law, István Tiborcz, and his former business associates play games with bid invitations from EU sources.

In 2014, Atlatszo was joined by Direkt36.hu, another online investigative startup put together by refugees from Origo.hu, Andras Petho and Gergő Sáling, which began a series of stories that, if anything, were more devastating to the government.

When Hungarian open society was facing its darkest hours—Orbán's dominance seemingly total, civil society under heavy attack, the opposition in disarray or bought off, the media system a giant propaganda operation, the U.S. embassy hobbled by Trump's ascendance—Hungary's independent media, its investigative sites in particular, kept democracy vital to a degree that only those who live here can fully appreciate.

The point isn't that independent journalism has been able to supplant pro-government public broadcasting and the FIDESZ-allied radio, TV, and newspaper empire, which produces a relentless stream of anti-immigrant messages and trumped-up conspiracy theories about George Soros. It is that independent journalism has managed to create a counternarrative to the government's propaganda.

And there have been signs that the ice encasing Hungarian democracy will one day finally break. In February 2018, voters in Hódmezővásárhely, a FIDESZ stronghold for two decades, overwhelmingly elected an opposition candidate—a political earthquake. Although it came too late for the opposition to organize to unseat the government, the aura of FIDESZ's inevitability slipped momentarily, only to be papered back over by the country's skewed electoral system, which gave the government a super majority with less than half the popular vote.

Bodoky says that Atlatszo has faced plenty of legal challenges from the government and its supporters, but there is no evidence of the tax authority's tampering with Atlatszo's one percent eligibility. Not that it's not possible for this to happen, he says. It just hasn't happened, and, given the fraught state of the rule of law in Hungary, that's saying something. "I don't remember a single case where the tax authority's decision was problematic," said Csaba Tordai, a legal scholar and senior official under Socialist governments.[31]

What About Us?

Can the one percent law be imported to the United States?

First, we recognize that a cadre of scholars and journalists, including Robert McChesney, John Nichols, Robert G. Picard, Victor Pickard, Rodney Benson, and others, have tirelessly promoted the idea of public support for journalism for years. The one percent idea, for instance, can been seen as a variation on the tax credit for journalism proposed by McChesney and others. We don't claim to be inventing anything.

But the beauty of the Hungarian model is that it's not a model anymore. It's a tried and tested program that has worked practically, financially, and politically for twenty years and is now part of the Hungarian landscape. It works. And it has continued to work under difficult circumstances that American journalists can only imagine.

We have no illusions about the political prospects for *any* public-policy idea—let alone one aimed at supporting journalism—in the current U.S. political environment, with Republicans set against government initiatives in general. But, in theory, an idea that takes funding discretion away from government in favor of taxpayers should have conservative appeal.

This very feature, we believe, also helps overcome many or most of the market-distorting effects described by Picard's "subsidy failure hypothesis" for news. Rather than rewarding noncompetitive firms and disadvantaging firms that don't receive subsidies, the one percent law would simply be an extension of a market system, with firms competing, as they do in Hungary, for the favor of readers.

And although we call our proposal "the one percent solution," the actual percentage can be tailored to circumstances. Still, one percent of personal income taxes collected translates into serious money. One percent of the estimated $1.89 trillion in personal income taxes the U.S. government collected in 2018 would have been $18.9 billion. Newspaper industry revenue is down more than $40 billion from its peak, but even only a portion of that is devoted to journalism.

Using U.S. Bureau of Labor Statistics data, we calculate, for instance, that it would cost $1.9 billion a year to cover the salaries and benefits of the 27,210 newspaper newsroom workers lost in the past decade. The infrastructure would cost more, but clearly that "more" is not a big number. Obviously, this very rough estimate doesn't include costs such as infrastructure and expenses such as travel. But it also likely overstates the amount required because it doesn't include efficiency gains or digital journalism jobs gains. We include this number mainly to put the scope of the problem in perspective: it is far from insurmountable.

Indeed, 0.1 percent would probably cover it.

The biggest challenge—one not encountered in Hungary but all but inevitable in the United States—will be in tax authorities' administration of the program, particularly in deciding who is eligible to receive the one percent funds and who is not. Our one percent plan is targeted for local news, but not only local. What if someone wanted to cover the Environmental Protection Agency? Or the Pentagon?

The InfoWars Problem

It's a safe bet that InfoWars, Gateway Pundit, and others that routinely traffic in misinformation and conspiracy theory will apply for one percent fund eligibility, not to mention those yet-to-be-created Russian-backed fake-news sites and other nefarious actors. So, too, one might anticipate, would Breitbart, Occupy Democrats, and other partisan messaging operations on both the left and the right.

But the fact is that the Internal Revenue Service (IRS) has already seen most of these issues before in determining who is eligible for 501(c)(3) tax-exempt status under the "educational" designation—an increasingly popular route taken by news organizations of many stripes since the 2007–2008 journalism bust.

As Picard and his colleagues note, the IRS in 1967 issued criteria for organizations engaged in publishing (e.g., "The preparation of the material must follow methods generally accepted as educational in character") and has been litigating the question ever since. "Although not-for-profit media outlets can convey a certain ideology, their journalistic activities and articles must be supported, fulfilling an educational message. While the IRS accepts organizations that have a point of view . . ., the IRS requires tax-exempt media outlets that are organized and operated for educational purposes, to present 'a full and fair exposition of the facts.' "[32]

In 1980, for instance, in *Big Mama Rag, Inc. v. United States* (631 F.2d 1030 [D.C. Cir. 1980]), a court overturned an IRS ruling that a free monthly newspaper had failed to satisfy the full-and-fair exposition requirement by printing unsupported opinion. The court found the standard unconstitutionally vague. In *National Alliance v. United States* (710 F.2d 868 [D.C. Cir. 1983]), the court agreed with the IRS that the publications of a white-supremacist group didn't qualify as educational because they promoted racial hatred and anti-Semitism. Since these cases, the IRS "has continued placing more emphasis on certain elements that might reveal that a certain organization does not have an educational purpose, such as the lack of support for the organization's viewpoints, distortion of facts, and the use of inflammatory language."[33]

And in 1994, when the constitutionality of IRS procedures themselves were challenged, a court sided with the agency, finding "tax exemption [was] a privilege derived from legislative grace, not a constitutional right" (*Nationalist Movement v. Comm'r*, 102 T.C. 558, 588–89).

Marcus S. Owens, a former director of the IRS's Exempt Organizations Division and a partner at the Washington law firm of Loeb & Loeb, cautions that although in reality the IRS can deal with extreme examples (*National Alliance* dealt with American Nazis), it still struggles to draw a line between organizations that tend to be factually accurate and those that do not. Rules still on the books from the 1960s tend to disfavor news organizations that raise money through commercial methods—ads mostly—while favoring those showing more revenue from charitable contributions, he adds. Further, he notes, rules forbidding political endorsements or attacks are so vague that even investigative reporting of true facts against President Donald

Trump could in theory be found to overstep IRS boundaries. "There really is no standard there," Owens says.[34]

Indeed, a U.S. version of the one percent law would require an IRS overhaul of its rules and procedures for tax-exempt status that are at times burdensome and at others wildly permissive. Citizens United, recall, is tax exempt. But if a one percent law focuses attention on bolstering the IRS, that's not a bad thing.

Besides, the IRS has already weathered similar storms. Everyone remembers the so-called IRS "targeting scandal," in which conservatives charged the Obama-era IRS with harassing and otherwise burdening Tea Party and allied groups applying for "social welfare" status under the code. Under political fire, the IRS issued a rare apology, though the charges largely were debunked by the agency's inspector general. The problems were mostly administrative and caught up many types of organizations, including, yes, nonprofit news organizations clamoring for 501(c)(3) status. As Owens says, the IRS was found guilty of "opening and sorting the mail."

Although the IRS isn't perfect, it is perfectly capable of dealing with these issues or can be made so with a little support.

So let's get started. The private market has failed. The one percent plan is needed. And if it works in Hungary, it can work anywhere.

NOTES

1. Paul Farhi, "What Happens to Local News When There Is No Local Media to Cover It?," *Washington Post*, July 17, 2017.
2. Danny Hayes and Jennifer L. Lawless, "The Decline of Local News and Its Effects: New Evidence from Longitudinal Data," *Journal of Politics* 80, no. 1 (October 2017): 1.
3. Vicki Mayer, "More but Softer: A Content Analysis of News Before and After the Digital Decision at *The Times Picayune* 2012," in *The* Times-Picayune *in a Changing Media World: The Transformation of an American Newspaper*, ed. S. L. Alexander, Frank D. Dunham, Alfred Lawrence Lorenz, and Vicki Mayer, 118–23. Lanham, MD: Lexington Books. 2014.
4. Ricardo Gandour, "Study: Decline of Traditional Media Feeds Polarization," *Columbia Journalism Review*, September 19, 2016, https://www.cjr.org/analysis/media_polarization_journalism.php.
5. Dean Starkman, "The Hamster Wheel: Why Running as Fast as We Can Is Getting Us Nowhere," *Columbia Journalism Review*, September–October 2010, https://archives.cjr.org/cover_story/the_hamster_wheel.php.
6. Monika Bauerlein and Clara Jeffery, "This Is What's Missing from Journalism Right Now: And a Slightly Scary Experiment to Try and Fix It," *Mother Jones*,

August 17, 2016, https://www.motherjones.com/media/2016/08/whats-missing -from-journalism/.

7. Paul Starr, "Goodbye to the Age of Newspapers (Hello to a New Era of Corruption)," *New Republic*, March 4, 2009, https://www.princeton.edu/~starr/articles/articles09 /Starr_Newspapers_3-4-09.pdf.

8. Starkman, "The Hamster Wheel."

9. Dean Starkman, "Major Papers' Longform Meltdown," *Columbia Journalism Review*, January 17, 2013, https://archives.cjr.org/the_audit/major_papers_long- form_meltdown.php.

10. Felix Salmon, "Elizabeth Spiers and the Reinvented *New York Observer*," Reuters, February 6, 2012, http://blogs.reuters.com/felix-salmon/2012/02/06/elizabeth-spiers -and-the-reinvented-new-york-observer/.

11. See Nicholas Carlson, "Leaked: AOL's Master Plan," *Business Insider*, February 1, 2011, https://www.businessinsider.com/the-aol-way.

12. Alex Wilhelm, "AOL's Patch Is the End of Nearly Every US Paper," Next Web.com, September 14, 2010, https://thenextweb.com/us/2010/09/14/aols-patch-is-the-end-of -nearly-every-us-paper/.

13. Mayer, "More but Softer ," 118–23

14. Ryan Chittum, "The Battle of New Orleans: Is Advance Publications Securing the Future of Local News—or Needlessly Sacrificing It?" *Columbia Journalism Review*, March–April 2013, https://archives.cjr.org/feature/the_battle_of_new_orleans.php ?page=all.

15. Campbell Robertson, "How a Newspaper War in New Orleans Ended: With a Baked Alaska and Layoffs," *New York Times*, May 12, 2019.

16. John Paton, quoted in Mathew Ingram, "For Newspapers, the Future Is Now: Digi- tal Must Be First," *Gigaom*, December 2, 2010, https://gigaom.com/2010/12/02/for -newspapers-the-future-is-now-digital-must-be-first/.

17. John Paton, "WAN IFRA International Newsroom Summit: How the Crowd Saved Our Company," *Digital First* blog, January 27, 2012, https://web.archive.org/web /20120209023004/http://jxpaton.wordpress.com/.

18. Joe Nocera, "Imagine If Gordon Gekko Bought News Empires," *Bloomberg*, March 26, 2018, https://www.bloomberg.com/opinion/articles/2018-03-26/alden -global-capital-s-business-model-destroys-newspapers-for-little-gain.

19. Ken Doctor, quoted in Julie Reynolds, "Layoffs, Buyouts Across DFM Newspaper Chain Follow Hedge Fund's Profit-Extraction Strategy," DFMworkers.org, n.d., https://dfmworkers.org/layoffs-across-dfm-newspaper-chain-are-part-of-hedge -funds-profit-extraction-strategy/.

20. Marc Andreessen, "The Future of the News Business: A Monumental Twitter Stream All in One Place," February 25, 2014, https://a16z.com/2014/02/25/future-of-news -business/.

21. *CB Insights*, "Venture Capitalists Are Bullish on News: Funding to Media / Fat Con- tent Startups Jumps 145% YoY," March 10, 2015, https://www.cbinsights.com /research/venture-capital-media-news/.

22. Emily Bell and Taylor Owen, "The Platform Press: How Silicon Valley Reengineered Journalism," March 29, 2017, https://www.cjr.org/tow_center_reports/platform -press-how-silicon-valley-reengineered-journalism.php.

23. Jack Shafer and Tucker Doherty, "The Media Bubble Is Worse Than You Think," *Politico*, April 25, 2017, https://www.politico.com/magazine/story/2017/04/25/media -bubble-real-journalism-jobs-east-coast-215048.

24. Ricardo Gandour, "Study: Decline of Traditional Media Feeds Polarization," *Columbia Journalism Review*, September 19, 2016, https://www.cjr.org/analysis/media _polarization_journalism.php.

25. Julie Reynolds, "Working Under a Hedge Fund: How Billionaires Made the Crisis at America's Newspapers Even Worse," NewsMatters, a NewsGuild Project for Digital First Media Workers, n.d., https://dfmworkers.org/working-under-a-hedge -fund-how-billionaires-made-the-crisis-at-americas-newspapers-even-worse/.

26. Robert Kuttner and Hildy Zenger, "Saving the Free Press from Private Equity," *American Prospect*, December 27, 2017.

27. Peter Molnar, "Transforming Hungarian Broadcasting," *Media Studies Journal*, Fall 1999, 90.

28. Ágnes Vajda and Éva Kuti, " 'Forint Votes' for Civil Society Organizations Studies," Nonprofit Sector Research Series, January 2000, http://www.nonprofitkutatas .hu/letoltendo/1%25_English.pdf.

29. Boris Strečanský and Marianna Torok, eds., "Assessment of the Impact of the Percentage Tax Designations: Past, Present, Future," *ERSTE Stiftung*, September 2016.

30. Tamás Bodoky, interviewed by Dean Starkman, March 13, 2018; statistics from Atlatszo.hu—Watchdog NGO and Center for Investigative Journalism, "Annual Report 2017," 2017, https://d357ur41rhr3vp.cloudfront.net/wp-content/uploads/sites /6/2018/07/atlatszohu_2017_annual_report.pdf.

31. Csaba Tordai, email interview by Dean Starkman, February 27, 2018.

32. Robert G. Picard, Valerie Belair-Gagnon, Sofia Ranchordas, Adam Aptowitzer, Roderick Flynn, Franco Papandrea, and Judith Townend, "The Impact of Charity and Tax Law/Regulation on Not-for-Profit News Organizations," Reuters Institute for the Study of Journalism, University of Oxford, and the Information Society Project, Yale Law School, Yale University, March 2016, 87.

33. Picard et al., "The Impact of Charity and Tax Law," 88.

34. Marcus S. Owens, telephone interview by Dean Starkman, March 26, 2018.

Chapter Fourteen

BUILDING TRUST (AND A TRUST)

ANDREW SULLIVAN

The nonprofit investigative-reporting industry has prospered and grown over the past decade. In terms of employees and stories, the nonprofit sector may even be larger than its commercial version. The sector is now in the midst of its greatest growth and biggest successes with more investigative centers and networks of centers forming worldwide. Meanwhile, commercial investigative reporting, along with commercial media, has been stagnant at best or shrinking. Nonprofit media has been especially important in developing countries where investigative reporting in the commercial sector never established itself or has been dismantled by the political takeover of media. Nonprofit media is often the only independent media left.

But the industry still faces an environment with limited sources of revenues and structural problems inherent in the nonprofit form of investigative reporting that makes it difficult to plan for a sustainable future.

That's a problem for all of us because investigative reporting is critical to current and future democracies. Its rapid growth might be exactly what is needed to understand and beat back the massive globalization of crime and corruption that is undermining democracies across the globe.

Yet there are solutions that could hold the promise of a sustainable future if donors and media organizations are willing to act aggressively and with vision. Such actions could help create a mechanism that permanently fosters investigative reporting even in the worst of times. However, creating such a sustainable solution will not be easy.

One such solution is a journalism trust that could remove many of the limitations that are keeping nonprofit investigative reporting from sustainability and the reaching of its full potential.

Also, a change in mindsets is needed. Donors and governments need to think differently about long-term sustainability of media that serves the public interest and to invest aggressively in the development of sophisticated direct-marketing skills needed to help the best of the investigative reporting centers achieve sustainability.

DECLINING REVENUES

Over the past decade, traditional mainstream journalism has suffered from plummeting revenues due to reduced income from advertising and circulation. According to a Pew Research Center study, the year 2016 saw an 8 percent drop in circulation, the twenty-eighth consecutive drop.[1] Only a minority of advertising revenue is made up from online circulation or advertising revenues.

Legacy media has responded to this revenue fall over the past two decades by relentlessly cutting costs and in the process cutting investigative journalism. Some of those downsized journalists quickly moved to a nascent nonprofit format that started to grow in the early 2000s.

Investigative reporting had always been a loss leader for traditional media. It is very expensive, often taking the most experienced (and expensive) journalists months or even a year to complete one project. It is not unusual for media to spend from $100,000 to well more than $2 million on one high-profile investigative series. Although these stories can sometimes lead to circulation increases, the conventional wisdom is that media never make up their costs from these short-term benefits. Instead, it is believed that investigative stories lose money in the short term but help the long-term image of media as holding government accountable. Although investigate reporting doesn't always bring in new readers, it may help maintain existing readers. Regardless of its effect on readership, it is often considered central to the identity of journalism organizations, and media organizations often use these projects to market and advertise themselves.

But when newspapers face short-term cash crunches or profitability problems, investigative reporting is often the first thing that is cut back. The decades-long contraction of the journalism industry has led to many of the best investigative reporters leaving their media organizations and starting nonprofits.

Although many legacy news organizations have shuttered their investigative teams, not all have. Some of the world's great newspapers have kept up their investment or even invested more in investigative reporting, including the *New York Times,* the *Washington Post,* the *Guardian, Süddeutsche Zeitung,* and others. These media are maintaining investigative teams who are doing some of the best work they have ever done.

It is the presence of these nonprofits that has contributed to what many believe is the golden age of investigative journalism.[2]

Starting in the early 2000s, many of these new centers embraced fully and even defined themselves by the public-service role of journalism. Their rank has now swelled by the more than 100 regional and international organizations that have sprung up over the past decade. There are more than 160 investigative-reporting organizations in the Global Investigative Journalism Network, and the network has tripled in size since 2012.[3] More than 100 of these organizations regularly publish investigative stories. The Institute for Nonprofit News in the United States boasts more than 250 nonprofit members, a number of which are geared toward investigative reporting.[4]

The new players are making a difference. A decade ago, no one would have believed you if you had told them that organizations such as the Organized Crime and Corruption Reporting Project (OCCRP) and the International Consortium of Investigative Journalists (ICIJ) would sport investigative teams that dwarf those of traditional media outlets. OCCRP has a staff of more than 140 people working on investigative stories, and the ICIJ sports investigative staffs of more than 30 people. And their work is having an impact. *Süddeutsche Zeitung* and ICIJ's Panama Papers project may have reached more people on earth than any other investigative project, and OCCRP has topped more than one hundred investigative projects in a year, the largest output of investigative journalism known.

Smart legacy media have co-opted the nonprofit model. The *Washington Post* and the *Guardian* raise money from donors for investigative content. The *Mail* and the *Guardian* in South Africa teamed up with reporters to start AmaBhugane, a nonprofit partially funded in part by the newspaper.

But most investigative-reporting nonprofits have decoupled from legacy media and are increasingly surviving without the traditional base of a daily media organization. Can they survive as nonprofits, and will the public continue to support them?

There is also a question of whether these new media can meet the growing global need for investigative reporting. America once was the bastion of great investigative reporting, but the field has suffered from decades of parsimonious funding doled out by penny-pinching managing editors in contracting newspapers. Reporters in many other parts of the world were often limited in what they could do because of repressive governments and no tradition of investigative reporting. But starting in the 1990s, journalists from Eastern Europe, Eurasia, the Middle East, and other locations joined the ranks of investigative reporters.

As these restrictions have been lifted in many places, investigative-reporting networks flush with donor money have blossomed all over the world. Global networks of investigative reporters such as the ICIJ, the OCCRP, Arab Reporting for Investigative Journalism, Forbidden Stories, and Connectas have sprung up, doing dozens of huge, complex investigations such as the Panama Papers, the Russian Laundromat, and the Daphne Project.

Throughout the world, there are investigative-reporting heroes, starting in the 1990s with the Philippine Center for Investigative Journalism, which helped bring down a president. In the 2000s, Novaya Gazeta in Moscow became the first sustained investigative-reporting organization in that country. Nonprofit centers in Armenia, Romania, Serbia, Bosnia and Herzegovina, Peru, Honduras, Burkina Faso, Kyrgyzstan, and other countries have redefined journalism in their regions.

There is a growing demand for investigative reporters to hold government officials accountable around the world. The increased globalization of trade, crime, and corruption has meant it is no longer possible to have just a good investigative reporter who knows how to watch over a city. To do stories, you must have a network with colleagues you can reach out to from Moscow to Manila.

The globalization of corruption and organized crime, one of the least-told stories of the past decade, has led to the greatest plundering of public resources in the developing world since colonialism. Trillions of dollars in ill-gotten gains have poured into the West from oligarchs, organized crime, autocrats, kleptocrats, and corrupt officials who have parked their assets in high-end real estate, hedge funds, and equities. Hidden behind offshores and protected by Western lawyers, these figures often continue their antidemocratic practices of corruption, bribery, tax evasion, and funding of extremist/nationalist political parties who cater to their wealth. Hidden money begets hidden power, which often seeks to turn their new home into a more plutocratic society that is even more responsive to their wealth.

Not enough investigative reporters are working on these complex global issues. Crime and corruption are a difficult beat involving a complex, transglobal industry designed to be opaque. That industry is beyond the reach of national law enforcement, which often is limited in its ability to cross borders. Despite the growth of such networked investigative reporting, journalists are still only superficially covering significant stories. A tremendous amount of work is needed but is not getting done.

Paul Radu, the cofounder of the OCCRP, estimates that funding for investigative reporting needs to increase a hundredfold for the craft to fulfill its public-service role of holding those in power accountable. Whether this is a good estimate or not, even doubling the amount of money now given would be extremely challenging. How can investigative reporting meet this need?

MISINFORMATION VERSUS JOURNALISM

Funding is not the only challenge investigative-reporting networks face. The successes of investigative reporting around the world have also led to a backlash in authoritarian regimes and wannabe authoritarian regimes. Independent media have been bought out by the state or oligarchs close to the state in many countries, especially in Eastern Europe and Eurasia. And laws have been propagated from Russia to the Philippines seeking to limit what money nonprofit organizations, especially media organizations, can take.

One of the leaders of the war against civil society and independent media has been Russia. It is interesting to note that Russia, which has almost no development or assistance programs, invests quite heavily in media around the world. Russia and Russian-aligned countries such as Hungary have spent billions in building out media enterprises that have been aggressively exported to other countries. Most of these media organizations can be charitably described as pro-government but are more accurately described as purveyors of Russian state propaganda and misinformation.

Much of this work is done through state enterprises such as Russia Today and Sputnik, but other efforts have been through state-friendly oligarchs who have bought out independent media in neighboring countries. Sputnik and Russia Today can be found now in many countries around the world where Russia has strategic interests.

In addition, it is believed that the Russian government supports a number of fake-news and propaganda sites and also operates troll factories to support these efforts. Although no one can know for sure how much Russia invests in all these media-related efforts, it is believed to be several billions of dollars—even more if you add in the investments by client states such as Hungary and Kazakhstan.

Meanwhile, in contrast, a total of $454 million is spent to support independent media and public-service media worldwide per year. That amount includes government and institutional support, but it is only about 0.3 percent of all development assistance. Investigative reporting accounts for just a small portion of that percentage.[5] By comparison, China allocated $2 billion in total media funding from 2010 to 2014. Figures are not available for Russia and its aligned countries, but it's likely all Western support for media is dwarfed by this spending by a factor of dozens.

Investigative reporting gets only one percent of media development assistance funding ($32 million) internationally, despite donors ranking it as their number one priority.[6] That priority hasn't shown up in actual funding. For example, media diversity and inclusion get almost eight times more funds than investigative reporting. Basic journalism skills get nine times more funding. Even access to information, which is arguably less important than the investigative reporters needed to use such information, gets more than twice what investigative reporting gets.

It is important that donors back up their priorities with real money. Unfortunately, funding of investigative reporting is often discouraged by media-development implementers, especially American organizations, who find investigative training difficult to do, legally and physically dangerous, and hard to be successful at. They often push donors toward simpler tasks

TABLE 14.1

Area of Funding	Funding 2010–2015 (US$)[a]	Percentage of Whole
Projects lacking adequate information to identify themes	1,909,785,398	64.7
Journalist skills and knowledge	297,357,482	10.1
Media diversity and inclusion	256,172,127	8.7
Communication/information for development	78,761,421	2.7
Access to information/transparency	70,942,343	2.4
Legal-enabling environment	59,093,838	2.0
Media in conflict and postconflict regions	46,675,784	1.6
Community media	39,496,623	1.3
Professional associations and press unions	33,257,190	1.1
Economic sustainability	32,822,669	1.1
Investigative journalism	**32,544,587**	**1.1**
Journalist safety, journalist defense	26,282,471	0.9
Digital rights, internet freedom	23,023,986	0.8
Research and engagement on media reform	12,129,846	0.4
Public-service broadcasting	11,975,759	0.4
Universities	11,015,249	0.4
Media monitoring	7,131,235	0.2
Media literacy	4,146,480	0.1
Fact-checking	560,073	0.0

[a] Myers and Juma, "Defending Independent Media."

and less-strenuous issues such as basic training and diversity and inclusion programs.

Table 14.1 shows where media money is spent, according to a Center for International Media Assistance report on media funding. For investigative reporting to grow globally means not only overcoming the lack of a sustainable financial models but also overcoming misinformation and the political headwinds in many parts of the world.

THE DIFFICULTIES OF GIVING

There is not enough funding in the traditional state and institutional donor pool to cover this shortfall. There is no indication that states or institutional donors will invest more. In fact, the funding from traditional donors has been static. Although donors haven't added more money, media outlets have shifted funds to investigative reporting, which promises more impact per dollar invested. Still, it's not enough.

To make up that overall shortfall, funds will have to come from donors that have not traditionally funded media, including corporations, governments, and high-net-worth individuals.

The good news is that there is money out there. According to the National Philanthropic Trust, Americans gave $410 billion in 2016 to charitable organizations, corporations $21 billion, and foundations $67 billion.[7] If investigative-reporting nonprofits were to capture just one percent of these funds, it would mean a massive increase in funding and a more equal footing against misinformation campaigns.

Almost half of philanthropic giving by individuals goes to religious and educational institutions, but there is a growing activism especially among younger donors, and there is a growing awareness that independent media and especially investigative reporting constitute a vital public service. Nowhere has that become more visible than in the United States after the election of President Donald Trump. Many people were concerned that without a strong media, misinformation will manipulate elections for years to come. Several organizations experienced a windfall of contributions in the months after the elections.[8] New large donors, especially from the technology sector, entered the media scene. Some of these new donors appear to be making long-term investments, but others made what are not just one-off investments.

But there are other problems in funding media organizations.

Anecdotal evidence suggests that many prospective donors did not know how to enter the space, and many were concerned about the nature of investigative reporting.

Many conservative donors may not like to fund investigative reporters. Investigative reporters are not as cuddly or as sweet as the panda bear marketed by the World Wildlife Fund or a cute village child advertised by Save the Children. Companies don't like the controversy that investigative reporting attracts, and many want to stay clear of anything that might make enemies.

For example, an aide to a well-known tech entrepreneur told me that her boss would love to contribute to investigative reporting, but they were worried about who they should support and how. Their concern was that the media organization receiving the donation would write an investigation that would be problematic for the entrepreneur.

Because of their ethics and mission, investigative reporters have problems taking money from such entities. High-net-worth individuals and corporations are not always free of bad politics or scandal.

Media is also a very difficult space to understand and to donate to. Established media donors have spent decades learning from expensive mistakes. Best practices have been learned, and a set of sophisticated implementers exist. But there is no system in place for new donors to share in that experience and easily tap into those best practices.

And although there was a small postelection bump in funding of media by traditional donors after 2016, much of the funding was aimed at addressing fake news and misinformation. These funds almost never went to actual media but rather predominately to American development implementers or specialized nonprofits. This development often took the form of programs for media literacy, anti-fake-news technology, fact-checking systems, and verification studies. Rather than supplementing independent media, funds were turned into new specialty or implementer websites that will never see much traffic and never sustain themselves.

In countries such as Russia, Serbia, Macedonia, and others where fake news is generated and propagated, no money went to the last remaining independent media. Had money gone into these media in sufficient quantities a decade ago when Russian misinformation first entered their media spheres, solutions could have been developed that would have mitigated the problem. The situation is the same in the Middle East, Africa, and Asia, where Russian-style misinformation programs have started to appear, but there is still not enough support for local independent media.

It's not clear if antipropaganda spending has had much impact. And the public's general awareness of this problem is largely due to the work of the independent media around the world and not to a fact-checking site or a media-literacy group.

GOVERNMENT FUNDING

Governments are the largest funders of global investigative reporting and the development of independent media. They have increasingly focused on investigative reporting, which is often believed to have the greatest impact in the media-development space.

They offer the deepest resources for helping combat the mismatch of independent media versus captured state media, but just adding more government money does not provide a complete solution.

Many investigative organizations, due to ethical constraints, cannot take any government money, especially from their own government. Others restrict what governments they'll take money from. For example, Arab Reporters for Investigative Journalism will not accept U.S. government funds, although it will accept Swedish government funds. The decision was made not just on optics but also on what governments are influential in the region and how they work.

OCCRP has taken funds from the U.S. government for work in Europe and Eurasia but has turned down funding from wealthy individuals from Russia—funds that other American organizations have actively sought. Some organizations will not take money from Open Society Foundations because its founder George Soros is often vilified by the leaders of some captured states and by the alt-right. These issues are complicated and often come down to each organization making individual decisions about individual donors, and those decisions may change over time.

One recent development has been that media outlets that accept government money have been targeted, especially in Eastern Europe and Eurasia. Media or civil society organizations that take funds from governments are now labeled foreign agents in some states. Even traditional foundations such as the National Endowment for Democracy and the Open Society Foundations, two of the rare organizations that work in the developing world, have been labeled enemies of the state in Russia and Hungary.

Government money could be quite helpful if a means could be designed so that more organizations could take it.

PROFESSIONAL CHARITIES AND CORPORATE GIVING

If one looks at how large American nonprofits survive, you will see that a significant amount of their money comes from individual and corporate sources. United Way, long the world's largest charity with $3.5 billion in annual receipts, has built itself up over decades using its deep ties to corporations. Those corporations sponsor United Way and allow it to collect from employees through payroll deductions.

Many charities in the United States also have sophisticated direct-marketing campaigns through automated mail or email systems. Most of these organizations will spend between 8 and 20 percent of their budgets on these campaigns. Media nongovernmental organizations simply have not invested these significant amounts of money. Through these techniques, corporate ties, and significant public outreach, organizations such as Human Rights Watch, Greenpeace, United Way, Save the Children, and others have become extremely sophisticated and successful in reaching the public and corporations. Why not nonprofit media?

Media nonprofits, most of which did not exist until the mid-2000s, have yet to develop the sophistication to become the fund-raising machines that large charities have become. They are often started by well-meaning journalists, not by professional charity experts.

Corporations, although the smallest of the major givers when compared to individuals and foundations, do play an important role. They often have corporate responsibility or accountability programs that would seem to make them match well with funding media work. But many large companies often have difficult relationships with investigative reporting. Investigative journalists often expose the wrongdoing of such companies, which makes corporate charity decision makers less inclined to donate to the journalists' work. But more problematic is that few investigative-reporting organizations will take money from Monsanto, Exxon, Siemens, British Petroleum, or other large companies that have or will be involved in large scandals. This scruple leaves out one of the best sources of funding.

CORPORATE FINES

Investigative reporting is hugely important in bringing cases against big corporations, kleptocrats, and other transglobal bad actors. A former FBI official told a meeting of journalists and donors that half of the cases in the kleptocracy branch where she worked were started from the work of investigative reporters. The work of journalists is often the catalyst that leads to indictments and large fines against corporations. Consider just one organization—the OCCRP. The OCCRP has been responsible for more than $7.3 billion in fines, seizures of assets, and fees against organized-crime figures, businessmen, companies, and other legal entities. In most of these cases, these fines would most likely not have been levied had it not been for the work of journalists. These fines are a huge boon to police and prosecutorial departments.

Yet journalists, again for ethical and legal reasons, do not get any return for this service to society.

If just 10 percent of the money accrued from fines, seizures, and fees could be allotted to journalists and nonprofit media organizations, it could permanently fund investigative reporting. The OCCRP would be permanently funded if it received only one percent of the fines and seizures it helped bring about.

The reality, however, is that the justice system would prefer not to share the funds with others, and there are few if any laws around the world that could be the basis of such petitions. In fact, U.S. law specifically forbids journalists from being whistleblowers and from making recovery claims on such funds.

Moreover, the truth is that most journalists would be very uncomfortable collecting funds from the targets of their stories. Doing so would create an inherent conflict of interest, wherein journalists might focus not on the most important story but rather on the story that would be more likely to return a large sum of money. Stories would tend to focus on deep-pocketed targets rather than on those that are causing the greatest harm to society.

Although corporate fines and seizures offer a tantalizing funding mechanism for investigative journalism, any such system would need to decouple the reporting from the fine collection. In such a system, a percentage of the fine may be returned not to the journalism organization that wrote the story but rather to a general fund that helps all investigative reporting.

In general, studies have shown that investigative reporting provides a significant benefit to society. James Hamilton shows in his book *Democracy's Detective* that each dollar spent on investigative reporting returns about \$100 in public good to a society.[9]

If investigative reporting is so valuable and pays for itself with such positive returns, why is it living in such a penurious state? How should society make sure it has a robust investigative-reporting sphere? What can the public, government, and businesses do to make sure investigating reporting is alive and healthy?

The answers to these questions are difficult.

To summarize, what is needed now in the investigative-reporting funding space is a system that

- Helps create a massive increase in funding levels that will pay for a robust investigative-reporting industry, including funding from individuals, corporations, and government;

- Creates additional funding not from overburdened donors but from new sources;
- Allows more organizations to take funds from businesses, controversial people, and governments;
- Allows for journalism to share in the bounty of fines and seizures from illegal acts;
- Helps media in developing countries avoid the stigma of accepting government money or money from organizations considered foreign agents.

DESIGNING A SOLUTION

Because of these unique problems, unique solutions are needed.

There are two clear ways investigative journalism can improve its funding levels:

- Funding to develop expertise in fund-raising
- An investigative-reporting trust

Solution: Funding for Fund-Raising Expertise

Clearly, contributions from the citizenry does hold a promise to help build up investigative-reporting organizations, especially in the United States and Europe but also potentially in other places. Subscriptions, membership systems, and crowdfunding systems are increasingly popular in many organizations, and some organizations earn significant portions of their income from such sites. There is even an organization called News Revenue Hub, which provides backend database support and expertise in implementing such programs.

Several organizations are quite successful in this type of fund-raising. De Correspondent, a slick Dutch site, raised more than €1 million in an initial crowdfunding effort. The site spends considerable time and effort marketing itself to readers often in a landscape normally reserved for news content. Reporters' faces are featured more prominently than news makers'.

Organizations such as ProPublica, the Center for Investigative Journalism, the Center for Public Integrity, and others have sophisticated direct-marketing and fund-raising skills. ProPublica earned $2.9 million in 2016 in small contributions to go along with its high-net-worth individual contributions and its blue-chip list of dozens of donors.

In general, this type of program works better with organizations in wealthier countries where readers have more disposable income and access to credit cards. But this needn't be the case. Two investigative centers in eastern Europe, RISE Project in Romania and Atlatszo in Hungary, cover more than half of their costs from individual contributors, often without any of the slick pandering done by De Correspondent and ProPublica.

What is often the problem for smaller organizations is the investment. Large charitable organizations will invest about 10 percent of the total funds they receive on fund-raising and marketing, which can constitute significant amounts of money. But investigative-reporting organizations can seldom do likewise because many of them have to dedicate a significant amount of staff time to addressing readers.

The new media nonprofits are just beginning to learn how the large-scale charitable-contributions industry works.

The most important area for journalists to improve on is direct marketing to readers of their publications. About 15 percent of Europeans and Americans pay for online news. Although that number seems low, it represents hundreds of millions of potential readers. If many nonprofits could turn 5 percent of their readers into contributors, that would go a long way to covering costs.

But as is the case for American charities, contributions from private individuals can never be relied on completely to cover all funding needs for media nonprofits. We know that additional funding is needed to narrow the funding gaps between independent media and media peddling misinformation. Contributions from individuals can offer basic survival for organizations, but it cannot close the gap.

To get to the next level, nonprofit media must access more corporate and institutional money, which will require growing that pool.

Solution: Building Trust Through a Trust

A trust fund for investigative reporting would be a very useful tool for investigative-reporting nonprofits. A trust can remedy some of the limitations these nonprofits face. Its main purpose would be to create an instrument so that journalists can accept governmental, corporate, or individual funds that they normally cannot accept.

For example, a trust can mingle funds that are not acceptable to some media organizations with funds that are. The trust can also assign management of the funds to a board of respected journalists and take management out of the hands of the problematic donor. If the donor has no say over the specific use of the funds, most media organizations will consider that as sufficient separation to allow them to take the funds. For example, if an organization cannot take Swiss government funds because it operates in Switzerland, the trust can protect the recipient by eliminating Swiss government control in the matter and mixing the funds so that Swiss government involvement is not material.

If the management also limits the amount any donor can give to the fund (say, less than 10 percent) and resists any restrictions on the usage of the funds, journalists will have greater confidence in taking the money. It may even be possible to make some of the funding anonymous to recipients.

The utility of such a trust is that it would allow for the taking of funds that an individual organization cannot take in the name of all journalism.

For example, such a trust could actively seek to get governments to deposit into the trust fund 10 percent of all recovered assets from settlements, fines, and seizures where journalism played a role in alerting law enforcement to the crimes. Governments can force guilty parties as part of settlements to contribute to the trust. Because the journalism organization that was responsible for the fines or seizures would not directly benefit from such funds entering the trust, there would be no incentive for media to prioritize stories that might lead to settlements.

Bad actors, as penance for their bad behavior, can be encouraged to contribute to the trust as a public-relations effort to show their good faith and reformed ways. They can turn the funds over to the trust, which will have greater expertise at distributing funds effectively and efficiently.

CHARACTERISTICS OF SUCH A TRUST

A trust can add significant funding to needy investigative-reporting organizations, but careful design is important. Many foundations and donors spend a significant amount of money on their own operations. It would be best to leverage existing experience in the news media and development industries rather than to re-create it.

Therefore, some practices that might be considered are:

- The trust should focus on investigative reporting. Although daily and other journalism organizations are important, they have more opportunities to cover costs through membership programs, micropayments, and other techniques. Investigative reporting is expensive and not adequately funded. Also, many of the conflicts of interests with donors and private donors' discomfort with journalism relate to the investigative space and not to the daily-news space. Furthermore, investigative reporting is more likely to lead to the fines and settlements that could fund such a trust. It is simpler and cleaner to put all the difficult eggs in one basket and support them.

- The trust should provide core funding to investigative media organizations that have proven to be successful rather than to individual stories or projects. By eliminating program funding that requires lots of monitoring, evaluation, financial tracking, and other tasks that swell donor structures, the trust would remain small and be inexpensive to operative.

- Committees of current donors can provide input to the selection committee that will choose recipients of the trust monies so that funding to organizations is done in a manner that works in harmony with current donor efforts and doesn't cause more harm than good to recipients.

- Trust funds could also be used to supplement successful programs of current donors and implementers, which would encourage active donors to play a role in contributing to the trust.

HOW TO START A TRUST

Although it's easy to conceive of a useful tool such as an investigative-reporting trust, starting one is far harder. Getting enough consensus among current donors, convincing new donors to join, and getting governments to change laws to allow donations to a trust from settlements, fines, and seized assets are especially difficult.

The elements needed to start such a trust would be:

- A working group of key recipients and stakeholders, including donors, governments, and media organizations to meet and strategize

- The hosting of a general donor conference to start initial funding of a trust
- The creation of a lobbying effort to convince key governments to create policies that might allow for contributions to the trust
- The funding of a small administrative staff to build the trust and to create appropriate policies and governing and decision-making bodies

Much of the last element listed could be done by using an adequately funded fiscal sponsor.

Two such efforts to build a trust were started in 2019. One effort led by BBC Media Action is working to get funds from global development programs. The funds would go to the media-development sphere, and some would be designated for investigative reporting. A separate but complementary fund effort led by the Global Forum for Media Development is following the fines model discussed earlier. Both face long uphill battles. In the end, even if they are successful, it is not clear if they can get enough money to be meaningfully important.

But if this problem is not solved, our complex world will be more and more prone to manipulation by misinformation. And that's dangerous for all of us.

NOTES

1. Michael Barthel, "Circulation, Revenue Fall for US Newspapers Overall Despite Gains for Some," Pew Research Center, June 1, 2017, http://www.pewresearch.org /fact-tank/2017/06/01/circulation-and-revenue-fall-for-newspaper-industry/.
2. For example, Anya Schiffrin, "We're Living in a Golden Age of Investigative Journalism," *Nation*, June 29, 2015, https://www.thenation.com/article/were-living -golden-age-investigative-journalism/; and Sheila Coronel, "Is It Really Investigative Reporting's Golden Age?," Global Investigative Journalism Network, October 28, 2014, https://gijn.org/2014/10/21/is-it-really-investigative-reportings-golden -age/.
3. Global Investigative Journalism Network, "Our Members," n.d., https://gijn.org /member/.
4. Institute for Nonprofit News, "Members," n.d., https://inn.org/members/.
5. Mary Myers and Linet Angaya Juma, "Defending Independent Media: A Comprehensive Analysis of Aid Flows," Center for International Media Assistance Defending Independent Media, June 19, 2018, https://www.cima.ned.org/publication /comprehensive-analysis-media-aid-flows/.
6. Myers and Juma, "Defending Independent Media."
7. National Philanthropic Trust, "Charitable Giving Statistics," 2019, https://www .nptrust.org/philanthropic-resources/charitable-giving-statistics/.

8. Nicholas Fandos, "Nonprofit Journalism Groups Are Gearing Up with Flood of Donations," *New York Times*, December 7, 2016, https://www.nytimes.com/2016/12/07/business/media/nonprofit-journalism-groups-are-gearing-up-with-flood-of-donations.html.

9. James Hamilton, *Democracy's Detectives: The Economics of Investigative Journalism* (Cambridge, MA: Harvard University Press, 2016).

Chapter Fifteen

DEFENDING VANGUARD JOURNALISTS

JOEL SIMON

In the 1990s, when I worked as a freelance journalist in Mexico and wrote frequently about drug trafficking, immigration, and human rights, I developed a network of Mexican reporters who generously hosted me and shared their knowledge as I traveled around the country. None was more important than Jesús Blancornelas, the editor and cofounder of the independent Tijuana weekly *Zeta*. Every time I visited his city, Blancornelas caught me up on the latest local skullduggery. He did the same for many other journalists, shaping perceptions about his troubled city and its relationship to national and global events.

When it comes to media capture, Mexico has been ahead of its time. Long before the term was even coined, the government and its oligarchic allies dominated and controlled the media through concessions, relationships, and commercial pressures.[1] In the 1940s, President Miguel Alemán granted a national broadcast monopoly to Televisa in exchange for the network's unstinting support for the ruling Institutional Revolutionary Party, or PRI.[2] The compact was reaffirmed each night when the network's sycophantic anchor Jacobo Zabludovsky came on the air. His nightly newscast consisted of innocuous interviews with government officials and warmed-over press releases. Televisa's owner, Emilio Azcárraga, once proudly described his station as "part of the government system."

FIGURE 15.1. One of the gunmen in the assassination attempt against editor Jesús Blancornelas in 1997 was hit by a ricochet and died propped up on his own gun.
Source: Photograph by Ramón T. Blanco Villalón/Zeta.

The government used a different system to manage the print media, which in general operated with more latitude. The control mechanisms were subtle, though hardly invisible. Until 1990, there was only one source of newsprint in Mexico, a parastate monopoly called Pipsa.³ Newspaper and magazines were exclusively distributed by vendors who were members of a government-aligned union. State advertising—from legal notices and appeals to visit this or that state-funded tourist development—filled newspapers and magazines. In a famous outburst following the publication of a critical article in the national news magazine *Proceso*, President José López Portillo declared, "No te pago para que me pegues," which translates as "I don't pay you so you can hit me."⁴

Zeta was structured to operate outside this system of pressure and control. When Blancornelas and his partner, Héctor "El Gato" Félix Miranda, founded the tabloid weekly back in 1980, they adopted the motto, "Libre como el viento," or "Free as the wind." In order to evade the government's newsprint monopoly, *Zeta* was printed across the U.S.-Mexico border in San Diego and shipped back into Mexico. It was sold not at the kiosks manned by the PRI-aligned newspaper vendors but by a small army of hawkers employed directly by *Zeta* who hit the streets each Friday and wove through the thousands of cars waiting to cross the border, a captive market. *Zeta* created a sales team and built a base of local businesses from auto-repair shops to taquerias, whose ads filled the paper each week.

These arrangements assured *Zeta's* independence, but it was precisely because Blancornelas could not be controlled by the usual means that the paper became a target of violent retribution. In 1988, *Zeta's* cofounder Héctor Félix was murdered by gunmen linked to Jorge Hank Rhon, the son of a prominent national politician who had relocated to Tijuana and ran the local racetrack. Even while Blancornelas fought for justice for his slain colleague, *Zeta* continued to cover the city aggressively, chronicling the rise of the Arellano–Félix drug cartel and its alleged ties to Hank Rhon, who was later elected mayor.

One notable scoop published in 1997 revealed that the cartel had recruited assassins from the street gangs in San Diego. The gunmen would cross the border into Mexico to carry out their crimes, then slip back into San Diego, safe from Mexican law enforcement, which would not be looking too hard in any case because it had been completely infiltrated and corrupted by the drug cartels. The leader of this transnational hit squad, *Zeta* reported, was named David Barron Corona and went by the nickname "CH."

On November 27, 1997, not long after I started a new job at the Committee to Protect Journalists (CPJ) as the Americas program coordinator, I got a call from a friend in Mexico to let me know that a team of assassins had ambushed Blancornelas on his way to work. His bodyguard, Luis Valero, was dead. Blancornelas was clinging to life and had survived only because the leader of the hit squad had been killed in the crossfire. Blancornelas's son, Cesár René, a photographer for *Zeta*, was first on the scene and captured an image of the dead assassin eerily propped up on his gun. He was later identified as David Barron Corona. The Blancornelas assassination attempt helped fuel the creation of Mexico's first national press freedom organization. But the violence continued.

In June 2004, I got another call. *Zeta* reporter Francisco Ortiz Franco, with whom I had become close, had been shot and killed while picking up his young children from school. With a CPJ colleague, Carlos Lauría, I flew to Tijuana to investigate. In a report published later that year, we disclosed that the murder had once again been carried out by the Tijuana cartel because Ortiz Franco had published photos of police officers who were working for the traffickers.[5]

"I regret having created *Zeta*," Blancornelas told me during that visit when we met him at the newspaper's fortified office. "After losing three colleagues, I believe the price has been too high. I would have liked to retire a long time ago,. . . [but] I cannot allow drug traffickers to think that they were able to crush *Zeta*'s spirit and our readers to believe that we are afraid." Blancornelas ran the paper for another decade, maintaining the same hard-hitting tradition, until dying of natural causes in 2006. Today, the paper is run by his son, René, and his former deputy and protégé, Adela Bella Navarro. They continue to carry on the paper's crusading tradition.

Journalists often work in packs, chasing the same story. What might distinguish one journalist from another is more stylish writing or production, nuggets of new information, or a more informed and critical analysis. Then there are what I call the vanguard journalists. They are journalists whose investigative skills, specialized knowledge, visibility, or courage set them apart from the pack. Vanguard journalists break stories and publish explosive information others are afraid to touch. This relatively small group of reporters has an outsize influence, not just on the way people understand events in their own communities but also on global perceptions.

When the international human rights movement began in the 1970s, it was in response to emblematic cases such as Jacobo Timerman, the Argentine publisher arrested and tortured by the country's military junta, and Andrei Sakharov, the Soviet nuclear scientist turned dissident. Over the intervening decades, as the human rights movement grew, its focus shifted from championing emblematic cases to creating structural change and legal regimes that institutionalize protections for vulnerable populations.[6]

CPJ and other press freedom organizations have also evolved to focus more on systematic change, such as eliminating criminal defamation laws and protecting journalists from government surveillance. But precisely because of the role played by vanguard journalists, defending the rights of individual reporters remains a crucial part of the day-to-day work toward change. Preserving the life of one such journalist or getting one such reporter out of jail helps ensure the flow of information at the global level. The imperative is all the more acute in an age of media capture. As the less-visible means of control grow, journalists who operate outside these systems must be championed and defended.

Examples of vanguard journalists who have had a transformational impact on their media environment include Veran Matić and Saša Mirković at the Belgrade-based radio station B-92, which they founded in 1989. During the Balkan Wars, the station provided an independent, critical perspective for a domestic audience and served as a tremendous resource for international journalists based in Belgrade.[7]

Peruvian investigative journalist Gustavo Gorriti provided groundbreaking reporting on the radical Marxist group Sendero Luminoso but also broke stories linking senior officials in the government of Alberto Fujimori to drug traffickers. In 1992, government security forces abducted Gorriti from his home in Lima. He was released after two days in response to an international outcry. He later took a job at the Panamanian daily *La Prensa*, where he published stories on the growing presence of the Cali cartel and its efforts to influence the Panamanian government.[8]

In Zimbabwe, as editor of the country's last independent tabloid, the *Daily News*, Geoffrey Nyarota withstood the withering assault on press freedom by the government of President Robert Mugabe. He was forced into exile in 2002 by two bombings, six arrests, and an alleged plot on his life.[9]

For two decades, Paraguayan journalist Candido Figueredo has covered organized crime for the national daily *ABC Color* from his base in the border town Pedro Juan Caballero. He has lived surrounded by armed guards, never leaving his home without his trusted Glock pistol. "It never passed through my head to arm myself," Figueredo told me in when I spoke with him in 2015. "But at the end of the day, you can't count on someone else to risk their life for yours. I understand people who criticize me for being armed. I just ask them to live with me for one week. I think they will change their opinion."[10]

All of these journalists have been subjected to repression. They all have relied on international pressure to protect them from powerful and violent forces that have grasped a terrible reality: in most cases, if a vanguard journalist is eliminated, there is no one who can step forward to take his or her place; thus, death equals censorship. In his book *Marked for Death: Dying for the Story in the World's Most Dangerous Places*, Terry Gould notes that journalists who are driven by a belief in their own power to right injustice are "unstoppable except by murder."[11]

It sadly sometimes comes to that. Mozambican journalist Carlos Cardoso, who was murdered in 2000, was a unique figure in that country's history.[12] The son of Portuguese exiles, Cardoso grew up in Mozambique's capital, Maputo. He was educated across the border in South Africa, where he battled against apartheid and became a supporter of FRELIMO, the Marxist guerrilla organization fighting for Mozambique's independence from Portugal. When Mozambique's colonial government was toppled on July 25, 1975, Cardoso joined the celebration. For more than a decade, Cardoso worked for a series of state-run media organizations, but his independent streak caused problems. He frequently butted heads because of his critical and aggressive journalism.[13]

In October 1986, Mozambican president and independence leader Samora Machel was killed in a plane crash in South Africa. Many believed he was murdered by the apartheid regime in reprisal for his support for the African National Congress. South Africa was also backing the anti-Communist RENAMO rebels who were waging a brutal insurgency against Mozambique's Marxist government.[14]

Cardoso eventually clashed with the FRELIMO government, which, following Machel's death, was led by President Joaquim Chissano. In 1997, Cardoso launched a new publication called *Metical*, a reference to the Mozambican currency. Precisely because he was denouncing the FRELIMO leadership for betraying their socialist ideals, he sought to live by example. At *Metical*, reporters and janitors were paid the same salary. But Cardoso stood out among Mozambique's small press corps not just because of his independence but also because of his incredible aptitude for financial reporting. The mass privatization of Mozambique's state companies, combined with the opening of the banking sector, fueled massive corruption and eventually turned Maputo into a regional money-laundering hub. A real-estate boom transformed Maputo's skyline, even as the country remained one of the poorest in the region.

In October 2000, two men began staking out *Metical*'s office. A month later, they cut off Cardoso's car in busy downtown traffic and sprayed gunfire from high-powered rifles. When the gunmen were eventually arrested, they led police to the two brothers Abdul and Momade Satar, who owned a series of the exchange houses and had been involved in a banking scandal that Cardoso had covered. In May 2001, I traveled to Maputo as part of a CPJ delegation to investigate Cardoso's murder. The city was beautiful and vibrant but also had a menacing atmosphere. Every well-placed source we spoke with pointed us to the possible involvement of President Chissano's son Nyimpine in Cardoso's murder. One day Nyimpine and his entourage showed up at our hotel. They sat conspicuously in the lobby and actively listened to our conversation. We viewed this behavior as a form of intimidation.

In a convoluted legal process that went on for years, the gunmen were put on trial, and the Satar brothers were convicted. A middleman, Aníbal dos Santos Júnior, was charged with organizing the murder but escaped twice from prison under highly suspicious circumstances. He was eventually extradited from Canada back to Mozambique, where he was sentenced to thirty years in prison.[15] Nyimpine Chissano died of a heart attack in November 2007. He was only thirty-seven. At the time of his death, he was under investigation for Cardoso's murder, but he was never brought to trial. The entire process was a mess, but it was hardly a whitewash. The international pressure helped to achieve partial justice. But what was never the same was the Mozambican press corp. The problem was not that journalists faced systematic repression but that no one could step into Cardoso's shoes and pursue the financial stories that needed to be told.

Another vanguard journalist whose murder left a permanent void in the global information landscape was Anna Politkovskaya. One of Russia's leading investigative journalists, Politkovskaya was shot dead in front of her Moscow apartment on October 7, 2006. If Cardoso was distinguished by his acumen for financial reporting, what set Politkovskaya apart were her deep compassion and fearlessness. She lived with constant threats and survived a poisoning attempt. She could not be deterred. She insisted on telling the stories of the victims of the brutal conflict in Chechnya, which pitted Islamist-inspired separatists against Kremlin-backed pro-Russian forces.[16] Politkovskaya chronicled the suffering of civilians murdered by militants and killed in indiscriminate bombing. She also told the stories of the Russian conscripts who endured constant abuse and deprivation at the hands of their superiors.[17]

After Politkovskaya's murder and the murder of her colleague, journalist and human rights activist Natalya Estemirova, the flow of information from the North Caucasus slowed dramatically. Politkovskaya's reporting had not only documented the systematic violations of human rights by Chechen forces but also exposed the web of business dealings and Kremlin-sponsored corruption that kept Chechen leader Ramzan Kadyrov in power. It is not a coincidence that following her murder and that of Estemirova, Kadyrov was able to consolidate political control over Chechnya. Today, with strong Kremlin backing, close ties to President Vladimir Putin, and very little media scrutiny, Kadyrov is virtually untouchable.

Vanguard journalists' ability to circumvent the mechanisms of media control is essential to their project. For *Zeta* and Blancornelas, the project was about finding alternative ways to print and distribute the newspaper. In other cases, circumvention has involved the exploitation of new information technologies.

For Cuban journalists working in the 1990s, that meant the internet. The irony was that because of state censorship the internet was not available in Cuba, but independent journalists found a workaround. Cuba is a highly repressive society, but it is also legalistic. One thing that is not illegal is talking on the phone, a loophole that independent Cuban journalists exploited.

Cuban journalists arranged to receive regular calls from colleagues in Miami who had set up a news website they called CubaNet. Journalists on the island would dictate their stories or share their experiences and observations. The resulting stories, posted online in the United States, were picked up by Radio Martí, the U.S. government–funded propaganda network, and broadcast back into Cuba, thus infuriating the regime. The Cuban government eventually found a way to stem the tide of embarrassing information. While the world was distracted by the U.S.-led invasion of Iraq, Cuban security forces rounded up dozens of journalists in a sweeping crackdown beginning in March 2003 that became known as the Black Spring. They were jailed on charges of acting against the "integrity and sovereignty of the state" and collaborating with foreign media for the purpose of "destabilizing the country." Many were held for years, until they were released as part of an agreement brokered by Spain and the Catholic Church and then forced into permanent exile.[18]

A more recent innovation came from a Syrian citizen journalism collective, Raqqa Is Being Slaughtered Silently, or RBSS. After fleeing their native city Raqqa, the group's leaders set up shop across the border in Turkey. They built up a network of anonymous correspondents inside Raqqa who smuggled out information using flash drives and an erratic internet connection. RBSS became a crucial source of information for international journalists unable to access Syria directly because of the risks. But the cost of its activism was high. At least four RBSS collaborators were murdered by the Islamic State, both inside Syria and in neighboring Turkey.[19]

Information technologies have in general made it more difficult for those in power to manage and control information. Only a few highly repressive countries, such as Cuba, North Korea, and Eritrea, fully control online access. Several others, such as China and Iran, have invested enormous resources to create permanent structures of information management. But in the rest of the world direct censorship has become obsolete.

Governments and other forces that seek to control and manage information instead tend to respond once news is made public. They have two primary means of doing so. One is direct repression. Imprisonment is a favored tactic. At the end of the 2017, 262 journalists were in jail around the world, the highest number ever recorded by CPJ.[20] (Over the next several years, the tally averaged around 250.)[21] The wave of repression can be directly correlated with the popular uprisings of the Arab Spring in 2011. Governments in the region and around the world understood that the public protests were fueled in part by new technologies that allowed people to share information and organize more readily. In China, Russia, and across the Middle East, repression increased as a result.[22] Turkey and Egypt have adopted an antiterror framework to justify their repressive actions and have made sweeping arrests to stem the tide of information. This type of mass repression breeds fear and self-censorship.

In areas under the influence of powerful nonstate actors, violence achieves the same purpose. People living under the authority of the Islamic State understood that the penalty for violating its information regime was death. The circumstances are not much different for those journalists living under the sway of the Mexican drug cartels.

For some journalists, the logical but painful choice is to leave the country and go into exile. In July 2016, when dissident soldiers launched an attempted coup against Turkey's president Recep Tayyip Erdoğan, Can Dundar happened to be out of the country. He never went home.

Dundar, the editor of the daily *Cumhuriyet*, had been arrested in November 2015 along with one of his reporters and jailed for several months. The imprisonment was in reprisal for reporting on a Turkish government effort to smuggle a convoy of trucks containing boxes of weapons across the border to Islamist militants fighting the Assad regime in Syria.[23] Today Dundar lives in Germany.

Meanwhile, Patricia Mayorga left her native Chihuahua, Mexico, after her friend and colleague Miroslava Breach was murdered in March 2017. Breach was gunned down in reprisal for her reporting on human rights violations, corruption, and illegal logging. Today, Mayorga continues to report on those same topics, but from outside Chihuahua. Mayorga knows she needs to stay alive to continue reporting but acknowledges that it is much more difficult to cover the story when she is far away and sources are scared.

In other instances, governments respond not with violence but with efforts to marginalize, undermine, or intimidate reporters who report critically. In Mexico, this tactic has a long history as well as a name, *ninguneo*, meaning "to turn a someone into a nobody." In Venezuela, Hugo Chávez and his successor, Nicolás Maduro, openly denounced critical journalists as corrupt, lazy enemies of the Venezuelan people (sound familiar?). They used state media and social media to undermine the credibility of the media and attack individual journalists. In Turkey and Egypt, the government routinely refers to journalists as terrorists.

The threat of marginalization is compounded by the media structure, which has been fragmented by technology. Many local media organizations have disappeared, and larger national organizations have fewer resources. Both make the remaining media organizations more vulnerable to media capture, such as takeovers by oligarchic interests sympathetic to governments, a favored tactic in Russia. Media organizations that retain their independence tend to have fewer resources to support the kind of in-depth, high-risk reporting that changes perceptions. Technology has also become a tool of repression. Governments use social media to monitor their critics and mobilize troll armies to attack and threaten them online. In repressive countries such as Egypt and Iran, they force imprisoned journalists to give up their passwords, then access their email and social media to track down their sources.[24] And they are increasingly able to achieve the same effect through malware implanted in journalists' devices.[25] This is why in the internet era, even as the barriers to publications have been reduced or eliminated, the risk of violence and repression to journalists has grown.

One way of keeping journalists safer is to create structures that support them in this new networked environment. One of the most successful efforts has been carried by the International Consortium of Investigative Journalists (ICIJ), publishers of the Panama Papers and the Paradise Papers (in which media organizations around the world collaborated to publish stories based on leaked electronic documents related to offshore investments and tax evasion). The ICIJ has built a community of international investigative reporters who collaborate and support each other. More visibility means more impact, and more impact can mean more safety. It's a virtuous cycle, until it isn't. The Organized Crime and Corruption Reporting Project (OCCPR) brings together the leading investigative journalists in the Balkans and central Europe. In February 2017, Slovak journalist Jan Kuciak was shot dead along with his girlfriend while he was working on a story for the OCCPR on the growing Mafia presence in Slovakia.[26]

The physical risk to journalists who operate outside systems of media control has been constant, so that supporting vanguard journalists means keeping them alive. According to CPJ data, 40 percent of journalists are threatened before they are killed.[27] Over the years, CPJ and the other press freedom groups have evacuated dozens of journalists facing imminent threat of violence. But this strategy also has its limits. After all, what makes vanguard journalists so special is their willingness to risk their lives, their stubborn belief that there are stories worth dying for.

In 2011, CPJ honored the Mexican journalist Javier Valdez Cárdenas with an International Press Freedom Award.[28] The award was given in recognition of his courageous reporting on drug traffickers and corruption in the state of Sinaloa. It was also a way, we hoped, to increase his security because international visibility can raise the political cost of violence.

For years, Valdez Cárdenas had lived in a state of heightened anxiety. He was constantly evaluating and recalibrating his reporting and his movements based on the changing threat environment in Sinaloa. He knew that cartel leaders didn't like his reporting, but he also knew that they were running a business and that murdering a journalist would not be good for their bottom line. On February 19, 2016, Valdez Cárdenas published a story in his newspaper *Ríodoce* based on an interview with a leader of the Sinaloa cartel. The story was so sensitive that members of the cartel bought up the entire edition before it hit the streets. On March 12, Valdez Cárdenas wrote to the CPJ to say that he felt vulnerable and planned to spend some time in Mexico City working on a book. We urged him to get out of the country for several months until the situation calmed down, but Valdez Cárdenas said he had work to do to inform his city, his country, and the world. He saw this work as a responsibility he couldn't turn his back on. And so he went back to Culiacán. On May 15, 2016, only a few weeks after returning home, Valdez Cárdenas was shot dead as he was walking from his car to the newspaper's offices.

Valdez Cárdenas's murder was devastating for the CPJ staff. I told my colleagues we had done all we could to support him while he was alive. Now that he was gone, we had to honor and respect his decision to take the risks he took. It was only later when I met with Valdez Cárdenas's widow, Griselda, and their children, that I fully grasped the devastation his murder had wrought.

I thought back to what Blancornelas had told me after the murder of his colleague Ortiz Franco: he regretted starting *Zeta* but carried on because he could not allow the forces of violence to prevail. That role for vanguard journalists is even more vital and important today as the strategies of media capture have spread around the world, transformed by technology, putting new constraints and limitations on media organizations that were once able to work the margins. The challenge ahead is clear and remarkably unchanged over the past three decades. We must fight against the systems of media control, but we also must defend those who exercise journalism with courage and integrity. Preserving press freedom means doing all we can do to keep them safe. It means rallying for justice when they are killed. And if we fail in that effort—as we too often will—it means doing all in our power to comfort the grieving and honor the sacrifices of all the vanguard journalists who have given their lives for the truth.

NOTES

1. On media capture in Mexico, see in general William A. Orme Jr., ed., *A Culture of Collusion: An Inside Look at the Mexican Press* (Miami: University of Miami North South Center, 1996).
2. Claudia Fernández and Andrew Paxman, *El Tigre: Emilio Azcárraga y su imperio Televisa* (Mexico City: Grialbo, 2013).

3. Reuters, "Mexico Ending Paper Control," April 21, 1990.
4. Joaquim Ibarz, "La prensa mexicana y el poder: 'No te pago para que me pegues,'"
   La Vanguardia, September 24, 2005.
5. Joel Simon and Carlos Lauría, "Mexico: Free Fire Zone," Committee to Protect Journalists (CPJ), November 2004, https://cpj.org/reports/2004/11/tijuana/.
6. See Aryeh Neier, *Taking Liberties: Four Decades in the Struggle for Rights* (New York:
   PublicAffairs, 2005).
7. CNN, "Government Takes Over Independent Yugoslav Radio Station," April 2, 1999.
8. European Journalism Centre, "Investigative Journalism According to Gustavo Gorriti," May 26, 2011.
9. CPJ, "Attacks on the Press 2002: Zimbabwe," March 31, 2003, https://cpj.org/2003
   /03/attacks-on-the-press-2002-zimbabwe/.
10. Candido Figueredo, quoted in Joel Simon, "A Gun-Carrying Journalist, and Rightly
    So," *Columbia Journalism Review*, November 16, 2015, https://www.cjr.org/first_per-
    son/gun_carrying_journalist.php.
11. Terry Gould, *Marked for Death: Dying for the Story in the World's Most Dangerous
    Places* (Berkeley, CA: Counterpoint, 2010), 321.
12. CPJ, "Mozambique Report: The Murder of Carlos Cardoso," May 2, 2002, https://
    cpj.org/reports/2002/05/moz-may02/.
13. CPJ, "Mozambique Report."
14. "Mozambique's Renamo: A Short History," *Mail & Guardian*, October 23, 2013.
15. "A Trial Ends in Mozambique, but Many Questions Hover," *New York Times*, Janu-
    ary 21, 2006.
16. See Anna Politkovskaya, *A Small Corner of Hell: Dispatches from Chechnya* (Chi-
    cago: University of Chicago Press, 2007).
17. See Anna Politkovskaya, *Is Journalism Worth Dying For?* (London: Melville House,
    2011).
18. Carlos Lauría, "Cuba's Long Black Spring," CPJ, March 18, 2008, https://cpj.org
    /reports/2008/03/cuba-press-crackdown/; CPJ, "Cuba Frees 17th Journalist Jailed in
    Black Spring," October 12, 2010, https://cpj.org/2010/10/cuba-frees-17th-journalist
    -jailed-in-black-spring/.
19. Zia Weise, "Isil Murders Five Media Activists for Exposing Syria Atrocities," *Tele-
    graph*, June 26, 2016.
20. CPJ, "Record Number of Jailed Journalists for Second Year, CPJ Census Finds,"
    December 13, 2017, https://cpj.org/2017/12/record-number-of-jailed-journalists-for
    -second-yea/.
21. Elana Beiser, "China, Turkey, Saudi Arabia, Egypt Are World's Worst Jailers of Jour-
    nalists," CPJ, December 11, 2019, https://cpj.org/reports/2019/12/journalists-jailed
    -china-turkey-saudi-arabia-egypt/.
22. Joel Simon, *The New Censorship: Inside the Global Battle for Media Freedom* (New
    York: Columbia University Press, 2017).
23. Agence France-Presse, "Turkish Journalists Charged Over Claim That Secret Ser-
    vices Armed Syrian Rebels," November 26, 2017.
24. Simon, *The New Censorship.*
25. See Azam Ahmed and Nicole Perlroth, "Using Texts as Lures, Government Spyware
    Targets Mexican Journalists and Their Families," *New York Times*, June 19, 2017.

26. Edin Pašović, "A Murdered Journalist's Last Investigation," Organized Crime and Corruption Reporting Project, February 2018, https://www.occrp.org/en/amurder edjournalistslastinvestigation/.

27. Elisabeth Witchel, "Getting Away with Murder," CPJ, October 27, 2016, https://cpj .org/reports/2017/10/impunity-index-getting-away-with-murder-killed-justice-2/.

28. Sara Rafsky, "Javier Valdez Cárdenas, Brave and Beloved Mexican Journalist," CPJ, May 15, 2017, https://cpj.org/2017/05/javier-valdez-cardenas-brave-and-beloved -mexican-j/.

Chapter Sixteen

DO TECHNOLOGY COMPANIES CARE
ABOUT JOURNALISM?

EMILY BELL

The extent to which technology platform companies have been able to integrate themselves into the fabric of the news industry is a concern for the accountability of both. At a relatively low cost, rarely exceeding $100 million a year, the largest and wealthiest technology companies have used their economic power to create a patronage system within news, which ties reporting organizations to these commercial entities in often opaque and subtle ways.

In a survey in 2019 of all journalism projects funded by Google, the Oracle-sponsored Google Transparency Project found that there were more than 3,700 separate instances of Google funding journalism projects or journalists at a total cost of around half a billion dollars.[1] The nature of how Google and Facebook make money from advertising, by collecting user data and tracking behavior and content, already embeds them within the field of practice for publishers. Their own content-moderation policies and terms of use are proxies for a new type of publishing standard, and yet the scale and scope of their activities mark them out as being nonjournalistic entities. The vast scope of their wealth and products mean technology platform companies that are funding journalism are simultaneously working with governments, commercial organizations, and other stakeholders in ways that might represent a conflict of interest.

Assessing the impact and influence of these interventions, either bene-ficial or detrimental, is difficult because neither Google nor Facebook has a consistent policy of sharing its data on funded projects or even of disclos-ing the terms or amount of the funding. Journalists (and academic researchers) are often asked to sign nondisclosure agreements as a condi-tion of receiving funding. Most of the time, journalistic organizations them-selves do not disclose the funding they have received. The governance and accountability process for how the funds are dispersed and what effects the funding has are either not tracked or not reported in every case.

Because the news industry is so weakened financially on the face of it, the offers of subsidy, partnership, and training represent welcome help from which valuable projects can emerge. However, the terms of the platforms' engagement with the news business are arbitrary and unregulated and lack both data and oversight. The frequent funding of news organizations that are already well supported (grants have been given to organizations such as the BBC, the *New York Times*, the *Economist*, and so on) suggests that the web of tech company patronage is not aimed simply at redressing finan-cial need. Research suggests that the spikes in funding journalism come from external regulatory pressure and can be seen as analogous to lobby-ing or marketing expenditure. There is also a substantial risk that funding creates direct relationships with the heart of the newsroom, thus giving plat-form companies a level of access to journalists that few other organiza-tions would have. This access is being gained at a time when the need for investigations into platform accountability is high and the arguments for regulation are growing.

Although a number of other technology companies, including Apple, Snapchat, LinkedIn, and Twitter, have products or services aimed at journalists, Google and Facebook in particular have been the focus of attention. From 2015 on, both companies directly aimed at subsidizing either individual news organizations or journalists through myriad dif-ferent initiatives. These initiatives included but are not limited to inno-vation projects, training and scholarships, conferences and direct pay-ments for content. Facebook famously provoked a rush to "pivot to video" in 2016 by pushing video production as an advertising priority. It launched Facebook Live as a video service, soliciting commissions from publishers with financial incentives. A number of newsrooms, including *Mic* and *Mashable*, significantly reshaped their newsrooms around video and in *Mic*'s case directly in response to the sums of money offered by Facebook. Then when the social media platform changed its mind about video two years later, many newsrooms had to lay off staff, and some—such as *Mic*—had to close altogether.

These collateral effects have so far, however, been indirect. A more recent trend is for platform companies to move in to much more direct support for news organizations. Google is leading this trend, and its deliberate policy of funding journalism directly is unprecedented and deserves further scrutiny.

In mid-2019, Google announced it would partner with the news chain McClatchy to fund three new local news entities in communities of less than five hundred thousand people. This marks a change in how quickly the news business is being absorbed into the fringes of large technology businesses. For the first time, a major technology company is working directly with news executives to set up local news operations, which it proposes to fund.

Craig Forman, chief executive of McClatchy, describes the effort as a true "collaboration" in which the McClatchy team will work with experts at Google. Though Google "is helping support the effort financially," Forman wrote in a press release on the *Google Blog*, "the sites will be 100 percent McClatchy owned and operated and McClatchy will maintain sole editorial control and ownership of the content." Just in case we are in any doubt, he reiterated that "Google will have no input or involvement in any editorial efforts or decision making."[2]

It is hard to know what it will look like to have experts from Google collaborating with McClatchy staff but without any editorial input. Everyone who has built a successful news product online knows that the technical architecture, tools, software, and analytics applied to journalism inevitably end up shaping aspects of editorial content. In fact, one of the most common errors in newsrooms is the failure to properly integrate "product" into the newsroom or to properly take into account the technological environment into which they are publishing.

No company has done more to fund and support journalism over the past decade than Google. It is almost impossible to attend a news conference, hear about experimentation in newsrooms, or even look at journalism research without seeing Google's name on the funding credits. The expansion into the United States of Google's Digital News Initiative, which has spent more than a hundred million euros on news innovations in

Europe, has so far included high-profile investments into Report for America and now the McClatchy initiative.

Because so little advertising money remains available to publications and reader revenue has not met that shortfall, the expensive job of innovation in newsrooms increasingly means asking, "What would Google want?," which influences what newsrooms choose to develop, from virtual reality to voice skills to photo libraries.

But to question Google is now frowned upon in many quarters in journalism. The company has received markedly better press than some of its competitors, notably Facebook. This is in part because it is more mature and handles relations with the press far better (it has not tried to hide its own influence campaigns, for instance). It also spends more money. The extra money Google provides to journalism is not directly buying favor or dampening dissent, but it is certainly making news CEOs and editors I speak to put Google in a subtly different category from other platforms. Their attitude is that "Google gets it." In the earliest days of Google News, when I was in charge of editorial for the *Guardian*'s websites and digital products, we benefitted from a close relationship with Google when it came to understanding how to optimize article metadata for Google's search algorithms. It is easy to see day-to-day "help" as beneficial to journalism if you are directly benefitting.

But Google's foray into local journalism is not just a matter of help. When the company launched the Digital News Initiative in Europe, it was a direct response to pressure by European Union regulators. The money was allocated from a marketing budget and amounted to a lobbying exercise. As Google moved its direct-funding efforts into the United States, it did so ahead of the presidential election in 2020 and at the point at which the Democratic field was being assembled. For the first time in a presidential contest, regulating technology platforms registered as an issue for the electorate, was on the agenda of at least one serious candidate, Elizabeth Warren, and has long been an area of interest for another, Amy Klobuchar. Bernie Sanders also announced a plan to fund journalism from hypothecated taxation of platform companies.

Those who would rethink antitrust law in order to break up the world's Facebooks, Amazons, and Alphabets (Google's holding company) are gaining traction. But the think tank that pioneered much of this work, the Open Markets Initiative, lost its perch at the New America Foundation in

2017 when it caused tension with major funder Google. But who would suggest that Google's increased funding of U.S. journalism is at all related to the first major initiatives to regulate technology platforms? This sounds like a conspiracy theory so rich it should be relentlessly promoted on YouTube.

The suddenness of technology companies caring about the financial stability of journalism is not at all coincidental. As *Columbia Journalism Review*'s Mathew Ingram reported, Facebook assembled its own local news conference in Denver recently (the conference Wi-Fi password was "movefast").[3] Tim "Apple" Cook spent several minutes of his opening speech during the company's semiannual marketing presentation in March 2019 proclaiming his love of journalism before launching Apple News+, a product that reduces your $8,000 magazine bill to $10.[4]

Having spent a lot of time with news executives who work for technology companies, I can say that plenty of people in those companies are knowledgeable about—and care about—journalism. Many of them are smart and accomplished journalists who have a genuine zeal for improving journalism. But they are relegated to marginal departments. The core of platform companies is software engineering; they are at the core of our business, but we are not at the core of theirs. Miles away from the ritzy conferences such as Newsgeist and the meetings for the Facebook Journalism Project, in the central loci of technology businesses, executives generally don't care that much about journalism. They see it as the Pluto in their solar system—a part of what they do, but rather small and very far away. They care about journalism in the same way I care about clean water and aircraft safety—deeply and often—but this does not qualify me to be involved in its development.

Facebook, Apple, and Google do things that journalists should be investigating, not profiting from. Google negotiates with the U.S. Department of Defense—albeit to the horror of half of Google's employees—and tries to cover it up; Facebook underpays and traumatizes employees who deal with blacklisting offensive content; Apple works with regimes that routinely jail journalists and construct ethnic concentration camps. All three have strategies for managing the press, and they publish very little data about what happens on their platforms or the effects of what they do. All of this makes tech reporting a vital form of accountability.

Although Google's partnership with McClatchy is unprecedented, non-journalistic organizations taking on the role of publishers and funding journalism directly are not new. What's new is the industry-wide acceptance of funding from Google and Facebook, in particular the funding of independent journalism at a local level. Individuals who have made money from technology have sometimes used it to support journalism; Jeff Bezos has been hailed for his salvation and resurrection of the *Washington Post*; Laurene Powell Jobs's Emerson Collective is supporting and expanding the *Atlantic*; Craig Newmark (who founded Craigslist) funds journalism schools and research, including parts of both the *Columbia Journalism Review* and the Tow Center.

In all of these operations, transparency and a commitment to editorial independence from funding makes for somewhat comfortable relationships. But when it comes to corporate interests, journalists have to be alert to agendas in conflict with their own. For technology to support journalism in a totally independent way—more than one way, in fact—is possible, for the record: it can be done through taxation and an expansion of civic media. It can be done through payments into arms-length endowments administered by separate bodies. It can even be done by changing the incentive structures on the digital platforms to elevate newsrooms and return more money to them.

Whether it can be done with the direct system of patronage that Google and other platforms are offering remains highly unlikely.

NOTES

An earlier version of this chapter was previously published in *Columbia Journalism Review*, March 27, 2019, https://www.cjr.org/tow_center/google-facebook -journalism-influence.php. The edited version here is published with permission by *Columbia Journalism Review*.

1. Google Transparency Project (n.a.), "Google's Media Takeover," October 2019, https://www.techtransparencyproject.org/sites/default/files/GTP-Media-Takeover .pdf.
2. Craig Forman, "McClatchy and Google Partner on an Experimental Lab for Local News," *Google Blog*, March 26, 2019, https://www.blog.google/outreach-initiatives/ google-news-initiative/mcclatchy-and-google-partner-experimental-lab-local- news/.
3. Matthew Ingram, "Facebook: We Care Deeply About Journalism. Please Believe Us," *Columbia Journalism Review*, March 22, 2019.
4. Apple, *March Event 2019—Apple*, YouTube, https://youtu.be/TZmBoMZFC8g.

CONTRIBUTORS

Emily Bell is founding director of the Tow Center for Digital Journalism at Columbia Journalism School and a leading thinker, commentator, and strategist on digital journalism.

Ryan Chittum is a journalist who has worked at the *Wall Street Journal*, *Columbia Journalism Review*, International Consortium of Investigative Journalists, and *Traffic Magazine*.

Noam Cohen is the author of *The Know-It-Alls: The Rise of Silicon Valley as a Political Powerhouse and Social Wrecking Ball*.

James Cusick is editor of openMedia at OpenDemocracy and a former political correspondent at the *Independent* and the *Independent on Sunday*. As an experienced member of the lobby, he has previously worked at the *Sunday Times* and the BBC.

Andrew Finkel is a correspondent and columnist who has been based in Turkey for over thirty years. He has worked for both international and Turkish-language media and is a cofounder of P24, an Istanbul-based NGO that defends freedom of expression and press integrity.

Mary Fitzgerald is openDemocracy's editor in chief. She has served on the editorial code committee of Impress, the UK press regulator, and is a former senior editor of Prospect magazine in London. Her writing has appeared in the *Guardian*, *New York Times*, *New York Review of Books*, *New Statesman*, *Project Syndicate*, and Al-Jazeera and has been syndicated globally.

Rana Foroohar is global business columnist and an associate editor at the *Financial Times*. She is also CNN's global economic analyst. She is the author of *Makers and Takers: The Rise of Finance and the Fall of American Business* and *Don't Be Evil: How Big Tech Betrayed Its Founding Principles and All of Us*.

Andrea Gabor is the Bloomberg Professor of business journalism at Baruch College/ CUNY and the author of several books, most recently *After the Education Wars: How Smart Schools Upend the Business of Reform*. She also writes a regular column on education for *Bloomberg Opinion*.

Peter Geoghegan is investigations editor of openDemocracy's main site and a founder of the cooperative investigative journalism project the Ferret. His most recent book is *Democracy for Sale: Dark Money and Dirty Politics*.

James Ledbetter is the editor and publisher of FIN and former editor-in-chief of *Inc*. He is most recently the author of *One Nation under Gold: How One Precious Metal Has Dominated the American Imagination for Four Centuries* (Liveright, 2017).

Josh Marshall is the founder, editor, and publisher of *Talking Points Memo*. He received the George Polk Award in 2007.

Philip M. Napoli is the James R. Shepley Professor of Public Policy in the Sanford School of Public Policy at Duke University, where he is also a faculty affiliate with the DeWitt Wallace Center for Media and Democracy. His most recent books are *Audience Evolution: New Technologies and the Transformation of Media Audiences* (2010) and *Social Media and the Public Interest: Media Regulation in the Disinformation Age* (2019), both from Columbia University Press.

Raju Narisetti is the founder of India's *Mint/LiveMint* newspaper and website. He has previously worked at the *Wall Street Journal*, the *Washington Post*, News Corp, Univision/Gizmodo Media Group, and Columbia Journalism School.

Mark M. Nelson is senior director at the National Endowment for Democracy, where he heads the Center for International Media Assistance. He previously worked on governance and development at the World Bank and as staff reporter for the *Wall Street Journal* based in Brussels, Berlin, and Paris.

Felix Salmon is the chief financial correspondent at *Axios* and host of *Slate Money*.

Anya Schiffrin is the director of the Technology, Media, and Communications specialization at Columbia University's School of International and Public Affairs. She teaches courses on media and development and innovation. She is the editor of *African Muckraking: 75 Years of African Investigative Journalism* (2017) and *Global Muckraking: 100 Years of Investigative Reporting from Around the World* (2014).

Joel Simon is the executive director of the Committee to Protect Journalists. Simon has written widely on press freedom issues for publications in the United States and around the world. He is a regular columnist for *Columbia Journalism Review* and the author of several books, including *The New Censorship: Inside the Global Battle for Media Freedom* (Columbia University Press, 2015) and *We Want to Negotiate: The Secret World of Kidnapping, Hostages, and Ransom* (Columbia Global Reports, 2019).

Dean Starkman is a senior editor for the International Consortium of Investigative Journalists. He is a fellow in residence at the Center for Media, Data, and Society in the Democracy Institute at the Central European University, Budapest. He is the author of *The Watchdog That Didn't Bark: The Financial Crisis and the Disappearance of Investigative Journalism* (Columbia University Press, 2014).

Andrew Sullivan is a social entrepreneur who cofounded in 2007 the Organized Crime and Corruption Reporting Program, where he serves as editor. Before that, he founded and edited the Center for Investigative Reporting, the leading investigative center in Bosnia-Herzegovina, in 2004.

Nikki Usher is an associate professor of journalism in the College of Media at the University of Illinois with affiliate appointments in communication and political science. She is most recently the author of *Interactive Journalism: Hackers, Data, and Code* (2016) and *News for the Rich, White, and Blue: How Place and Power Distort American Journalism* (Columbia University Press, 2021).

INDEX

strategies for, 119; fundraising amounts for, 117–18; through No Child Left Behind policy, 118; during Obama administration, 117; Teach for America, 118; transparency laws and, 126; *Vergara v. California*, 124, 128–29; through vouchers, 135–36; in *Washington Post*, 135. *See also specific philanthropic organizations; specific topics*

Egypt, social media in, 219

8-chan, 40

Eli and Edythe Broad Foundation: education reform and, 117, 122–33; *The Founders*, 131; Great Public Schools Now initiative, 122–23; influence of, 124–26; *LA School Report* and, 126–32

Engadget, 95

Entman, Robert, 32

Erdoğan, Tayyip, 141, 143–46, 153, 157n12, 158n30; attempted coup against, 285; as authoritarian leader, 214; on social media, 146; Trump and, 146

ESI Media, 192–93, 195, 198

Estemirova, Natalya, 283–84

ethics, for journalists, media capture and, 76

European Union (EU): Anti-Fraud Office, 251–52; Brussels bureaucrats, 3; Civitates in, 17; Digital News Initiative in, 293–94; Media Pluralism Monitor in, 216; unified media policy in, 220

Evening Standard, 188–92, 205

Every Student Succeeds Act, U.S. (2015), 119

Facebook: blogs and, 99–100; in Brazil, 35; Cambridge Analytica scandal, 36, 112; exemptions for Trump, 69; financial support for media outlets, 25; in Germany, 225; Google compared to, 87; in India, 225; influence peddling by, 12; investment in, 236; journalistic productivity negatively influenced by, 242; in Libya, 225; as monopoly, 220; in

Myanmar, 225; as news platform, retreat from, 74–75; in Philippines, 225; in Sri Lanka, 225; user growth for, 33

Facebook Journalism Project, 295

Facebook Live, 292

fact-based reporting, 73

Federal Communications Commission (FCC), 5, 219–20

Federal Trade Commission (FTC), 109; Cambridge Analytica scandal and, 112; digital payola guidelines, 111–12

Federated Media, 96

Ferret, 202–4

FIDESZ. *See* Alliance of Young Democrats

Figueredo, Candido, 281

filtering: in blogs, 51–52; in local journalism, 51–54; in online news, 51–52; in print media, 53

Financial Times, paywall for, 244

Fleet Street, 197–98

Florida, education reform in, 133–36

Flynn, Mike, 112–13

Follow the Money (Reckhow), 117

Forbes (magazine), 115n3

Forbes.com, 106

Ford Foundation, journalism and, 14

Forman, Craig, 293

for-profit journalism, 236–44

Founders, The (Eli and Edythe Broad Foundation), 131

4-chan, 40

Fourth Estate, 4; captured, 195–96; media capture and, 213. *See also* journalism

Fox News, Trump election and, influence on, 3, 5

France: public broadcasting in, 16; value added tax rates in, 16

free and independent media: governmental support of, 15–16; in India, 160; in United Kingdom, 198–201

Freed, Allan, 105

FTC. *See* Federal Trade Commission

Talking Points Memo (TPM): Google and, as revenue source, 84–91; violations for hate-speech bans, 88

Tampa Bay Times, 135

Tanzania, blogger taxes in, 219

tax credits, 234, 253

Teach for America, 118

Teles, Steven, 118

television: in India, 161; private, in Turkey, 157n8. *See also* broadcast media

television advertising, digital advertising compared to, 24–25

Thailand, non-coercive media capture in, 5

Thiel, Peter, 70; *Bollea v. Gawker*, 102; Gawker Media and, 8, 92, 101–2

Tiborcz, István, 252

Times of India, 165

Timmerman, Jacobo, 280

Tolentino, Jia, 103

Tordai, Csaba, 249

tower stations, 52

TPM. *See* Talking Points Memo

transparency: data, Big Tech and, regulations for, 34; Google Transparency Project, 291; in India, 163; under Law on the Transparency of Organizations Funded from Abroad, 251

transparency laws, education reform and, 126

True/Slant, 106

Trump, Donald: as authoritarian leader, 214; election of, media influenced by, 7; Erdoğan and, 146; Flynn and, 112–13; Fox News and, 3, 5; Google and, bias claims by, 37–38; Internal Revenue Service and, 255–56; journalistic productivity and, 234–35; misinformation by, 266; Modi and, 183; right-wing press and, 11–12; Sater and, 111; Silicon Valley and, role in election of, 23; social media exemptions for, 69

trust funds, for investigative reporting, 272–75

Türfent, Nedim, 155

Turkey: banking systems in, 148–49; cognitive capture in, 147; Doğan Holding in, 141–42, 149; financial crisis in, 144; Gezi generation, 142–43, 152; Gülenist movement in, 149–50, 158n20; Justice and Development Party in, 141–42, 145–46, 148–49, 157n12; Law Number 5651, 154; media capture in, 141–56; media plazas in, 151–52; minority rights in, 143; news media in, 141–43, 145, 149–50, 152–53; newspapers in, 141–42, 145, 149–50, 152–53, 286; private television channels in, 157n8; protocol news in, 144; redistribution of economic benefits in, 215; social media in, demographics for, 154; Welfare Party in, 145–46

Twitter: blogs and, 99–100; exemptions for Trump, 69; shadow banning, 39

2016 presidential election, in U.S., media influenced by, 3, 5

Uber, in United Kingdom, 189–91

Uganda, social media taxes in, 219

U.K. *See* United Kingdom

Ukraine, media reform movement in, 223–24, 227–28

uncaptured media, 7; in United Kingdom, 206

uncaptured news, in U. K., 206

United Kingdom (U.K.): advertising revenues in, changes in, 199; BBC in, 196, 275; Brexit and, 188, 193, 207; *Buzzfeed* in, 193–94, 201; *Cairncross Review*, 207; Competition and Markets Authority, 17; *Daily Express*, 197; *Daily Mail*, 192–93, 197; *Daily Telegraph*, 193–94, 205; Digital News Initiative, 190; editorial independence for press in, 198–201; ESI Media, 192–93, 195, 198; *Evening Standard*, 188–92, 205; *Ferret*, 202–4; Fleet Street, 197–98; Future London project, 192; Google in, 189–91; *Guardian*, 115n3, 120, 148,

204–5; Guardian Labs in, 200–201; Guardian News & Media in, 201; *Huffington Post* in, 201; *Independent*, 192; media capture in, 204–7; media fund in, 203; media ownership in, 195–96, 198; *Mediapart*, 202; news deserts in, 204; newspapers in, 115n3, 120, 148, 188–94, 197–98, 204–5; *openDemocracy* and, 189–92, 194–95, 201, 207; philanthropy in, 206; press barons era in, 197; prization of news media in, 192–95; public broadcasting in, 16; self-censorship in, 197–98; Sky in, 196; stakeholder media in, 203; *Sun*, 76, 197–98; Uber in, 189–91; uncaptured news in, 206; value added tax rates in, 16; *Vice* in, 201; war reporting in, 194–95
United Nations, establishment of, 227
United States (U.S.): Every Student Succeeds Act, 119; Federal Communications Commission, 5, 219–20; Federal Trade Commission, 109; Internal Revenue Service in, 254–55; media capture in, 8; media regulation mechanisms in, 219–20; Modi in, 182–83. *See also* Congress; *New York Times*; 2016 presidential election; *Washington Post*
United Way, 268–69
Universal Declaration of Human Rights, 227
Ünker, Pelin, 155, 159n39
U.S. *See* United States

Valdez Cárdenas, Javier, 286–87
Valero, Luis, 279
value added tax rates (VAT rates), 16
Venezuela, 286
venture capital investment, journalistic productivity influenced by, 241–42
Vergara v. California, 124, 128–29
Vice, 201
Villaraigosa, Antonio, 125–26
violence, against media: Committee to Protect Journalists, 177; in India,

163; against journalists, in India, 176–77
vouchers, education reform through, 135–36

Wall Street, corporate mythology for, 23
Wall Street Journal, 97, 114, 175, 234; decline in stories published in, 237; paywall for, 244
Walton Family Foundation, 117, 127, 132–33
Warren, Elizabeth, 294
war reporting, in United Kingdom, 194–95
Washington Post: advertising policies at, for employees, 9; Bezos and, 3, 8; declines in stories published in, 237; education reform stories in, 135; liberalism of, public perception of, 37; on local journalism, crisis in, 48
Wasserman Foundation, 123
Weingarten, Randi, 126–27
Welfare Party, in Turkey, 145–46
West Africa, civil society organizations in, 223
Whitmire, Richard, 131
Wilhelm, Alex, 238
WordPress, 98
World Development Report, 222

Yahoo, 25–26
yellow journalism/yellow press, 12, 69; Big Tech and, 70
Yglesias, Matthew, 102
YouTube: exemptions for Trump, 69; user growth for, 33

Zabludovsky, Jacobo, 277
Zaman (Turkish newspaper), 149–50
Zeta, 277–80, 288
Zimbabwe, 281
Zimmer, Steve, 129
Zuckerberg, Mark, 3, 40–41, 69; Congressional questioning by, 72; on news media, public importance of, 73–74. *See also* Facebook
Zuma, Jacob, 214